THE MESSAGE MATTERS

THE MESSAGE MATTERS

THE ECONOMY AND PRESIDENTIAL CAMPAIGNS

LYNN VAVRECK

PRINCETON UNIVERSITY PRESS   PRINCETON AND OXFORD

Published by Princeton University Press, 41 William Street, Princeton, New Jersey 08540
In the United Kingdom: Princeton University Press, 6 Oxford Street, Woodstock, Oxfordshire
OX20 1TW

Library of Congress Cataloging-in-Publication Data
Vavreck, Lynn, 1968–
The message matters : the economy and presidential campaigns / Lynn Vavreck.
      p.   cm.
Includes bibliographical references and index.
ISBN 978-0-691-13962-3 (hardcover : alk. paper) — ISBN 978-0-691-13963-0 (pbk. : alk. paper)
1. Presidents—United States—Election.   2. Political campaigns—United States.   3. United
States—Economic conditions—Public opinion.   4. United States—Politics and government.
5. Public opinion—United States.   I. Title.
JK528.V38 2009
324.973'092—dc22

                                                                        2008053045

Dedication page "1952 Vincent Black Lightning"
Written by Richard Thompson
© 1991 Beeswing Music (BMI) Administered by Bug
All Rights Reserved. Used by Permission.

British Library Cataloging-in-Publication Data is available

This book has been composed in Minion

Printed on acid-free paper. ∞

press.princeton.edu

Printed in the United States of America

10   9   8   7   6   5   4   3

To Jeff

... but he smiled to see her cry,
and said I'll give you my Vincent to ride.
  —Richard Thompson,
    "1952 Vincent Black Lightning"

CONTENTS

LIST OF FIGURES   xi

LIST OF TABLES   xiii

ACKNOWLEDGMENTS   xvii

PROLOGUE   xxi

CHAPTER ONE
Presidential Campaigns   1
  Basic Questions   2
  What's Coming   3

PART I

CHAPTER TWO
How and Why Campaigns Matter   9
  The Challenge   10
    Something's Happening in America   11
    The Importance of the Economy   12
    The Importance of the Media   14
  A Theory of Campaign Effects   15
    Integrating Literatures   16
    Spatial Voting: The Past as Predictor of the Future   18
    Retrospective Voting and Campaign Effects   22
    Individual-Level Characteristics and Campaign Effects   23

CHAPTER THREE
Context Matters: A Campaign Typology   26
  Theoretical Predictions   28
  A Campaign Typology   31
    Clarifying Campaigns   31
    Insurgent Campaigns   32
    When the Economy Is Mixed   33
  Predicting Campaign Types, 1952–2000   35

PART II

CHAPTER FOUR
The Media Disconnect: Media and Candidate Messages   43

Candidates' Messages and How to Measure Them   46
  Advertisements and Speeches   46
  Newspaper Coverage   48

Coding the Ads, Speeches, and News Coverage   53

The Content of Modern Campaigns   57
  The Media Disconnect   58

CHAPTER FIVE
The Message Matters: Candidate-Level Tests of the Theory   67

Clarifying Campaigns: Dominating Economic Discussion   69

Insurgent Campaigns: Issue Selection Matters   71
  Stevenson 1952 and 1956: Second Time Same as the First   76
  Goldwater 1964: Just Enough Power to Get the Job Done   78
  Carter 1980 and Mondale 1984: War through Strength   80
  Dukakis 1988: An Unfocused American Dream   82

Insurgent Candidates Making Wise Choices   83
  Kennedy 1960: High Hopes   83
  Nixon 1968: Freedom from Fear or Racial Appeal?   86
  Carter 1976: Outside and Honest   90

Two More Tests of the Theory at the Candidate Level   105
  A More Rigorous Test of Compliance   105
  Explaining the Errors in Forecasting Models   107

PART III

CHAPTER SIX
The Message Matters: Microlevel Tests of the Theory   113

*Clarifying Candidate Campaign Effects: Do Campaign Messages
Shape Voters' Evaluations of Candidates?*   115
  High Fidelity?   116
  Ads: Messages That Matter   120

*Clarifying Candidate Campaign Effects: Do Campaign Messages
Help Voters Learn about Candidates' Issue Positions?*   123
  Measuring Uncertainty   125
  Reducing Uncertainty   128
  Campaign Learning about the Economy   131

*Insurgent-Candidate Campaign Effects: Changing the Debate
by Increasing the Importance of Issues*   134

The Most Important Problem in the Nation   137
Most Important Problem and Vote Choice   140

*Insurgent Candidate Campaign Effects: Being Closer to
Most Voters on the Insurgent Issue*   144
The Difference in Distances   144
Differences in Distances and Vote Choice   151

The Message and Its Effects   155

CHAPTER SEVEN
Candidates Creating Context   159

Can Candidates Create the Context?   160

Creating Salience: Finding the Right Insurgent Issue   163

Appendix   167

References   191

Index   199

LIST OF FIGURES

FIGURE 2.1   A Theory of Campaign Effects Derived from
              the Spatial Voting Model   19

FIGURE 4.1   Number of Campaign Advertisements, Speeches,
              and Articles by Campaign Year   50

FIGURE 4.2   Percent of Candidate-Based Coverage Compared
              to All Stories about the Campaign   52

FIGURE 4.3   Fidelity between Candidate Content and News
              Coverage: Traits and Foreign Policy   64

FIGURE 4.4   Fidelity between Candidate Content and News
              Coverage: Economy and Domestic Policy   65

FIGURE 5.1   Campaign Messages in Ads, Speeches, and News, 1952   92

FIGURE 5.2   Campaign Messages in Ads, Speeches, and News, 1956   93

FIGURE 5.3   Campaign Messages in Ads, Speeches, and News, 1960   94

FIGURE 5.4   Campaign Messages in Ads, Speeches, and News, 1964   95

FIGURE 5.5   Campaign Messages in Ads, Speeches, and News, 1968   96

FIGURE 5.6   Campaign Messages in Ads, Speeches, and News, 1972   97

FIGURE 5.7   Campaign Messages in Ads, Speeches, and News, 1976   98

FIGURE 5.8   Campaign Messages in Ads, Speeches, and News, 1980   99

FIGURE 5.9   Campaign Messages in Ads, Speeches, and News, 1984   100

FIGURE 5.10   Campaign Messages in Ads, Speeches, and News, 1988   101

FIGURE 5.11   Campaign Messages in Ads, Speeches, and News, 1992   102

FIGURE 5.12   Campaign Messages in Ads, Speeches, and News, 1996   103

FIGURE 5.13   Campaign Messages in Ads, Speeches, and News, 2000   104

FIGURE 6.1   Fidelity between Candidate Messages and Voters'
              Evaluations   118

FIGURE 6.2   Changes from September to Election Day in Mean
              Levels of Issue Uncertainty by Candidate Type   126

FIGURE 6.3   Changes in Mean Levels of Uncertainty from
              September to Election Day for Clarifying Candidates
              by Dominant Topics of Campaign Messages   127

FIGURE 6.4   Changes in Mean Levels of Uncertainty from September to Election Day for Insurgent Candidates by Dominant Topics of Campaign Messages   128

FIGURE 6.5   Changes in Predicted Probability of Issue Nonplacement over Course of Campaign by Levels of Attention to Campaign in Media   133

FIGURE 6.6   Mean Percent of Respondents Who Offer Insurgent Issue as Nation's Most Important Problem over Time for Different Classes of Insurgent Candidates   138

FIGURE 6.7   Change in Insurgent Candidate Vote Share Depending on Whether Respondent Named Insurgent Issue as Most Important Problem in Nation for Each Class of Insurgent Candidate by Levels of Political Information   141

FIGURE 6.8   Mean Differences in Squared Distances on Insurgent Issues over Campaign Period for Each Class of Insurgent Candidate by Levels of Political Information   146

FIGURE 6.9   Mean Differences in Squared Distances on Insurgent Issues over Campaign Period for Each Class of Insurgent Candidate by Respondent's Party Identification   149

FIGURE 6.10   Predicted Vote for Clarifying Candidate at Varying Differences in Distances on Insurgent Issues by Levels of Political Information   153

FIGURE 6.11   Change in Predicted Probability of Voting for Insurgent Candidate by Levels of Information for Varying Degrees of Differences in Distances   154

LIST OF TABLES

TABLE 3.1   Percentage of People Believing Foreign Policy and the Economy Are Nation's Most Important Problem, 1952–2008   29

TABLE 3.2   A Campaign Typology: Clarifying and Insurgent Campaigns   34

TABLE 3.3   Range of Economic Forecasting Predictions and Actual Two-Party Vote Share from Four Popular Forecasting Models   37

TABLE 3.4   Predicted Clarifying and Insurgent Candidates   38

TABLE 3.5   Predicted Campaign Types by Electoral Success   39

TABLE 4.1   Campaign Ads, Stump Speeches, and *New York Times* Coverage by Year and Candidate   51

TABLE 4.2   Content of Campaign Ads, Speeches, and News Coverage   58

TABLE 4.3   Dominant Subjects of Campaign Advertisements, Speeches, and News Coverage by Year   60

TABLE 4.4   Dominant Subjects of Campaign Advertisements, Speeches, and News Coverage by Candidate and Year   61

TABLE 5.1   Dominant Subjects of Campaign Ads and Speeches by Campaign Type   68

TABLE 5.2   Theoretical Predictions and Election Outcomes   70

TABLE 5.3   The Behavior of Clarifying Candidates and Their Electoral Success   71

TABLE 5.4   The Behavior of Insurgent Candidates and Electoral Success   72

TABLE 5.5   Theoretical Predictions and Election Outcomes, Strict Test   106

TABLE 5.6   Forecasting Models, Explained Variation, RMSE, and Accuracy   109

TABLE 6.1   Do Ads, Speeches, or News Affect Voters' Evaluations of Candidates?   121

TABLE 6.2   Effects of Campaign Messages about Economy on Evaluations of Candidates   122

TABLE 6.3   Reductions in Mean Levels of Issue Uncertainty
for Eight Issues   129

TABLE 6.4   Summary of Individual-Level Campaign Effects for
Clarifying Candidates and Messages   156

TABLE 6.5   Summary of Individual-Level Campaign Effects for
Insurgent Candidates and Messages   157

TABLE A1   Forecasting Models 1952–2000 (Table 5.6)   169

TABLE A2   Media Attention and Uncertainty (Figure 6.5)   170

TABLE A3   Media Attention and Uncertainty (Figure 6.5)   171

TABLE A4   Media Attention and Uncertainty (Figure 6.5)   172

TABLE A5   Media Attention and Uncertainty (Figure 6.5)   173

TABLE A6   Mean Percent of Respondents Who Think Insurgent
Issue Is Nation's Most Important Problem by Time
of Interview (Figure 6.6)   174

TABLE A7   Non-Independence of Vote and Whether Respondent
Thinks Insurgent Issue Is Nation's Most Important
Problem (Figure 6.7)   175

TABLE A8   Non-Independence of Vote and Whether Respondent
Thinks Insurgent Issue Is Nation's Most Important
Problem (Figure 6.7)   176

TABLE A9   Non-Independence of Vote and Whether Respondent
Thinks Insurgent Issue Is Nation's Most Important
Problem (Figure 6.7)   177

TABLE A10   Non-Independence of Vote and Whether Respondent
Thinks Insurgent Issue Is Nation's Most Important
Problem (Figure 6.7)   178

TABLE A11   Mean Differences in Distances on Insurgent Issue
over Campaign by Type of Insurgent Candidate,
All Respondents (Figures 6.8 and 6.9)   179

TABLE A12   Mean Differences in Distances on Insurgent Issue
over Campaign by Type of Insurgent Candidate,
High-Information Respondents (Figures 6.8 and 6.9)   180

TABLE A13   Mean Differences in Distances on Insurgent Issue
over Campaign by Type of Insurgent Candidate,
Low-Information Respondents (Figures 6.8 and 6.9)   181

TABLE A14   Mean Differences in Distances on Insurgent Issue
over Campaign by Type of Insurgent Candidate,
Independents (Figures 6.8 and 6.9)   182

TABLE A15   Mean Differences in Distances on Insurgent Issue
over Campaign by Type of Insurgent Candidate,
Clarifying Partisans (Figures 6.8 and 6.9)   183

TABLE A16   Mean Differences in Distances on Insurgent Issue
over Campaign by Type of Insurgent Candidate,
Insurgent Partisans (Figures 6.8 and 6.9)   184

TABLE A17   Importance of Differences in Distances to Vote for
Clarifying Candidate by Insurgent Candidate Type,
All Respondents (Figures 6.10 and 6.11)   185

TABLE A18   Importance of Differences in Distances to Vote for
Clarifying Candidate by Insurgent Candidate Type,
High-Information Respondents, (Figures 6.10 and 6.11)   186

TABLE A19   Importance of Differences in Distances to Vote for
Clarifying Candidate by Insurgent Candidate Type,
Low-Information Respondents, (Figures 6.10 and 6.11)   187

ACKNOWLEDGMENTS

IT HAS BEEN MORE than ten years since I first thought about making this argument. But the roots of the project go back much farther than that—the beginnings feel like a lifetime ago, and yet, I can't believe it's finished. The hours spent watching campaign ads in Harkness Hall, the weeks and months spent coding newspaper coverage in the dusty attic of Rush Rhees and ultimately Young Library, the days spent staring at the pages of results pasted up on my wall in Silsby, Bunche, and Hoover, and it all comes down to this. I'm going to take these last moments and I'm going to go slowly through them. We so rarely have the time to tell the people who shape, change, and inspire us how much they have done, and so, in the last hour of this project, I'm going to linger over that list. I hope you'll forgive me the indulgence.

If John Geer had not repeatedly belittled me for deciding to go to law school (he really believes this negativity stuff!) I would never have found the courage to leave after the first day. Because of John, I read Downs, Fiorina, Fenno, and Schattschneider, and I got to work as Warren Miller's research assistant. If not for John's encouragement and confidence in me, I would not have applied to Rochester and I certainly would not have had the nerve to show up. John changed everything—and I am forever grateful.

Rochester was chilly when I arrived, but the people and environment were warm. My work on the economy and presidential approval reminded Dave Weimer of one of his former students, and he said these six words to me: "You should talk to Simon Jackman." And so I did. That conversation has lasted sixteen years and in one way or another, it shapes a lot of what is on the pages to come.

It was Simon who introduced me to Larry Bartels and John Zaller, both of whom became coauthors of mine, but more importantly, enduring friends. And it was Larry and John who invited me, in my second year of graduate school, to a meeting they were hosting on how best to measure campaign effects. At this meeting I met Doug Rivers and a few years later, Doug and I sat across the table from each other at Stanford, and on a series of napkins, I sketched out my ideas for how to bring spatial modeling, economic forecasts, and campaign effects together into one argument. For this, and so much more, I "generally speaking" thank Doug.

John, Simon, Larry, and Doug, along with my dissertation advisor at Rochester, Dick Fenno, are the reasons I kept working on this project even when I thought I would never finish. The project is a tribute to them and their interest in my intellectual and professional development at moments when it mattered most. If the work is good, it is because they inspired it. If it is not good, it is because I did not listen.

In 1997 Larry Bartels offered me a postdoc at Princeton as part of a project investigating reforms to the presidential campaign process. So many wonderful things came out of that year. Larry and I found (and still find) countless delightfully amusing things to share with each other—from articulating the campaign reform attributes of Chicken George to hosting a press conference in DC about our book on the same day the Starr Report was released, we never lack for laughter. Still, and I think always, simply having him around brings me quiet comfort.

In 2001, I took a job at University of California Los Angeles that came with a new tenure clock. While I don't recommend this strategy to everyone, the new clock gave me just the flexibility I needed to do something I really wanted to do: directly test the power of advertising. When Don Green approached me at a meeting in 2001 and asked if I wanted to get involved with the second stage of his GOTV research, I knew instantly I wanted to do it. We made our own TV ads and we aired them on shows like *Law and Order* and *Monk*. The project was a labor of love and extremely rewarding, but the biggest payoff (aside from the three-point increase in turnout!) was working with Don and getting to know him. His generosity, across multiple dimensions, has given me a career that is orders of magnitude more rewarding than I ever imagined.

Others along the way provided feedback, support, laughter, and friendship: At Rochester, Dick Niemi, Lynda Powell, Renee Smith, Jim Johnson, and Jeff Banks helped me sharpen the overall story and the argument. My Harkness Hall partners in crime Mitch Sanders, Georg VanBerg, Lanny Martin, and Randy Stevenson set a high bar for my work and for all colleagues to come. At Dartmouth College, Linda Fowler, Dean Spiliotes, and Dick Winters surpassed that bar and broke the news to me gently that the presidential candidates probably wouldn't just *show up* at my door for coffee and I should probably stop waiting. Linda directly sponsored my work through her directorship of the Rockefeller Center and shared her research budget generously during the 2000 primary.

Along the way, I benefited from participants in seminars at Columbia University, University of California San Diego, the University of Pennsylvania, Princeton University, UCLA, and the University of Michigan. Skip Lupia read an early draft of the manuscript and significantly changed the way I thought about testing the theory. And Sam Popkin supported my work over the years in ways that have to be experienced to be believed. A personal favorite was the time he told George Stephanopoulos to call me to talk about the New Hampshire primary and I was so sure it was my colleague Dean playing a practical joke on me, I "played along" by answering "George's" questions with the most surly and absurd things I could think to say. Ooops. A very Sam moment.

The Rockefeller Center at Dartmouth College supported this work with a Junior Faculty Development Grant and with the Wilson Faculty Research Fellowship. The UCLA Faculty Senate did the same with an Assistant Professor Career Development Award and numerous Faculty Senate Grants; and the UCLA Center for American Politics and Public Policy recently honored me with its research award. Danielle Montgomery, Jenny Blake, and Margaret Coblentz provided excellent research assistance with the content analyses. Marty Cohen made the NES likes/dislikes data intuitive and tractable. Michael Tesler helped to put the finishing touches on the references and the text. And Brian Law provided keen "insight" (read: luck) into the workings of the ever-mysterious Microsoft Office.

Mike Lofchie, my department chair at UCLA has gone to bat for me more times than I can recall, and Bret Nighman solved more than one financial wrinkle by magically extending me credit that never got billed. There simply is no more supportive and productive research environment than UCLA. My colleagues here make coming to work everyday a pleasure—and their accomplishments motivate me to do my part to increase the department's reputation. Foremost among people I look forward to talking to every day is John Zaller. I consider the times I've spent thinking with him some of the finest moments of my career. And although he is no longer at UCLA, I still claim Marty Gilens as a colleague and deeply regret that most of our joint work was done after he left for Princeton. My UCLA graduate students push me to learn along with them—and to them I owe a nonquantifiable debt. Ryan Enos, Seth Hill, Brian Law, Matt Atkinson, James Lo, and Michael Tesler are simply the best parts of my job. Both smart and creative, they keep me sharp and make me think about things in all sorts of new ways. I can't wait to watch them develop in the profession, but I will so miss them when they are gone.

In the last year several people and institutions have transformed this project in extremely important ways. Mo Fiorina and David Brady gave me an office and research support at the Hoover Institution at Stanford, and that time was essential in finishing chapter 6. While there, I benefited greatly from conversations with both of them and many of their colleagues about my work. Paul Sniderman listened to me talk about the project and instantly saw connections across ideas that I had missed. Paul's enthusiasm and encouragement gave me the confidence to rewrite the beginning of the manuscript in a way that I recognize now is a tremendous improvement. I cannot thank him enough for sharing his mind with me in this way.

One week after I left Hoover, I arrived in Oxford, England, at a meeting that Ray Duch organized on context and election outcomes. The meeting was the final turning point this project needed. Presenting the new work from chapter 6 along with the new introduction led Jamie Druckman to see other connections in the project and he pushed me to think about the argument in a bigger way. The time he spent discussing my work at that meeting changed this book. Michael Lewis-Beck, Ray Duch, and Ken Scheve also encouraged me to see the connections the argument had to non-campaign-effects research, and for that, and their enthusiasm for the project, I am thankful.

Finally, my friends Jill, Susan, Maren, and Angi are my lifelong confidantes and role models. I know not a single one of them thought this book actually existed! Hah! These women are incredible and the best of me is just a collection of each of them. Life is hard—but mine is easier because of them.

My interest in politics comes from my parents—Walter and Jane Vavreck. Not because we ever had a single political conversation at home, but because they raised me in the white, ethnic suburbs of Cleveland and sent me to Ukrainian School to learn the language, even though we were not Ukrainian. Along with the language, and thirteen years of reading, writing, and thinking in Ukrainian, I soaked up the culture—and a lifetime of hearing people talk about communist oppression affects a young girl. Coupled with routine trips to Mexico with my parents—where I saw poverty, structural breakdown, and campaigns that quite literally *couldn't matter*—my interest in politics was cemented at an early age. That so many years later, my mom is beginning to pay attention to the presidential campaign ("They say that Hillary isn't going to make it, Lynn") is a great delight to me. Although I rarely tell her, I am so proud of her and everything she has learned in the last six years. My single and biggest regret about this project is that my dad is not here to open this book and read these pages.

It would have thrilled him so.

And so I turn finally to the part of the acknowledgments in which people usually thank their non-political science spouses for reading drafts and catching errors. Ironically, Jeff Lewis, my political science spouse, may have done less of this than most, although he was extremely helpful in mass-producing the figures at the end of chapter 5 and beginning of chapter 6. Mostly, though, Jeff taught me that life is too short to wait to do the things you love to do. He never once, not a single time, suggested that I better finish this book. He didn't pressure me, he didn't judge me, and he never so much as intimated that I might have been making the wrong choice in letting it stew for so long. Instead, he bought me a horse and told me to ride it every chance I could. He bought me musical instruments and told me to play them. Jeff makes me laugh—every day—and the best parts of any one of my days are the moments when we laugh together.

Lastly, I thank Chuck Myers at Princeton University Press, who is easily the most patient person I know.

PROLOGUE

O
N OCTOBER 5TH, 2008 John McCain, the Republican nominee for president of the United States said these 12 words, "If we keep talking about the economic crisis, we're going to lose." Meanwhile, his opponent, Barack Obama, kept repeating the phrase "we can't afford more of the same." So went the presidential campaign of 2008, arguably one of the most compelling contests of the last half-century. In raw numbers, more people voted in 2008 than in any previous election. The candidates raised and spent an unprecedented one billion dollars. And, more people tuned in to watch election night coverage than ever before (71.5 million), making it the second most watched television broadcast in 2008 after the Super Bowl.

Yet, despite these astonishing markers, the 2008 presidential match delivered an unexceptional election outcome. Economic forecasting models predicted a Democratic party win long before Hillary Clinton dropped out of the race. And the lack of a focal candidate on the Republican side underscored the notion that Republican up-and-comers knew it wasn't the party's year. To the long list of presidential elections correctly predicted by the state of the nation's economy in advance of the election (12 of the last 15), we add another year. National economic conditions matter to aggregate election outcomes.

But, if the state of the economy predicted Democrats would win long before the candidates were even known, how much of a role could the billion-dollar campaign have played in the outcome? It should come as no surprise that in a book called *The Message Matters* I argue that even in the face of strong structural conditions like a declining economy and a lengthy war, what candidates say and do in their campaigns can affect outcomes. The message matters, too.

The 2008 election delivered an archetypical outcome alongside a remarkable campaign in an extraordinary context. Every passing day of the campaign brought more devastating economic news. Beginning with the mysterious collapse of Bear Stearns in the spring and culminating in the closure of Lehman Brothers, the effects of a shrinking credit market were ubiquitous. As an increasing number of family homes slipped into foreclosure, the price of a gallon of gasoline inched higher and higher, reaching its zenith at nearly $5.00 a gallon in California in the middle of June. The context of the 2008 election was not subtle. And it's the context that shapes the candidates' messages.

The Democrats relished their spot as beneficiaries of this serious national (even global) economic crisis. In a clever turn of Ronald Reagan's 1980 phrase, Obama asked voters at a campaign rally, "are you better off today than you were four *weeks* ago?" As Obama moved from place to place, he assumed the role of clarifying candidate with agility. The theory laid out in the pages that follow defines a candidate as a clarifying candidate if an economic forecast done well before the election predicts that his or her party will win. Obama was the beneficiary of national, even global economic stagnation.

What better backdrop for his well-branded tagline of hope and change than an increasingly gloomy economic climate? Obama talked about the economy more than anything else in his campaign and more than McCain talked about it—clarifying his role as the man who would change the course of the economy. Just slightly more than 60 percent of the appeals in Obama's general election ads were about the economic crisis. Obama ran a classic clarifying campaign.

Second to the economy, Obama's campaign message centered on his character, upbringing, and optimism. On Election Day, Obama joined a long list of clarifying winners (Dwight Eisenhower, Lyndon Johnson, Richard Nixon, Ronald Reagan, George H.W. Bush, George W. Bush 2004, and Bill Clinton). And those who were members of the out-party when they won, like Obama (Eisenhower's and Reagan's first elections), fared well enough vis-à-vis the economy to run a second time as incumbent-clarifying candidates and win.

But as you will learn in the pages to come, it's the insurgent candidate, the one predicted to lose based on the state of the economy, who can affect the outcome by choosing his or her message wisely. The challenge for insurgent candidates sounds straightforward: refocus the election off the economy and onto something else; but, not just anything else. The winning insurgent issue is something on which the insurgent candidate is closer to most voters than the clarifying candidate, and on which the clarifying candidate is committed to his or her unpopular position. This latter part is the hard part, at least historically.

Insurgent candidates as varied as Walter Mondale and Barry Goldwater have failed to find dimensions of politics on which they were more popular than their opponents and on which their opponents were stuck in an unpopular spot. A few (George McGovern, George H.W. Bush 1992, and Bob Dole) didn't even try to refocus the election off the economy and onto something else—they just focused on the economy even though the national economic conditions helped their opponents. To this trio of failed insurgent candidates, add John McCain.

McCain's campaign advertisements focused mainly on the economy. Nearly half of all the appeals he made in advertisements were about the economy. The second most popular theme in McCain's ads was experience or readiness for office. In McCain's ads as in Obama's, these two sets of ideas worked together to form the message. Through these appeals, McCain defined Obama as "ready to tax, not ready to lead." The post-convention trait appeals claimed Obama was a risky choice because he was unknown. McCain's ads (*Dangerous* and *Hypocritical)* asked, "Who is Barack Obama?" And in another (*Special)* the male narrator says, "behind the fancy speeches, grand promises, and TV specials, lies the truth . . . Barack Obama lacks the experience America needs." These messages, coupled with the tagline "Country First" provided a subtle, implicit cue to make viewers draw the inference that Obama put country second . . . or perhaps last.

As McCain and Palin honed their joint message, they talked about "real change" and started calling themselves "the original Mavericks"—original as in first (in McCain's case), but also as in authentic (in Palin's case).

As an insurgent message, the economy fails by definition—insurgent candidates should never focus their campaign on the economy. Empirically, all of the insurgent candidates in the last 60 years who ran on the economy lost their elections. Among those insurgents who focused on something else, roughly one-third won—even though the economic forecasts predicted they would lose. The message matters.

Unfortunately, even McCain's "Maverick" theme failed to meet the criteria of a winning insurgent issue. Was McCain preferred to Obama as an agent of change? To argue that you are the candidate who has the *experience* to bring change is demonstrating that you are something *old* when the point of this argument is to sell yourself as something *new*. Further, was Obama committed to his position as a newcomer, a politically inexperienced novice? On the one hand, this is exactly the kind of constraint a good insurgent issue exploits—there is nothing Obama can do about the fact that he is young and has not held political office for very long. On the other hand, couching the experience constraint in *change* draws attention to the hard facts that Obama was the embodiment of change. He changed the way candidates campaign and raise money. He beat party insider Hillary Clinton. And his candidacy alone hinted at changing racial attitudes across the country. Saying you've been around long enough to know how to really change things doesn't work in this context—and in fact, may underscore the fact that you've been around long enough.

John McCain said if he kept talking about the economy he would lose. He seemed to understand that despite economic reality, despite the structural conditions, he had a choice about whether to talk about the economy or talk about something else. He should have listened to himself. Insurgent candidates *can* overcome structural conditions, but it is rare and it is hard. Further, when insurgent candidates win elections it is by the narrowest of margins (Kennedy, Nixon 1968, Carter 1976, and Bush 2000). In McCain's case, given the intensity of the economic collapse during the fall campaign, refocusing the election off the economy might have been impossible. But focusing his message *on the economy* was only going to do one thing—help elect Barack Obama.

THE MESSAGE MATTERS

Chapter One

PRESIDENTIAL CAMPAIGNS

I N 1976 JIMMY CARTER ran for president of the United States as a trustworthy Washington outsider. He was elected by defeating an opponent who was the consummate Washington insider—a man who pardoned Richard Nixon and who was appointed to the vice presidency and the presidency. Gerald Ford was as inside the Washington Beltway as one could get—and he could not get out. Similarly, John F. Kennedy in 1960 recognized his opponent's culpability in what was called "The Missile Gap"—the alleged fact that America had fallen behind Russia in weapons development. Richard Nixon, whose administration had presided over this "slump" in American productivity, had no evidence it did not exist and could not counter Kennedy's claim. Thus, he too, was stuck—although the economy was doing well and the War in Vietnam had not yet escalated.

What Carter and Kennedy both recognized and exploited was a dimension of electoral politics on which their opponents faced constraints. Although Ford and Nixon were members of incumbent administrations and the nation's economy was growing over the course of their stewardships, their challengers defeated them. This book is about how candidates campaign, what effects these campaigns have on voters, and how the context of elections conditions all of these things in important ways.

What we know about why presidential candidates lose elections mostly centers around campaign strategies or candidate style. Pundits are quick to blame electoral losses on a poor campaign strategy or a candidate's inability to connect with voters on the stump. Journalists, however, are rarely heard suggesting that a candidate lost because his or her policies were unpopular. Why did Michael Dukakis lose the 1988 presidential election after a seventeen-point lead coming out of his convention? It must be because George Bush outcampaigned him, say the experts. The *New York Times* Editorial Board wrote:

> He [Dukakis] was not destined to lose at all, and did so only because he ran a dismal campaign. . . . "Why didn't he say . . ." became a virtual motto of endless exasperation—when the Dukakis campaign gave leaden answers or no answers at all to accusations about the Pledge of Allegiance or prison furloughs or to questions like, "How would Governor Dukakis feel if his wife were raped and murdered?" (November 9, 1988, p. A34)

Similarly, why did Bill Clinton win the 1992 election at a time when the incumbent Bush was popular and the economy was recovering from a recession?

Many pundits answered that it was Clinton's "War Room" campaign strategists who outmaneuvered the Bush campaign on a daily basis, or that Bush himself was somehow a "bad" campaigner:

> Something odd happens to Mr. Bush when he vaults into "campaign mode." His good manners fall away and he stands revealed as Nasty-man. . . . this time it went from Red-baiting to juvenile expostulations like, "My dog Millie knows more about foreign affairs than these two bozos." (November 5, 1992, p. A34).

What exactly is a good campaign or a good campaigner? These concepts have certain ephemeral qualities about them. Experts cannot precisely detail what makes a campaign "good," except maybe that it produced a winner; and, they know a good campaigner when they see one. Such explication is not helpful. Most notably it ignores the fact that one candidate can be a good campaigner in one year (Bush in 1988) and a lousy one in a later year (Bush in 1992). If campaign success were merely a function of the candidate's ability to strategize about how to beat the opponent and then execute that strategy effectively, we would not expect to see such differences in the successes of candidates like Bush (1988, 1992), Carter (1976, 1980), and Nixon (1960, 1968, 1972).

There must be more to the story about why campaigns are successful than strategy and execution. My aim in this book is to explore more systematically the types of campaigns run by candidates for president of the United States by paying special attention to the messages they send and the constraints candidates face when running their campaigns.

The most important constraint for all candidates is the condition of the nation's economy. Others include previously taken issue positions or personal characteristics. I focus on illustrating why candidates like Carter and Kennedy exploit their opponents' weaknesses, while Reagan and Eisenhower talk mainly about a booming economy, largely ignoring their opponent's presence in the race—and why these campaign strategies are predictable well in advance of the election, and ultimately successful. My hope is that presidential campaigns may come to be viewed not as exercises in strategy executed by idiosyncratic candidates whose personal capabilities and whims influence success, but as logical, rational and often predetermined means toward an end.

BASIC QUESTIONS

Much attention has been given recently to presidential campaigns because they are "too negative" or "too long" or cost "too much" money. Proposed reforms include removing or lessening the role of money, giving candidates free television advertising time, urging newspapers to report when candidates are lying or misleading voters in their advertisements, and asking candidates to sign "codes of conduct" or compacts to promise "good behavior." These complaints and reforms presuppose that money, ads, newspaper coverage, and campaign tone all matter to voters on Election Day. Or more generally, that what goes on during campaigns for the presidency matters to voters at all. The extent to which discussion about these reforms increases in the absence of scholarly understanding about whether and how campaigns "matter" to voters is striking. While journalists, pundits, and voters may be confident that presidential campaigns influence election outcomes, political scientists have not always been so sure.

Party identification is still the greatest and most powerful predictor of vote choice across any demographic group (Miller 1994; Bartels 2000b). Most people do not pay much attention to politics or campaigns, even when faced with making a decision about their president. And, worse yet, perhaps because of their lack of attention, it seems that many voters are uninformed about where the candidates for president stand on various and important issues. Some argue that since party identification is known, presumably, before the campaign starts, and voters do not attend to campaigns when they are happening, campaigns must not matter to voting outcomes.

The study of campaigns, however, is not that simple. What does it mean, for example, to say that a campaign "matters"? Does a campaign matter if it changes someone's choices or vote decision? This is simple—probably so. However, does the campaign matter if it reinforces a voter's decision—if it makes the voter more confident of his or her choice? What if campaigns change the focus of national discussion; do they matter then—even if a campaign does not produce a winning candidate or change people's minds? If campaigns teach voters about the current state of the economy or of education policy or of trade policy in America, does it matter that voters have learned during the campaign even if their voting decisions were left unaffected? Any sophisticated and systematic analysis of campaigns and their effects must deal with these questions before moving on to assess whether the process is in need of change.

Many have argued that investigating the effects of campaigns is so complex as to be nearly impossible. Campaigns, because of their dynamic, contemporaneous, competitive, and cumulative nature take place in a research environment that is difficult to control. My own view is slightly more optimistic. If political scientists can theorize about voting behavior then we can theorize about campaign behavior and effects. Moreover, starting from a theory about how and why campaigns can matter, we can observe patterns of behavior among candidates that add to our understanding of the dynamic, contemporaneous, competitive, and cumulative nature of the campaign environment. That is what I attempt to do in the pages that follow.

WHAT'S COMING

This book is divided into three parts. Part I sets the stage for the other two by introducing theories of voting behavior and extrapolating them into a theory of how and why campaigns can matter (chapter 2). From this theory, a campaign typology is developed that introduces two types of campaigns, distinguished by their messages: the clarifying campaign (in which candidates clarify their position on an already important issue—the economy) and the insurgent campaign (in which candidates attempt to reset the agenda from the economy and onto an issue about which their opponent has previously committed to a position less popular than their own). Each campaign type consists of unique messaging by candidates and unique effects on voters (chapter 3). For example, in the clarifying campaign I expect candidates to talk mainly about the economy—simply taking credit for the good economic times or laying blame for the bad. Voters, then, should be very certain of the candidate's positions on economic issues by the end of the campaign as they learn about them throughout the process. In the insurgent campaign the candidate is expected to talk mainly about an insurgent issue (one on which his opponent is less popular then him). If the insurgent candidate is successful, voters, over time, should begin to believe that this issue is more important to their voting decision.

In chapter 3 I also explain how the theory suggests candidates sort themselves into these two categories. Of critical importance here is the state of the nation's economy. The candidate who is predicted to win the election based on a simple economic forecast runs the clarifying campaign. This could be the incumbent in a good economy or the challenger in a bad economy. The predicted economic loser runs the insurgent campaign. I use a simple economic forecast to predict what types of campaigns the theory suggests candidates will run over the period 1952–2000.

Part II begins in chapter 4 in which I detail the content of modern presidential campaigns by conducting an analysis of campaign advertisements, stump speeches, and campaign news coverage for every presidential election between 1952 and 2000. The data reveal a great divide between what candidates say and do and what the media report about them. In chapter 5 I explain candidate behavior in campaigns using the theory and typology as foundations. Using content analyses from the *New York Times*, candidate advertisements, and candidate stump speeches, I am able to compare what candidates actually talked about during their campaigns with what the theory predicts they should have talked about. The analytic power of the theory is tested as I discover that eventual winners are most often those candidates who behave as the theory and typology predict they should. Candidates who violate the typology's prescriptions lose elections.

In chapter 6, Part III, I turn the investigative light onto the behavior of voters in elections, searching for the unique effects associated with the clarifying and insurgent campaigns. Using public opinion data from 1952 to 2000 provided by the National Election Study, I assess whether candidates who conform to the typology's prescriptions are able to influence voters in specific and meaningful ways. Finally, in chapter 7 I engage larger theoretical questions about context and constraints. Can incumbent presidents manipulate national context? Is there an insurgent issue for every insurgent candidate or are some candidates just lucky? And, finally, how do these findings fit with common notions about elections?

Much of the theorizing and analyses in the beginning and latter parts of the book are based upon the use of statistical and mathematical models. As much as possible I have tried to present material in the main sections of the book in terms that citizens interested in politics can understand. The nuances of mathematics and modeling, along with detailed information on the data, models, and estimates from which my conclusions are drawn can be found in the book's Appendix.

PART I

Chapter Two

HOW AND WHY CAMPAIGNS MATTER

THERE IS LITTLE DOUBT that candidates, consultants, and journalists believe presidential campaigns have consequences. In other words— campaigns matter. It is never quite clear the way campaigns matter to these professionals; but the energy, money, and time they put into running and reporting on presidential campaigns suggests that somehow they must have a keen understanding of the importance of campaigns to election outcomes.

The Federal Election Commission (2008) reports that through October of 2008, spending by presidential candidates totaled nearly $1 billion, 143 percent more than comparable activity during the 2000 campaign. Additionally, parties and special-interest groups spent nearly $1 billion more on behalf of candidates. Of candidate spending, nearly 92 percent was spent on operating expenses, and a large portion of that went to political consultants—experts who "know" how to manage a campaign and produce a winner. In fact, political consultants are so convinced that campaigns matter to voters (and that they understand how they matter) that there is respect among some of them for the very best among them. This sentiment is summarized nicely in this exchange between Michael Dukakis's 1988 campaign manager, Susan Estrich, and George H. W. Bush's campaign manager, Lee Atwater, at a postelection conference held at Harvard's Kennedy School of Government in 1989 (Runkel 1989, 7):

> *Susan Estrich:* I'd like to . . . congratulate the Bush campaign. I think no one knows better than the person who's trying to figure out a way around your strategy when someone's got a good strategy. . . . you had a clear strategy. You executed it well. It was very tough running against you, and I guess it's the first time I've seen Lee [Atwater] and Roger [Ailes] since, so I just want to take a minute before I begin on our strategy to congratulate you for yours.

> *Lee Atwater:* Thank you.

Later in the conference, Atwater discusses his two most important strategic decisions in Bush's 1988 presidential campaign (Runkel 1989, 31):

> *Lee Atwater:* Decision number one was media, which is all-important; early strategy decision: hire Ailes. Number two was the debates, which we knew were going to be all important in the primaries; strategy decision: hire Ailes.

Candidates and consultants believe something important happens during presidential campaigns and that some of them, more than others, understand how to win.

There is some political science evidence to support the notion that something interesting happens to voters during presidential campaigns. From Labor Day to Election Day, people's level of interest in the presidential campaign changes (Bartels 2000, 23–26). In 1960, 1980, 1984, and 1992, people became more interested in the campaign as it progressed to Election Day. In the other years from 1952 to 1996, interest in the campaign declined. Similarly, in all presidential election years, people's overall evaluations of the candidates change during the Labor Day–Election Day period, implying that voters learn new things or update their beliefs during the campaign. In 1960, 1968, 1980, and 1984, people's evaluations of the candidates generally got better, and in the other years, the changes were mostly declines. Consultants, candidates, and journalists may be right—campaigns matter in important ways. Political scientists, however, are not sure.

The Challenge

It may seem unchallenging, at first glance, to uncover the ways that presidential campaigns affect people. The difficulty for political science, however, lies in the competitive, cumulative, and contemporaneous nature of campaigns. It is impossible to isolate the cause-and-effect pattern of one campaign event or one campaign decision, because of the highly interactive nature of the campaign environment. Furthermore, we cannot suspend the passage of time, which itself may cause changes in voters' attitudes and behavior that have nothing to do with things the candidates are actually doing during the campaign. As the first scholars of voting wrote in their landmark book, *The People's Choice* (Lazarsfeld, Berelson, and Gaudet 1944, 101):

> The proper perspective on a presidential campaign is gained only by a consideration of the changes from one presidential election to another. Only then can one basic question be answered: does the formal campaign during the summer and fall of an election year simply extend the long-term voting trend evident from election to election? Or does the campaign hasten or retard the trend line? In other words, what does the campaign do that would not have been done by the mere passage of time?

What these authors were getting at is simple: things happen in the world between presidential elections (and even during them) that might cause a person to change his or her party affiliation or even make a voter change his or her mind about a likely vote intention. Such changes should not be attributed to presidential campaigns. In fact, what Lazarsfeld and his colleagues discovered was that all the events that occurred between two elections (1936 to 1940) changed "over twice as many votes as all the events of the campaign" (102). The country was becoming more Republican all along, the campaign intensified the shift, but the majority of the changes in people's party affiliation happened during the three and a half years between elections, not during the six weeks before the election. What was happening in the nation and in the world seemed to affect people's political beliefs—the context of elections mattered, and campaigns, it seemed, weren't so important after all. Thus, the "minimal effects" hypothesis was born, and scholars spent decades trying to demonstrate that a presidential campaign has more than these narrow effects.

The idea that campaigns only mattered marginally to voters was counterintuitive, thus the Columbia University team of scholars investigated the nature of decision-making among voters further in 1948 (Berelson, Lazarsfeld, McPhee 1954). The results, however, did not change much. Even when they isolated voters during the campaign period to discover what moved them, they learned that the media did not matter very much, that voters often projected their own issue positions onto the candidates, and that, to the extent that voters were converted from one candidate to another (which was not much), it was most often due to the intervention of a friend, colleague, or family member. Not only did voting decisions seem to have little to do with campaign information explicitly, but Angus Campbell and his colleagues (Campbell, Converse, Miller, and Stokes 1960) confirmed what the Columbia research team had suggested: stable factors such as group membership and party identification were the things that best explained people's decisions during campaigns. The campaign seemed to have little if any effect. Even worse, Campbell et alia discovered that there was a great divide between average citizens and political elites in terms of their engagement in politics, levels of political information, and ideological connectedness (Campbell, Converse, Miller and Stokes 1960, 216).[1] Voters were not well equipped to deal with the information presented to them in campaigns.

Something's Happening in America

Nevertheless, as political scientists were moving on to answer questions about why voters were unenlightened, politics was stirring anew in America. In 1964 Lyndon Johnson won in a landslide and then in 1968 decided not to run for reelection. Hubert Humphrey had an astoundingly dismal campaign season in 1968 but barely lost that election and George McGovern was rejected by moderate Democrats in 1972. Could it be that the stable forces identified by scholars in the 1940s and 1950s weren't as solid as once thought? Maybe the decade of the 1960s had changed people—made them more aware of issues and candidates' policy agendas, gotten them to engage in identity politics and shake off old allegiances? People seemed, after all, to be responding to the candidates and their positions on crises that were unfolding nationally and internationally. As the conformity of the 1950s passed, perhaps so too did the conformity of stable political and structural forces.

[1] One might imagine the pioneers of voting research releasing a grand sigh of relief upon the realization that campaigns did not matter much to an electorate that could not or would not process political information in a sophisticated manner anyway.

By the middle of the 1970s, political scientists were interested in figuring out exactly what role issues played in helping voters make up their minds in presidential elections. Having been persuaded by the Columbia and Michigan teams that party identification and other psychological and sociological factors explained voters' decisions very well, scholars were not so much directly interested anymore in how campaigns might factor into the decision, but wanted to know if party identification would maintain its stability in the face of the alleged rising importance of issues in elections.[2] As the theatrics and volatility of the 1960s came to a close, political scientists believed that issues and policy mattered to voters in important ways. What would it mean, after all, if topics like civil rights, the War in Vietnam, women's rights, the spread of communism, and the use of illegal substances did not affect people's political attitudes? Taking the investigation farther back on the causal chain, some researchers wanted to know what processes were identifying the issues that were influencing vote decisions.[3] As researchers labored away on questions about party identification and issue voting, the search for direct campaign effects was cast aside.

The Importance of the Economy

The scholarly interest in issues during the 1960s and 1970s was fertilized by the rise of a clever and promising paradigm in political science—rational choice, which viewed economic decision-making and political decision-making as similar. Rational choice theorists used the notion of utility maximization to explain behavioral outcomes in both disciplines. In describing Downs's work, Stanley Kelley Jr. wrote (Downs 1957, x):

> Downs assumes that political parties and voters act rationally in the pursuit of certain clearly specified goals—it is this assumption, in fact, that gives his theory its explanatory power. . . . just as firms that do not engage in the rational pursuit of profits are apt to cease to be firms, so politicians who do not pursue votes in a rational manner are apt to cease to be politicians.

Downs's economic theory of democracy was the first formal description of how voters and parties behave. While the Columbia and Michigan scholars had done great work in describing and explaining vote decisions (and making positive predictions) using empirical findings, Downs's work was different because it started with clearly stated assumptions about behavior and deduced logical conclusions. To argue with Downs's approach, one had to choose between two basic critiques: the assumptions were wrong or the conclusions did not follow logically.

[2] See Converse and Markus (1979).
[3] See Goldberg (1966); Brody and Page (1972); Page and Brody (1972); Jackson (1975).

An Economic Theory of Democracy spawned a great deal of research about voting.[4] One of the products of this research was a synthesis of work on retrospective voting and incumbents' performances in office (Fiorina 1981). Retrospective voting was a way for voters to cut the costs of becoming informed, as Downs suggested they should. Fiorina argued in *Retrospective Voting in American National Elections* that even the least interested and informed voters have one solid piece of data on which to base their vote: they know what their own lives were like during the previous administration's tenure in office. This idea conjures up images of politicians prodding voters to ask themselves, "What has so-and-so done for me lately?" Or, in perhaps the most obvious example of trying to cue voters to think retrospectively about his time in office, Ronald Reagan asked voters at the end of the 1980 debate in Cleveland, "Are you better off today than you were four years ago?" While many political factors could be evaluated retrospectively, Fiorina's work helped to make sense of how important the nation's economic situation could be to voters in elections.[5]

Gelman and King (1993) gave retrospective voting on the economy a twist by suggesting that people might not be perfectly informed about such things as the state of the nation's economy and that campaigns could go a long way toward actually informing people about such conditions (people certainly were well enough informed about their own economic condition). Indeed, their hunches were confirmed as voters in countries with longer campaign periods were shown to be more likely to use correct economic information in their vote decisions when compared to voters in democracies with short campaigns (Stevenson and Vavreck 2000; Arceneaux 2005). The nation's economy mattered to voters, but campaigns could have an effect on the economic information brought to bear on the vote choice.

The work of election forecasters, copious during this period, supports the notion that the nation's objective economic conditions are important to election outcomes (Kramer 1971; Tufte 1978; Rosenstone 1983, 1985; Abramowitz 1988; Campbell and Wink 1990; Fair 1978; Hibbs 1982; Lewis-Beck and Rice 1992; Campbell 1992). On the one hand, the role of the campaign was never more clearly minimized—for forecasters to generate correct outcomes about which party would win, they did not even need to know the names of the party nominees, let alone be sure that voters eventually learned their names. The "enlightenment" that Gelman and King identified seemed immaterial. On the other hand, the role of the campaign was never more clearly *defined*—the three-, four-, and five-point errors in these forecasting models, and the occasional years in which the models were wrong, pointed to a role for the campaign that

---

[4]For example, Black 1958; Plott 1967; Davis and Hinich 1966; Shepsle 1972; Page 1976; Enelow and Hinich 1984; Calvert 1985; Wittman 1977, 1983; Alesina 1988.

[5]Others also contributed to this line of research: Kinder, Adams, and Gronke 1989; Lewis-Beck 1988; Markus 1988; Kiewiet and Rivers 1985.

could be deterministic, even after indicators such as presidential popularity or approval ratings were factored into the prediction. While objective measures of national economic conditions do a very good job of predicting winning parties long before candidates have even been named, if voters do not understand what the objective economic conditions actually are, the forecasts will fail. It is possible that campaign learning is necessary in order to generate the regularity of success the forecasting models enjoy. And it is also possible that the candidates have something to do with this learning.

The Importance of the Media

At about the same time forecasters were celebrating the successes of their models and empirical implications from Downs's theory were being carried out, public opinion scholars began to uncover important media effects (McCombs and Shaw 1972; Iyengar and Kinder 1987; Robinson and Sheehan 1983). Their findings showed that the media had lasting effects on people's perceptions about issue importance. Thus, while news or other media programming was not successful at making people change their opinions on various topics, the media were able to make people change the relative importance of different issues (agenda setting). Further, the media could suggest the criteria on which government, elected officials, or candidates should be evaluated (priming).

Oddly, this public opinion work, coupled with the robust success of forecasters and the focus of rational choice scholars on the role of candidates in shaping voters' levels of uncertainty, breathed new air into the search for campaign effects. If the media could influence people in these subtle yet important ways, candidates could accomplish the same sort of thing through the media. Could this explain the four-point errors in the forecasting models? Or help voters become "fully informed" or confused (Shepsle 1972; Page 1976) about election choices? It was only a matter of time before Larry Bartels (1986) synthesized rational choice work and public opinion research into an empirical test for the effects of issue-position uncertainty on voting. It turned out that voters did have uncertainty about candidates' policy positions and that this uncertainty did have a (negative) influence on vote decisions (additionally, see Franklin 1991; Alvarez and Franklin 1994; Alvarez 1997). Interest in campaign effects was reborn. Nevertheless, this time, the larger theoretical construct was clear: campaigns mattered because issues mattered in elections. If uncertainty about candidates' policy positions was important to voters as they made up their minds (even subconsciously), then candidates could do things in their campaigns to help voters understand issue positions clearly. Some candidates, for example, might be better communicators; some might have clearer campaign plans; others might try to be too much to too many and suffer on Election Day. The possibilities for campaign effects were many.

A Theory of Campaign Effects

The marked progress in the search for campaign effects, however, did not constrain scholars to investigate these specific theoretical implications. What emerged from the decades of work on voting behavior and the rebirth of campaign studies in the 1980s was a proliferation of miscellany—and a stark lack of any theoretical focus (although see Popkin 1991; Johnston et al. 1992; Bartels 1986, 1988, 1996; Johnston et al. 2004; and Marcus, Neuman, and MacKuen 2000). The most prodigious area has been the study of advertising (Kern 1989; West 1993; Ansolabehere and Iyengar 1995; Finkel and Geer 1998; West 1997; Kahn and Kenney 1999; Freedman and Goldstein 1999; Wattenberg and Brians 1999; see Lau et al. 1999 for complete list of citations). In addition, media studies have been numerous (Freedman and Goldstein 1999; Just et al. 1996; Patterson 1992; Page 1996; Hetherington 1996; Paletz 1999; Sparrow 1999; Cook 1999). Debates (Hart 1984; Kahn and Kenney 2007), campaign events or visits (Holbrook 1996; Shaw 1999a, 1999b; Holbrook 1994, 1996; Campbell, Cherry, and Wink 1992; Geer 1988; Vavreck, Spiliotes, and Fowler 2002), and candidate discourse (Hart 2000; Vavreck 2001; Spiliotes and Vavreck 2002) have also received mainly independent attention from scholars. These discrete analyses each suggest important elements of a theory of presidential campaign effectiveness, and my goal is to position this vast collection of findings in the context of a parsimonious theory about how and why campaigns matter to voters—and to discuss and test the implications for candidate behavior in campaigns.

This book is about more than just whether campaigns for the presidency *matter*. My aim, intellectually, is to be more interesting than that. I want to demonstrate that we know, and have known for a long time, that campaigns are important and sometimes determinative in presidential elections; but we have missed the forest for the trees—so many trees. We publish study after study showing that the economy matters, that ads matter, that the news matters—yet there has been so little effort to integrate them into one theory about campaigns and candidate behavior; so little attention to the forest.

In his posthumous book, *The Strategy of Rhetoric: Campaigning for the American Constitution*, Bill Riker (1996) laments the fact that political scientists cannot tell candidates and campaign professionals what they really want to know, which is "what to say in campaigns" if they want to win elections. Riker argues further that contemporary forms of content analysis enhanced by spatial modeling will provide the answers to this essential question about politics. Although my efforts are different from Riker's, my mission is similar—to bring spatial modeling and content analysis together in a way that has not been done in order to blend theories of public opinion and voting behavior into a theoretical model of presidential campaigns that can be tested "by the accuracy of its predictions" (Downs 1960, 21), or more aptly in this case, the completeness of its explanations.

Political scientists know a great deal about elections, about forecasting winners, about partisanship, about decision-making, and about media effects, and yet, we have no coherent theory of campaign effects that integrates existing knowledge on these topics. Given what we know about what affects people and how they make decisions on Election Day, what can we say about how presidential campaigns can influence people? And, further, what are the implications for candidates and the way they campaign?

Integrating Literatures

The literature on forecasting elections shows that the state of the nation's economy matters a great deal in determining presidential-election outcomes in the aggregate. But the errors in these models are not inconsequential. Four percentage points has determined more than a few presidential elections in the last sixty years. What do the results from the forecasting literature imply about the behavior of candidates in campaigns? Perhaps nothing useful when taken alone—if you are not a member of the incumbent party in a good economy or a member of the out-party in a bad economy, the forecasting literature provides no counsel for you. But, microlevel findings suggest opinions of candidates change during campaigns (and even aggregate polls show this), so what drives shifting opinions? Public opinion research (McCombs and Shaw 1972; Iyengar and Kinder 1987; Iyengar 1991) provides a clue.

Television and newspaper coverage affects what voters think are important issues or problems (agenda setting), and helps to determine the criteria by which voters evaluate political leaders (priming). The extant research on the effectiveness of campaign advertising and effort illustrate that these mechanisms work. Combine this literature with the forecasting literature, and a story begins to emerge—candidates, through TV and newspapers, may be able to affect the criteria on which they are judged. More specifically, they may be able to make the nation's economy a more or less important criterion of judgment among voters. If candidates can prime the economy, voters may respond.

Much is known about voters' willingness to consider economic conditions when making a vote choice, too. Theories of retrospective voting (Key 1966; Kramer 1971; Tufte 1978; Fiorina 1981) demonstrate that voters think about the economy in routine fashion, sometimes without even knowing or understanding they are doing it. The past, it turns out, is a good predictor of future behavior by presidents—and it is a signal that is easily accessible to voters (Downs 1957; Fiorina 1981; Popkin 1991). Candidates have an incentive to remind voters about past performances of their administrations or parties when conditions favor them—particularly on economic issues.

But what about those parties that do not benefit from economic conditions?

What can they prime in voters' minds? Rational choice theory and spatial voting (Downs 1960; Shepsle 1972; Enelow and Hinich 1984) coupled with notions of issue salience (RePass 1971; Page 1976; Pomper 1975; Nie, Verba, and Petrocik 1976) and issue ownership (Petrocik 1980) suggest that voters can evaluate candidates on important issues, and some issues will naturally advantage one party over the other. For example, if a candidate is successful at priming an issue during the campaign, one implication of the spatial model is that in order for the candidate to get maximum gains from priming this issue, it ought to be an issue on which most voters' positions are closer to the priming candidate's position than to the opponent's position. It does not help to prime issues in a campaign if increasing the importance of these issues encourages people to vote for the opposition.

The importance of these noneconomic issues is something that political scientists have written about on occasion but not regularly (Page 1976; Franklin 1991; Hammond and Humes 1993; Glazer and Lohmann 1999; Carsey 2000; Simon 2002; Brasher 2003) except to note that parties tend to associate with a set of issues on which they are seen as being more competent than the opposition (Petrocik 1980; Spiliotes and Vavreck 2002; Powell and Whitten 1993; but see Sides 2006). Foreign policy, crime and safety, candidate traits, and domestic policy are the most often studied noneconomic campaign issues.

The synthesis of this existing literature suggests the following: If you are advantaged by the economy, prime that. If you are not advantaged by the economy, prime an issue you "own"—whether ownership means your party is favorably associated with the issue or you have an electoral advantage on the issue.

Finally, not every voter is movable in the same manner—the long literature on party identification (Campbell, Converse, Miller, and Stokes 1960) reminds us that a majority of voters identify with one of the two major parties and that this identification drives their vote choice in perhaps a psychological, not political, way. But partisans, even strong ones, have to be mobilized, and weak ones may have to be activated. Campaigns can do both these things (Hillygus and Jackman 2003), but in terms of persuasion, we might expect the most susceptible voters to be those with low to mid levels of political sophistication (Converse 1964; McGuire 1968; Zaller 1992). Zaller argues that these people are likely to receive campaign messages and unlikely to have strong enough predispositions to cause the immediate rejection of new information. Campaigns may work on some voters more than others.

Each of these sets of findings is important to motivating a theory of presidential campaigns, but each is also central to explaining the individual-level mechanisms that drive aggregate- or candidate-level results about campaign effectiveness. Too often we think of the work in voting behavior as a set of discrete findings—perhaps even each in competition with the other over which model identifies the "true" state of the world. This approach is not productive. By coupling rational choice theories about proximity and retrospective voting with theories of priming, attitude change, and partisan activation, an understanding of individual-level voting behavior in campaigns begins to emerge that has very specific implications for the behavior of candidates in campaigns.

My plan in the pages that follow is to start with an established model of voting behavior and deduce a new theory of campaign effects born from models of public opinion and voting, taking account of the existing implications mentioned above. One of the simplest expressions of voting behavior is Downs's notion that people vote for the candidate who will deliver the most benefits to them under certain specific conditions.[6] This is certainly not the only compelling model of voter decision-making, but it is a simple, well-known model and a good place to begin thinking about why and how campaigns might matter to voters. Extending the spatial model's predictions to candidate behavior in this way yields more power to the theory of campaigns by generating scientific predictions about what candidates can do to maximize votes. The model's logical and formal setup also enables me to use inference as I evaluate the past behavior of candidates in campaigns, making it a productive apparatus for explanation as well as prediction.

Spatial Voting: The Past as Predictor of the Future

Downs's original assumptions in the spatial model were admittedly narrow. He assumes that candidates want to maximize votes, and voters want to maximize the benefits they get from government. These assumptions have two important implications for the way parties compete and the way voters gather information. Primarily, the assumptions imply that with a unimodal distribution of voters on an ideological dimension, if parties want to win elections, they will evaluate the positions of voters and take a position that will maximize votes. This is an important element of the model: parties or candidates take policy positions in order to win elections, not vice versa. Secondarily, because voters do not have perfect information about candidates, parties, and politics, they need help learning about these things during elections. They need, Downs argued, shortcuts to cue them about how candidates or parties are likely to behave if elected. While early voting-behavior researchers suggested that these cues come from other voters—from family, coworkers, and friends—it is possible that such cues come from the candidates themselves (Page 1976; Bartels 1986; Franklin 1991; Alvarez 1997) as they reset the agenda and prime favorable dimensions in their campaigns. These two implications of Downs's assumptions—that candidates adapt policy positions or priorities to suit the voting public and that voters search for cues and signals during elections to reduce the costs of gathering information—form the basis for a formal and positive theory of campaign effects.

---

[6]The assumptions are: voters are utility maximizers, preferences can be expressed with a Euclidean distance measure, and voters' preferences are single-peaked.

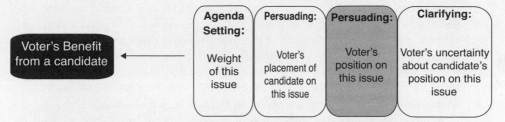

Figure 2.1 A Theory of Campaign Effects Derived from the Spatial Voting Model
Unshaded cells above (Agenda Setting, Persuading, and Clarifying) represent the three
things candidates can do to influence their vote share.

Downs's theory of voting assumes that voters have single-peaked preferences
over policy positions (or party platforms); in other words, candidates' positions
on issues that move away from a voter's preferred position in absolute terms are
increasingly less appealing to voters. Downs further assumes that voters know
and understand their own policy positions with certainty. Enelow and Hinich
(1981) adapt the basic spatial voting model by assuming a specific shape for the
loss function—a quadratic form, or basic concave shape. The spatial model, as
presented by Enelow and Hinich, has important implications about why and
how campaigns can matter.

Complete details of Enelow and Hinich's model and the derivations that
form the basis for my argument about campaign effects and candidate behavior
can be found in the Appendix to this chapter. The simple graphic presented in
figure 2.1, provides the intuition about the features of the spatial voting model
that can be directly influenced by candidates in campaigns. As you will see, the
spatial voting model actually provides considerable counsel to candidates about
how to win elections, although political scientists have mainly used it to explain
and predict the behavior of voters and parties. In the pages that follow, I extend
its application to explain the behavior of candidates in campaigns.

In figure 2.1 the dark square represents a voter's overall evaluation of a candidate. Ultimately, voters compare these evaluations or utilities across candidates
as they decide whom to cast their ballot for. The unshaded boxes above are the
three terms that can be influenced by the campaign as a result of spatial voting.

My interpretation of the model leverages the fact that each issue has a weight
or level of importance associated with it and that this weight multiplies the
effect of how close a voter is to a candidate on this issue. In Enelow and Hinich's
(1984) adaptation of the model, issues are conceived of as having potentially
draining effects on a candidate's vote share, so weights are represented as negative effects.[7] A voter's position on an issue is differenced from where that voter

---

[7]Actually, it is not vote share that the spatial model predicts, but an individual voter's benefit from
a candidate, or that voter's utility for that candidate. Voters then compare utilities across candidates
to make a vote choice. For simplicity's sake, I use the term vote share here to describe the model.

thinks a candidate stands on that issue, and this difference is squared in order to keep the numbers positive (and keep the math tractable). This squared distance is multiplied by the weight of the issue (which, in this construction, is negative). You can see how large distances between voter and candidate positions result in bigger losses to candidates than smaller distances—or no distance, which results in no loss for the candidate. There is one additional element of the spatial model that gets multiplied by the weight of the issue and that is a term representing how sure the voter is of where the candidate stands on this issue. If a voter is very sure of the candidate's position, this uncertainty term will be quite small, making it a minimal drain on candidate vote share. If the voter is very unclear about the candidate's position, the uncertainty term will be large, and when multiplied by the weight of the issue, it will become a substantial drain on potential votes. Thus, the important candidate-influenced terms in the spatial voting model are the weight of the issue, the candidate's perceived position on the issue, the certainty with which the voter can place the candidate on the issue, and finally, the benefit this voter gets from this particular candidate. Candidates can affect all of these terms.

My theory of campaign effects suggests candidates can engage in three behaviors in order to affect voters' assessments. The first is simply agenda setting—an attempt to refocus an election or change the weights associated with certain issues. In other words, this kind of candidate behavior is a direct attempt to tell voters what should be important in their voting decisions, but it is done implicitly by talking repeatedly about the things the candidate believes should be most important to vote choice. The second behavior is persuading—an attempt to educate voters that a candidate holds a specific position on an issue, regardless of whether that is truly the candidate's position. Persuasion can be done by a candidate about his own positions, but is also used by candidates to paint their opponent's positions as unpopular.[8] The third and final thing that candidates can do in campaigns to influence votes is to clarify their positions on already important issues.[9] If a candidate is lucky enough to hold a popular position on an issue that is of great importance to voters, that candidate can benefit from making it clear to voters that he or she holds this very popular position.

The idea underlying the spatial voting model is that voters know their own positions on issues, that is, they know the ways they would like the government to address issues; and they know where the candidates' positions are on these same issues, or they can at least make a guess as to the candidates' positions with some associated level of uncertainty about that guess. The final step, then, is for

---

[8]Usually we think of persuasion as altering the voters' *own* issue positions; in this case, I use it to refer to voters' placements of *the candidates* on the issues.

[9]The candidate must clarify a position on an already important issue because to do so for an issue about which no one cared would be a waste of effort. This observation is derived directly from the expectation of the spatial model, which shows that the uncertainty term is eventually multiplied by the weight of the issue.

the voters to compare the candidates and vote for the one they are closest to on these issues.

All of this implies that policy positions mean something to voters about policy outcomes—that voters can make the connection between a policy position and what the *likely* government outcome will be if that position is enacted into legislation or if a particular candidate is elected. This is a prospective type of voting because voters are making decisions about whom to vote for based on what they believe the future will be like under each candidate's presidency. The kind of electorate needed to carry out such a task would have to be sophisticated enough to make the connection between policies and outcomes, in general, but more to the point, it would have to be able to make this connection between stated policy positions by candidates known with some uncertainty and *future* outcomes. That requires a pretty sophisticated voter, and some scholars (Achen and Bartels 2002) have cited early voting (Campbell et al. 1960) and public opinion evidence (Campbell et al. 1960; Converse 1964) to argue that American voters are not equipped to make such prospective evaluations.[10] How can an electorate of mainly unsophisticated, politically uninterested voters make connections between their own policy preferences, the preferences of candidates, and likely outcomes in the future? This seems more a task for political junkies or hobbyists, people who read about politics on a regular basis and tune in to hear George Stephanopoulos or John King talk about politics.

What average voters seem better able to do is evaluate incumbent parties retrospectively on their tenure in office. This mechanism requires no policy orientation, only a results orientation that almost every voter is inclined to have. In the aptly titled *Retrospective Voting in American National Elections*, Fiorina writes (1981, 10):

> Retrospective voting requires much less of the voter than prospective voting. The retrospective voter need not spend his life watching "Meet the Press" and reading the *New York Times*. He can look at the evening news and observe the coffins being unloaded from Air Force transports, the increasing price of a basket of groceries between this month and last, and the police arresting demonstrators of one stripe or another. . . . he can go to the polls and indicate whether or not he likes the way those who can "cognize the issue" are in fact doing so. He passes judgments on leaders, not policies.

Instead of guessing about voters' preferences on issues, then, politicians need only anticipate voters' reactions to the *conditions* brought about by the policy instruments they enact. If you believe Fiorina, this is a pretty easy job. Fiorina suggests that large majorities of people prefer "peace to war, high employment

[10]Downs got around the problem by assuming voters made evaluations based on current times not future ones. In other words, voters simply ask themselves if the policies of the out-party would have been better than the current policies.

and stable prices to unemployment and inflation, social harmony to social tension, energy self-sufficiency to dependence on imported oil" (11). It is not hard for candidates to know voters' preferences over these kinds of results. They are what Stokes (1966) called "valence issues"—issues on which no one disagrees about the desired outcomes.

This retrospective model of voting is not intended to imply that voters live entirely in the past, evaluating candidates and parties based only on the conditions present during their terms in office. Voters, even unsophisticated ones, may be somewhat more concerned about the future than that. Thus the simple results-oriented retrospective model may not be as compelling as a more nuanced retrospective model that works in concert with the spatial voting model and allows voters to make judgments about the future by considering the outcomes of the past.

Downs's spatial model can be thought of as retrospective, albeit one that maintains the importance of the connection between policy positions and real-world outcomes. For Downs, retrospective voting is a cost-cutting mechanism. Knowing what conditions are like under the incumbent party is easier than figuring out what the future might be like under one or the other of the parties. Since we live under the conditions set by the incumbent party every day, we can easily be sure, more sure than we are about future conditions, what life is or was like under the party's rule. If a party's positions are consistent over time, a voter can use the past as a guide to the policies the parties would implement in the future. Thus, Fiorina writes, "Downsian retrospective voting is a means to prospective voting" (13). The spatial model allows for both retrospective evaluations and prospective projections. As candidates reset the agenda, persuade voters, and clarify positions, they may be doing so on retrospective dimensions of valence issues (like the state of the nation's economy) or on prospective dimensions of more spatial issues (whether to have free trade within North America).

Retrospective Voting and Campaign Effects

What does the retrospective or prospective nature of voter decision-making in campaigns have to do with a theory of campaign effects? It shows clearly how retrospective evaluations of valence issues can be thought of in spatial voting terms. Thus, we can theorize about how these types of issues can be expected to affect the way candidates campaign. Whether voters are merely rewarding the incumbent during an economic boom for providing desirable outcomes, or making projections based on the past about what the future will be like under this party if it is re-elected, incumbent parties can be expected to try to reset the electoral agenda onto issues from which they will benefit from voters' retrospective judgments.

Voters, however, may not be aware of good conditions and may need candidates to tell them how good things are—this is the argument first posed by Gelman and King (1993), tested by Stevenson and Vavreck (2000), Arceneaux (2006), Bartels (2006), and strengthened by Zaller (2002). Gelman and King asked the simple question, why are election outcomes so predictable well in advance of Election Day (based only on economic forecasts) when poll results during the campaign are so volatile? Their answer was that based on objective economic conditions, we can predict election winners easily months before the campaign, but voters are generally not aware of these objective conditions until about six weeks prior to the election. At that point, Gelman and King argued that voters begin to pay attention to their upcoming vote decision and to learn about objective political and economic conditions, thus the polls begin to resemble the earlier prediction and the eventual outcome. Stevenson and Vavreck (2000) bolstered this finding with evidence from thirteen democracies around the world and 113 election periods. In countries with longer campaigns, in which voters have more time to learn about objective conditions, real economic indicators are better predictors of outcomes than in countries with very short campaign lengths (some as short as three weeks). Campaigns, and more to the point candidates, can prime voters to think retrospectively about objective, fundamental conditions such as the economy (agenda setting) and *what those conditions are* (persuasion). Candidates may even compete over getting their interpretations of the fundamental national conditions to voters, as many pundits believe Clinton and Bush did in 1992 (see Hetherington 1996 for a rich discussion of this). Voters need the past to make decisions about the future; and even though they just lived through it, voters' views of the past may need some shaping and sharpening from political elites.

Individual-Level Characteristics and Campaign Effects

Incumbents in good economies do not always win, and challengers in good economies do not always lose, and while some of this may be due to successful resetting of the electoral agenda or persuading voters about the real conditions of the country, it is quite likely that there are other factors influencing voters in elections that have little to do with the issues and where the candidates stand on them.

Voters are not blank slates, aliens come down from another planet every four years to make decisions in elections. To the contrary, they are people playing the roles of family members, neighbors, colleagues, and friends—all of whom have different experiences with politics and a unique political history. For some people, their political histories are empty. They have never been interested in politics, never voted, and never want to. For others, their political identities are wound up in a complex amalgam consisting of everything from eavesdropping on their parents' postdinner conversations about foreign wars to the realization that taxes were taking away a solid chunk of their first paychecks to wondering when Social Security will dry up. To believe that presidential campaigns affect the people in these groups and everyone in between in the same way would be a crude attempt to show that campaigns matter.

Some people are interested in politics and gather lots of information about it. Others are happy enough not to know much, as long as the garbage is picked up and schools stay open. There may be some who remain blissfully ignorant of politics even when these things cease to happen. For those who are interested and aware, their political experiences or predispositions may color the way the presidential campaigns affect them. Their political beliefs may limit their willingness to accept new information about objective conditions or anything else that might be relevant to the campaign.

Since the beginning of voting research, party identification has been a powerful force. The Michigan team of researchers investigating the elections of the early 1950s thought of party identification as a psychological attachment (Campbell et al. 1960). In this view, party identification truly is an *identity*, and people use it in much the way they use other identifications, like woman and black. This identification, they wrote,

> can persist without legal recognition or evidence of formal membership and even without a consistent record of party support. Most Americans have this sense of attachment with one party or the other. And, for the individual who does, the strength and direction of party identification are facts of central importance in accounting for attitude and behavior (121).

The concept of party ID characterizes the individual's affective orientation to an important group-object; it serves as the supplier of cues by which the voter evaluates the elements of politics. The argument put forth by Campbell et alia (1960) suggests that people have an attachment to one of the parties and that this helps them to organize and understand political information—and this ultimately affects their behavior. Thus, the behavior of candidates in campaigns and its effect on voters may be mitigated by the party identification of voters. For example, if a candidate is successful at refocusing the election off of retrospective evaluations of the economy and onto some other issue, say foreign policy, the candidate may find that the "refocusing" works very well for voters who are affiliated with his own political party and less well for voters who are members of the other party.

Another way in which party identification or other political predispositions may mollify the behavior of candidates in campaigns is through informational effects. The effects of what candidates do in campaigns may be moderated by how much political information a voter possesses. John Zaller re-introduced this idea to political science in 1992 in *The Nature and Origins of Mass Opinion*.

Zaller's work was built on four simple axioms, the first two of which illustrate how attitudes can condition behavior. Zaller posits that politically aware people are more likely to be exposed to and comprehend political messages, and that people tend to resist arguments that are inconsistent with their political predispositions, although they have to know enough to be aware that the argument is inconsistent with their views and be aware enough that they are exposed to arguments at all (1992, 42–44). In other words, most attitude change comes from the middle levels of political awareness because low-awareness people, the blissfully ignorant, are never exposed to new arguments, and high-awareness people, the *Meet the Press* crowd, can successfully filter out political arguments that conflict with their preexisting opinions. Thus, the effects of candidate behavior in campaigns may be different for people with differing levels of political awareness.

Zaller argues that the effect of persuasive messages depends on exposure to messages, the other ideas already present in a person's mind, and the opposing ideas to which the person is concurrently exposed (266). For presidential campaigns, in a country with many partisan identifiers and pervasive news coverage of politics, maybe it is difficult to believe that attitudes are changed at all. There is high exposure to two competing messages, and many people have strong predispositions to limit their attitude change. "But," Zaller writes, "if a person has little prior information and little access to alternative communication flows, information reaching him from a . . . campaign will have a large effect" (267). A single stream of campaign information to a political novice can make a difference. This could happen in presidential campaigns in places where one candidate advertises or visits and the other candidate does not, or when a candidate or party reaches out to a previously disinterested group of voters.

More important for a theory of campaign effects is the filtering effect of a person's values, or predispositions. These are the things that enable a voter to sort through the many campaign messages sent by candidates and choose which ones to believe, which to ignore, and which will lead to changes in opinions or attitudes. Zaller calls this kind of filtering "partisan resistance," when the values that act as the filter are based on partisanship or ideology. He writes, "Democrats and Republicans tend to reject messages from the opposing party, and liberals and conservatives reject persuasive communications that are inconsistent with their ideologies" (267). Even the most well-articulated political campaign might have different effects among voters of different parties or ideologies.

In the pages that follow, I account for these individual-level differences as I examine whether the behavior of candidates in campaigns is consistent with my theory of campaign effects. I expect to find candidates engaging in agenda setting, persuasion, and the clarifying of their positions whether the issues candidates talk about are valence or positional in nature, and regardless of whether voters make decisions prospectively or retrospectively. Further, I expect these campaign activities to affect voters with different ideological, partisan, and awareness profiles in different ways.

Chapter Three

CONTEXT MATTERS: A CAMPAIGN TYPOLOGY

IF VOTERS BEHAVE THE way Downs describes, comparing the positions of candidates across issues to their own positions on the same issues, then how do candidates decide which issues to stress and which to remain silent about? When candidates sit down at the table, how do they think about their campaign's message?

Political scientist Bill Riker (1996, 106) suggests candidates look for issues that are ripe for "domination" (because when one side has an advantage on an issue, the other side ignores it). This is not unlike John Petrocik's (1980) answer to this question, which is that candidates' campaign issues are made up of those issues on which the candidate is deemed more competent than the opposition.

In practice, there are a variety of answers to these questions. At American University's Campaign Management Institute, a session on "Strategy, Theme, and Message" is taught in which participants are told that the most important thing about a candidate's theme and message is that it not contradict who the candidate actually is. For example, if a candidate is twenty-seven years old and running for Congress for the first time, he would not choose a theme and message that stresses his wisdom and experience. Similarly, a candidate who likes to dress in dark pin-striped suits and wear glasses should probably not have a campaign theme centered on progressive ideas. But this is just one notion about how to generate a campaign message. When I asked Michael Dukakis (2002) how he came up with his campaign message in 1988, his answer was simple:

> You don't come up with new ideas when you run for president, you've been in government for a long time and you stand for things. These are the things you believe in and the things you've worked for already. You run on those things.

My hunch is that there are as many answers to the question about generating a campaign message as there are candidates running for office and consultants looking for work. This is not a book about how candidates come up with their campaign messages. Instead, I explain the choices candidates have already made in light of the assumption that candidates want to win elections and voters want to maximize the benefits they get from government. In this chapter I answer a simple question: how might a rational candidate act, given the assumptions of the spatial model and my theory of campaign effects, in order to win an election?[1]

[1] I use the word "rational" in the economic sense. It refers to the way in which decision-makers

Surprisingly, the answer to this question is also simple: a rational candidate will exploit the electoral context to his or her advantage—the rational candidate pursues an efficient path to victory. The most efficient path to victory is going to be different for different candidates—as each possesses a unique set of policy positions and characteristics. When these candidate-level specifics are coupled with the nature of the times, efficient paths to election begin to take shape. One obviously efficient strategy is for a candidate to leverage his or her existing strengths. Or as Riker (1996) might have said, to engage in "heresthetics"; or using Schattschneider's language (1975), to displace and replace conflicts.[2] While the general theories laid out by Riker and Schattschneider are appealing, I would like to be more specific than merely suggesting that candidates leverage their strengths. In order to say anything more specific than that, however, knowledge of the actual electoral context is needed. This may seem unsatisfying to people who believe that it is akin to saying, "the right strategy depends on the times." A strategy that depends on context, however, is not one that is unpredictable. What kinds of contextual things are important to candidates as they make their plans? Very specific kinds of things.

For starters, national conditions such as economic prosperity and decline, or war and peace; and even certain characteristics of candidates can be important contextual variables. Specifically, compelling candidate characteristics are those to which a candidate is inescapably wedded. A candidate who took bribes in a prior office, one who flew to a foreign country to sign a peace treaty that bears his name, or one who comes into the political system from outside it are solidly associated with these characteristics. These events cannot be erased or reinvented the way other candidate characteristics can. For example, a candidate who states publicly that he is pro-choice is not inextricably linked to this position forever. He can change his mind somewhat reasonably. But there is nothing the first list of candidates, can do to change the noted characteristics. The first candidate, described above, who took the bribe, is not going to win an election that turns on honesty. The second candidate cannot be painted as a warmonger, and the third candidate, the outsider, can easily win an election when voters are feeling cynical about Beltway politics. This is the difference between

---

evaluate the alternatives they face by the relationship between the choice and the goal. Rationality refers to the decisions about the *means* of achieving a goal. A rational candidate moves toward victory in a way that, to the best of his or her knowledge, uses the least possible input of scarce resources; rational decision-makers are efficient pursuers of their goals. Rationality refers to the processes of action, not to the ends or even the success at reaching desired ends.

[2]Riker's term, "heresthetics," is the process of structuring a contest to leverage preexisting dimensions on which advantages are already held. Riker argued in his work on campaign strategy that candidates should not spend time trying to persuade voters that their positions are better than the opposition; nor should they converge to the median voter's position on issues. Instead, candidates should refocus the election onto a dimension on which they are already advantaged. This is similar to Schattschneider's (1975) idea of "displacing" conflicts.

a characteristic that can matter and one that cannot. For something about a candidate to be important to the electoral context, it must be something that the candidate cannot change or manipulate easily; and obviously, it must be something about which the voters care or can be made to care.

Saying context matters is not the same as saying campaign themes have to be decided on a case-by-case basis. If we know what issues or ideas are regularly important to voters during elections (or can be made important) and how pub- lic opinion typically reacts to these issues, we can characterize campaign mes- sages that help candidates efficiently win elections. I start with a campaign ty- pology that is general enough to be applied to all presidential elections and apply it more specifically to actual candidates over the course of the book. Throughout the remainder of the book I use language suggesting that the the- ory is useful as a predictive tool, however, I examine past campaigns to highlight the explanatory power of the theory. To be clear, my interest is in explanation *and* prediction. It is not enough for this theory to generate accurate predictions about what types of campaigns candidates are likely to run and whether those campaigns will win elections. I also want to know why these predictive relation- ships work—thus in chapter 6 I focus on the individual-level mechanisms driv- ing the aggregate- and candidate-level results.

THEORETICAL PREDICTIONS

My theory of campaign effects suggests three ways that candidates can increase votes: agenda setting, persuading, and clarifying. Clearly, it is much easier for a candidate to take advantage of an issue that is already important to voters than for a candidate to have to *convince* voters of an issue's importance. But in order to run this type of clarifying campaign, a candidate must be on the right side of the issue. To complicate things even more, in order to get any kind of significant increase in votes from this issue, public opinion on it should be one-sided—the more one- sided the better. This already sounds like a challenging task. Are there any issues with consistently lopsided public opinion about which voters routinely care?

According to the Gallup Organization, which has been asking people about the nation's most important problem since 1946, there are a couple of issues that are consistently on the minds of voters during election years. These include foreign policy, the economy, crime and safety, and health care. Two of these is- sues stand out for their prominence within years and steady presence over years: the economy and foreign policy (Smith 1985). Table 3.1 presents the percentage of Americans who named foreign policy and the economy as the nation's most important problems in the first quarter of election years since 1952.[3] Foreign

---

[3]In 1988 I had to use data from later in the year as Gallup did not ask this question in the first quarter.

TABLE 3.1
Percentage of People Believing Foreign Policy and the Economy Are Nation's
Most Important Problem, 1952–2008

Poll Date	Foreign Policy	Economy	Number of Respondents
Jan. 6, 1952	4	29	1500
March 8, 1956	36	31	1559
Feb. 4, 1960	37	17	1638
March 27, 1964	38	14	1676
Jan. 4, 1968	57	15	1502
Feb. 4, 1972	32	38	1502
Jan. 2, 1976	9	71	1572
Jan. 25, 1980	48	43	1597
Feb. 10, 1984	22	38	1610
Sep. 7, 1988	9	40	1003
March 26, 1992	3	95	1004
Jan. 12, 1996	4	35	1039
March 10, 2000	4	25	1006
March 11, 2004	19	53	1005
March 9, 2008	26	55	1012

Source: The Gallup Organization.

policy is mentioned more often than the economy from 1956 to 1968, but in 1972 the tide begins to change (along with the world), and the economy becomes more of a concern to people throughout the latter part of the decade. This culminates in 1992, when nearly every person Gallup polled mentioned the economy as the nation's most important problem. Foreign policy and the economy are good possibilities for issues on which candidates can leverage their popularity.

There is, however, something special about the economy as a campaign issue. Not only do voters think about the state of the nation's economy as an important problem during election years, the weight of existing evidence showing the important role of economic conditions on electoral outcomes is extraordinary. The simplicity of the relationship between public opinion and the nation's economy also makes it attractive as a campaign issue. Public opinion on retrospective evaluations of the economy is easy to predict—prosperity is always good, and further, opinion on this issue is incredibly one-sided—everyone prefers prosperity to decline.[4]

Foreign policy does not provide the same clarity, stability, or transparency in terms of the preferred opinion over time or the percentage split between opinions. While it is true that everyone prefers peace to war, opinion is much more divided about how to achieve or maintain peace than about how to do the same for prosperity. Consider the history of incumbency during war. Voters rarely dismiss an incumbent president during times of war, but sometimes (as for Truman and Johnson) things are going so badly that incumbents decide not to run for a second term. We rarely see cases of incumbents in good economies deciding not to run for office again. There is more stability and predictability in public opinion about the economy than there is in attitudes about foreign policy.

In the fall of 1952, the Gallup Organization asked Americans whether the United States should have sent military forces into Korea. Forty-three percent of Americans said yes and 37 percent said no (the Gallup Organization, October 17, 1952). The same divided opinion existed in the winter of 1968 when Gallup asked about the use of military force in Vietnam—42 percent thought it was a mistake and 46 percent thought it was not (the Gallup Organization, February 1, 1968). Even though this issue is important to voters during the 1968 election, a candidate who thinks he can win on this issue is mistaken, since roughly half of all Americans are on each side. What is further interesting about public opinion on war and foreign policy is that it changes as the wars change. Support for the use of force in Korea grew over the course of 1952, while support for Vietnam shrank during 1968. Candidates cannot know what is going to happen in a war, or in the world, that might change public opinion about the use of military force, making this issue a relatively risky one on which to base a clarifying campaign. A candidate could find him- or herself clarifying a position on this important foreign policy issue only to find public opinion on the issue changing in the middle of the year or campaign, along with the candidate's benefits from being on the "right side" of this issue.[5]

The way the media cover war and foreign policy in recent years also complicates the use of this as a clarifying issue. Daily or even hourly pictures from the battlefield are now the norm. The instant something happens, Americans know

[4] The reason I use retrospective evaluations of the economy here instead of economic policy is because when people report the economy as one of the nation's most important problems to Gallup, they are not referring to the president's tax policy or budget proposals, but to the state of the nation's economy or how well they are doing individually. When people do state a specific policy directly, Gallup represents it as its own category. The fact that people use general valence language when describing economic problems, however, does not mean that these retrospective evaluations implicitly lack specific policy content. They should be viewed as a proxy for the continuation (or discontinuation) of the incumbent party's economic policy, even though voters do not explicitly use this language.

[5] Unlike economic downturns, a solid case can be made for going to war (or increasing troop and spending levels), and has been made during this time period.

about it and are reacting to it. It is very difficult for candidates to predict the quantity of information to which voters will be subjected on this issue.

It is also true that the economy can change over the course of an election year; however, two things mitigate the risk associated with this issue. Primarily, changes in the economy happen gradually and progressively, barring some unusual occurrence. This gives candidates confidence that the state of the economy in the second quarter of the election year is a good predictor of the state of the economy during the summer and in to the election (or at least a good predictor of the trend). Additionally, the way voters experience the economy helps to make it a much wiser choice as a clarifying issue. The economy has an ethereal quality to it—it is housing starts, consumer confidence, unemployment, and inflation all wrapped into one experience. Most people do not have direct exposure to these things, except when things are going particularly badly, making ongoing evaluations of the economy by voters difficult. In fact, Americans mostly learn about the state of the economy when quarterly (or monthly) statistics from the Bureau of Labor Statistics or some other executive branch agency are reported on the news. Since this information is only released a few times a year and usually takes some time to compile, voters are learning in October about the state of their economy during the preceding summer months. There are no "this just in . . ." updates on the economy as there are about foreign affairs. Candidates know exactly how much information voters will have on the economy at all times during the campaign. In short, public opinion on the economy is highly weighted, its direction is easy to predict, and candidates can know whether the state of the nation's economy will benefit them or hurt them very early in the election year, when they are putting together their campaign plans. All of these factors make the economy critical to candidates' decisions about the issues and ideas on which they will campaign.

A Campaign Typology

Clarifying Campaigns

Candidates who are helped by the state of the nation's economy should run campaigns in which they simply clarify their positions or their role in fostering the good economic times or their lack of a role in bringing about bad times.[6] These candidates are clarifying candidates, and the economy is the clarifying issue. Since this issue is always important to voters in presidential elections, the

---

[6]Duch and Stevenson (2008) introduce an interesting idea into the individual-level modeling of economic voting and suggest that voters reward or punish parties in terms of economic performance by figuring out to what extent the incumbent party has control over the economic conditions. This raises an interesting role for the campaign as a set of messages aimed at helping voters extract that competency signal about the incumbent party.

candidate who benefits from the economic context need only clarify this link to win favor among voters. This is the first deduction from the theory of campaign effects and it has two corollaries: clarifying candidates should talk about the economy more than any other issue in their campaigns, because they get easy benefits from doing so, and they should talk about it more than their opponent talks about it. In the latter case, if a clarifying candidate does not dominate the discussion of the economy, his opponent may be able to convince voters that the clarifying candidate is incapable of sustaining the economic boom or digging out of the slump.[7] The effects of this type of campaign among voters ought to be observed as a decrease in the uncertainty measure associated with economic evaluations as voters become more certain that things are "good" or "bad" (and that the incumbent party is linked to that condition) depending on what the clarifying candidate is telling them.[8]

Insurgent Campaigns

Candidates who will not be helped by the state of the nation's economy have to find something else to talk about in their campaigns. Quite naturally, these candidates ought to try to refocus the election off the economy and onto an issue from which they can benefit. These types of candidates are insurgent candidates and the issues on which they run are called insurgent issues.[9] It is the insurgent candidate who is engaging in Riker's classic heresthetic effort. These candidates try to leverage current conditions and opinions on issues in a way that will benefit them to the detriment of their opponents. In Riker's work on political manipulation, the act of heresthetics always seems effortless (beyond

[7]The clarifying candidate's opponent may also want to talk about the economy to claim that he or she, too, can continue the prosperity, but economic evaluations in the Downs and Fiorina framework are made retrospectively about the incumbent party. Downs goes so far as to say explicitly that voters know what life is like under the incumbent party, therefore there is no ambiguity associated with generalizing about the future from the present. In evaluating the opposition party, even if it claims the same positions on economic issues (or the same valence signal), it is more difficult for voters to know with certainty what life under an out-party administration (given current conditions) would be like. This ambiguity makes voters less likely to believe the opposition party can deliver the same benefits that the voter *knows* the incumbent party can deliver.

[8]Alvarez (1992) finds that a reduction in uncertainty will also lead to an increase in the weight of the issue as voters weigh more heavily those issues on which they have less uncertainty. This may or may not be the case for retrospective evaluations of the economy, which are already highly important to voters on Election Day.

[9]I realize the use of the word "insurgent" to describe candidates who need to refocus the election off of the economy is a nonstandard use of the word, especially since we typically think of an insurgent as someone who rebels against the government or the leadership of their party. In my usage here, think of the insurgent candidate as rebelling against the structural conditions that predetermine the contest in which he or she is about to compete. The insurgent candidate is striking out against power—the power of the economy as a structural feature of American presidential elections. He or she has to battle general political rhythms and redefine the election on new terms.

identifying the strategy). In reality, these candidates have their work cut out for them.

There are two corollaries to the theory of campaign effects that describe the insurgent campaign, and they have to do with issue choice. The choice of insurgent issue is critical. The issue must be one on which the insurgent candidate benefits from the state of public opinion more than the clarifying candidate does (and the more one-sided opinion is on this issue, the better). More important, the insurgent issue should be one on which the clarifying candidate has previously taken, or is constrained in some way by, an unpopular position or characteristic. This is vitally important. If the insurgent candidate successfully resets the electoral agenda onto this other issue from which he hopes to benefit, and then the clarifying candidate can come along and take the exact same position on this issue as the insurgent candidate, then the latter can split the votes on this issue with the insurgent candidate, and the insurgent candidate will not win. If the clarifying candidate is not constrained in some way on the insurgent issue, he or she can change or restate his or her position on this issue and steal votes away from the insurgent candidate. Insurgent candidates ought to pick issues that directly exploit the weaknesses or constraints of their opponents—who should all be running on the state of the nation's economy. Among voters, the effects of the insurgent campaign will be seen as the weight of the insurgent issue gets bigger over the course of the campaign. This is the evidence that insurgent candidates have refocused the election onto this issue. They should also decrease voter's levels of uncertainty about their position on this issue as they discuss it repeatedly. Table 3.2 presents the campaign typology derived from the theory of campaign effects and the corollaries of each type of candidate behavior.

It is worth noting at this point that campaign types are determined *before* elections begin by the state of the economy *not* by the behavior of candidates once they start to campaign. For example, a candidate who tries to reset the electoral agenda onto the issue of global warming is not the insurgent candidate just because he or she is trying to reset the agenda. Similarly, a candidate who talks mainly about the War on Terrorism is not a clarifying candidate because he is clarifying his position on an important issue in this election. The behavior of candidates in campaigns does not predict the type of campaign a rational candidate should run, the objective state of the nation's macroeconomy determines candidates' campaign types. Their behavior in campaigns is data with which evaluations can be made about whether they ran the type of campaign the theory predicts.

When the Economy Is Mixed

In an ideal setting, there would be one clarifying candidate and one insurgent candidate in every presidential election. The candidates may not behave this way, but the campaign typology describes mutually exclusive types of cam-

TABLE 3.2
A Campaign Typology: Clarifying and Insurgent Campaigns

Economy Helps Candidate	Economy Does Not Help Candidate
Incumbent party in good economy or challenging party in bad economy.	Incumbent party in bad economy or challenging party in good economy.
Clarifying Campaign	**Insurgent Campaign**
Talk about economy more than anything else in the campaign to reduce voters' uncertainty about your relationship to current economic situation.	Choose an issue on which insurgent candidate benefits from public opinion more than clarifying candidate (the more lopsided the distribution of opinion, the better).
Talk about the economy more than the insurgent candidate to prevent him or her from increasing voters' uncertainty about your relationship to current economic situation.	Must be an issue on which clarifying candidate is committed to or constrained by previously taken unpopular position.
Individual-Level Effects	**Individual-Level Effects**
Decreasing uncertainty about retrospective economic evaluations over course of campaign.	Increasing weight of insurgent issue over course of the campaign.
Possible increase in weight of retrospective economic evaluations.	Decreasing uncertainty about insurgent candidate's placement on insurgent issue.

paigns with distinct and specific candidate behavior associated with each type. Since the initial step in deciding to run a clarifying campaign is whether a candidate benefits from the state of the nation's economy, it stands to reason that only one candidate can be in this category during a presidential general-election campaign. Since the other candidate does not benefit from the economy, he or she must focus on something else. This simple rule may not work so well once we take the theory out into the real world, where, sometimes, the state of the nation's economy is stagnant—not necessarily growing, but not in decline either.

How many elections in the last half century have been conducted during times of a mixed economy? Not many. In fact, evaluating Hibbs's (2000) model, which uses economic data (real disposable income per capita) from every part of a president's term in office except the first quarter, only three elections are held during times when the economy is not clearly helping one candidate.[10] Even so, when the economy is teetering on the edge of decline, what is a candi-

[10] I generated predicted values using two-party vote shares and Hibbs's average change in RDI over the course of each incumbent's tenure in office, used the predicted values to generate z-scores, and calculated probabilities of winning for each incumbent party. Only 1976, 1996, and 2000 generated predictions between 40 and 70 percent. The rest were decidedly high or low.

date to do? Should a clarifying candidate talk about a marginally decent economy that might just turn bad any day? Should an insurgent candidate ignore this economy?

In these situations there are two things that can happen. Both candidates can behave like insurgent candidates, and try to refocus the election off of the economy and onto something else that benefits their fortunes. The insurgent candidate would be doing this anyway, so this scenario only entails a shift by the clarifying candidate, away from talking about the marginally good economy and toward some other issue that he or she feels will bring more voters to the polls.

The other possible scenario is that both candidates talk about the economy, both behaving as if they were clarifying candidates. In this case, the out-party-insurgent candidate decides that the economic situation (small increase in growth) is so fragile that he or she can persuade voters the clarifying candidate's stewardship has not been well handled, or in the opposite situation (a slight decline in growth), the incumbent-insurgent candidate argues that things are not as bad as the clarifying candidate says they are.

The campaign theory laid out here assumes only one candidate can benefit from the economy and this one candidate should capitalize on that. In reality, these strict assumptions can be relaxed to accommodate situations in which it may not be clear which way the economy is going to go by election day.

Predicting Campaign Types, 1952–2000

Do candidates sort themselves as the typology predicts? Simply put, is there usually one presidential contender talking about the economy and one talking about something else? As a first step toward answering this question, I use economic forecasting data to predict campaign types. I use these data to make the predictions because campaign types are assigned based on incumbency and the state of the nation's economy. Because the economy is the reason these candidates are predicted to win elections, predicted winners should run clarifying campaigns and their opponents should run insurgent campaigns.

The economy has a long and successful history as a predictor of vote choice in both political science and political reality. On his War Room wall in 1992, Bill Clinton's strategists posted the sign: "It's the economy, Stupid." And indeed, by August of 1992, most American voters (60 percent) thought the economy was getting worse (ABC News/ *Washington Post*, August 14, 1992), and equally as many thought the economy had gotten worse in the previous year (NBC News/ *Wall Street Journal*, February 28, 1992). That so many people had cynical views of the nation's economy clearly worked to Clinton's advantage in 1992.

Political scientists have taken the individual-level connection between the economy and elections a step backwards and employed aggregate real economic data in order to forecast election winners long before the party nominees are even known. Early work by Kramer (1971) and Tufte (1978) sparked a cottage industry in predicting elections, and subsequent work produced highly accurate forecasting models (Abramowitz 1988; Campbell and Wink 1990; Fair 1978; Hibbs 1982; Lewis-Beck and Rice 1992; Holbrook 1996, 2001; Lewis-Beck and Tien 1996, 2001; Lockerbie 1996; Norpoth 1996, 2001; Wlezien and Erikson 1996, 2001; Bartels and Zaller 2001) based on fundamental political and economic variables that could mainly be known before the political conventions were held. For example, using change in GNP between the fourth quarter of the year before the election to the second quarter of the election year, presidential approval in July, and an interaction of the change in GNP with incumbency, a simple regression model generates an accurate prediction of the outcome of thirteen out of fifteen elections since 1952 (the misses are 1960 and 1976, both extremely close elections with no incumbent candidate running).

Although they are all trying to do the same thing—predict an election winner in advance of the election—all of these models are different. Some of them include presidential popularity, some do not. Some include indicator variables for years in which wars began (1952 and 1968), some do not. Some include the length of time the incumbent party has been in office, and some do not. They vary on the kinds of economic information they use as well. Most models use a measure of growth (GDP) to capture economic performance, but others use measures of disposable income (RDI). Some models track GDP change or RDI change per capita over a year's time, and other models use a shorter time period of two or three quarters. Some of them ignore the per-capita modifier. Some use trial-heat poll results. Some account for who won their party's first primary election.

The striking thing about these forecasting models is that despite their differences they almost always generate the same predicted winner. Certainly they produce different estimates of final popular vote counts, but with the exception of a single election, 1976, all of these various forecasting models pick the same candidate as a winner, and they are correct in their estimates in all but two other cases (1960 and 1968). In table 3.3, I provide the actual two-party vote share for incumbent parties and the range of forecasting predictions for four popular forecasting models for which time-series data are available from 1952 through 2000.[11]

Table 3.3 shows that the election forecasters, based on only a few political and economic variables, can accurately predict the outcome of modern presidential elections, whether the winner is likely to be a Democrat or Republican, or an incumbent party or out-party member. The forecasts generate mixed predictions in 1976, some predicting incumbent party wins and others not. Of the four models I have used to make this table, in 1976, two of them, Campbell's and

[11]These four models are from Wlezien and Erikson, Campbell, Abramowitz, and Holbrook. Each model can be found in *American Politics Quarterly*, vol. 24, no. 4, October 1996.

TABLE 3.3
Range of Economic Forecasting Predictions and Actual
Two-Party Vote Share from Four Popular Forecasting Models

Year	Actual Incumbent Vote Share	Range of Predictions
1952	44.6	42.5–47.5
1956	57.8	54.7–57.3
1960	49.9	50.4–52.6
1964	61.3	57.8–63.6
1968	49.6	50–51.7
1972	61.8	54.2–62.2
1976	48.9	47.7–53.7
1980	44.7	39.8–49
1984	59.2	57.2–60
1988	53.9	51.4–54.6
1992	46.5	46.2–47.1
1996	54.6	53.9–58.1
2000	50.3	52.8–60.3
2004	51.2	51.4–56.1
2008	53.4	44.3–52.7

Note: Range of forecasts includes predictions from models of Wlezien and Erikson, Campbell, Abramowitz, and Holbrook.

Holbrook's, predict an incumbent party loss while the others predict an incumbent party victory.[12] Holbrook's model is different from the others in that he uses voters' perceptions of the nation's economy instead of measures of the real economy, which may explain the difference. Campbell's model likely predicts a Carter victory due to its use of trial-heat poll data from September of the election year—perhaps too close to the actual election day not to be influenced already by people's final preferences.[13] In 2008 only Campbell's model produces an incumbent victory.

[12]When other forecasting models not included in table 3.3 are consulted, most predict an incumbent party victory in 1976, making Holbrook and Campbell outliers (for example, see Bartels and Zaller 2000; Norpoth 1996; Lewis-Beck and Tien 1996).

[13]The September Gallup Poll had Gerald Ford's estimated vote share at 41 percent. In March Ford's share was 40 percent.

TABLE 3.4
Predicted Clarifying and Insurgent Candidates

Year	Clarifying Candidate	Insurgent Candidate
1952	**Eisenhower**	Stevenson*
1956	**Eisenhower***	Stevenson
1960	Nixon*	**Kennedy**
1964	**Johnson***	Goldwater
1968	Humphrey*	**Nixon**
1972	**Nixon***	McGovern
1976	Ford*	**Carter**
1980	**Reagan**	Carter*
1984	**Reagan***	Mondale
1988	**Bush***	Dukakis
1992	**Clinton**	Bush*
1996	**Clinton***	Dole
2000	Gore*	**Bush**
2004	**Bush***	Kerry
2008	**Obama**	McCain*

Notes: Asterisk (*) denotes incumbent party.
Underline denotes Republican.
Bold denotes eventual election winner.

Even when the simplest of all forecasting models is estimated, one using only growth in real GDP per capita from the fourth quarter of the year preceding the election to the end of the second quarter of election year, the same predictions as in table 3.3 are given (with a Republican victory in 1976). The real state of the nation's economy and, in most cases, even people's perceptions of the economy do a very good job of predicting which party is going to win presidential elections, even months before the election will be held and before the candidates are known.

This information is surely not lost on candidates. The question is, do candidates who are predicted to benefit from economic conditions run clarifying campaigns about the economy? After all, holding a popular position on something that is already vitally important to voters is the surest way of increasing vote share as heresthetics, the spatial model, theories of issue ownership, or a retrospective voting model would suggest. Thus, the clarifying candidates

TABLE 3.5
Predicted Campaign Types by Electoral Success

	Clarifying	Insurgent
Won	Eisenhower (52)	Kennedy
	Eisenhower (56)	Nixon (68)
	Johnson	Carter (76)
	Nixon (72)	Bush (00)
	Reagan (80)	
	Reagan (84)	
	Bush (88)	
	Clinton (92)	
	Clinton (96)	
	Bush (04)	
	Obama	
Lost	Nixon (60)	Stevenson (52)
	Humphrey	Stevenson (56)
	Ford	Goldwater
	Gore	McGovern
		Carter (80)
		Mondale
		Dukakis
		Bush (92)
		Dole
		Kerry
		McCain

Note: Campaign type based on predictions from economic forecasting models.

should be talking about the economy more than anything else in their campaign and talking about it more than their opponent. In table 3.4, I list the theory's predictions for clarifying and insurgent candidates based on the economic forecasts in table 3.3.

Based on the economic forecasts for election years 1952–2008, eleven incumbents are predicted to run clarifying campaigns and four are not. Similarly, nine Republicans (not always also incumbents) are expected to run clarifying campaigns. There is variation among party incumbency status and type, and further, there is variation between campaign type in terms of success. Four insurgent candidates go on to win presidential elections. Although many more clarifying candidates win elections, it is clear that insurgent candidates can beat the economic favorite—and not just in times of war or foreign crisis. In table 3.5, I present a simple two-by-two table that places campaigns on two dimensions: predicted clarifying or insurgent campaign type and whether the campaign won or lost the presidential election.

As expected, most predicted election winners based on an economic forecast go on to win presidential elections, but what we do not yet know is if their campaigns had anything to do with that. As Gelman and King posited, maybe candidates have to remind voters of the objective conditions in order to cue retrospective voting, even on something like the economy. A measure of campaign content and focus is needed. That is the work of the next chapter.

PART II

Chapter Four

THE MEDIA DISCONNECT:
MEDIA AND CANDIDATE MESSAGES

I N ORDER TO ASSESS the theory's predictive and explanatory power, I need to compare candidate messages with what the theory predicts candidates should talk about. This means I need a measure of campaign message for presidential elections going back to 1952. While a good deal of research has been conducted on the importance of campaigns to election outcomes, no one has systematically analyzed the content of major candidate presidential campaigns over the last half century.

It may seem obvious that if you want to know whether a presidential campaign had any effects on voters, you ought to know what that campaign was about so you would know where to look for interesting and important effects. The campaign message, however, has been a missing element from investigations of campaign effects. Instead, scholars have looked at campaign treatments, such as conventions, advertisements, or visits, and evaluated their effects at both the macro- and microlevels. This body of work, which shows that campaign *effort* can have important effects, is an excellent set of ideas from which to begin thinking about how to incorporate a measure of campaign content into the search for campaign effects.

Tom Holbrook (1996) searched for the effects of major campaign events like conventions and debates on voters, while controlling for the nation's economic situation. He did not actually measure the content of conventions or debates, but made the assumption that a party's convention boosts support for its nominee. Holbrook let the data paint the picture of electoral support before and after each of these events and inferred whether the debates or conventions "mattered" to voters in terms of support for the candidates. If support for one candidate goes up after the debate or convention, these campaign moments are assumed to cause the change in support.[1] These major campaign events, it turns out, had very little lasting impact on support for the candidates. Nonetheless,

---

[1] The design is problematic in the following sense: There are many points in time over which opinions change during the campaign and no discernible campaign event has occurred. If the changes in support are evidence for the treatment's effectiveness, what should be made of changes in support during times when no treatment is delivered? Changes in support from before events to after events seem meaningful, but only if similar changes are not observed at other times when no intervening event exists.

Holbrook's work confirmed an important finding in the search for campaign effects: the state of the economy matters to voters and it is hard to get them to react to other campaign events—even major campaign moments like conventions and debates.

Daron Shaw (1999a, 1999b) similarly approached the search for campaign effects by looking at two different campaign activities—advertising buys and campaign visits. Like Holbrook, he did not actually measure the content of the ads or what candidates said or did during their visits, but assumed that more advertising and more visits benefit a candidate. Breaking his analysis into many different geographic areas—counties, media markets, and states—Shaw found support for the idea that candidates' activities do affect voters. Increasing advertising by 500 gross rating points increases candidate support in a given state by about 2.5 points. Over many campaign years Shaw systematically and convincingly demonstrates that there are bona fide effects from campaign effort.

There may be reasons to be concerned about endogeneity in these situations, and Shaw discusses this but does not account for it in his modeling. The essential problem is that candidates are likely to visit places where the crowd is potentially friendly—people who either like them a little already or can easily be persuaded to like them. Candidates are unlikely to visit places where the voters are decidedly unfavorable toward them. This means that support for candidates in the places they visit or advertise is likely to be higher to begin with than support in the places they do not visit or advertise, and also that the movement toward the candidate may be biased upward since the people who are being "treated" may be predisposed to like the candidate more after they meet him or learn more about him. The problem with the real campaign world is that the selection of treatment areas by candidates is not random, it is endogenous to the outcome we are interested in measuring.

In work on the New Hampshire primary, my colleagues and I tried to account for this endogeneity and found positive reinforcing effects on knowledge and approval from candidate contact (Vavreck, Spiliotes, and Fowler 2002). Recent work has taken this problem seriously and used the discontinuity between media markets and state boundaries to estimate the effects of advertising *alone* on the votes of people who happen to live in the geographic boundary of a media market experiencing a lot of advertising even though their own state is uncontested (Krasno and Green 2008; Huber and Arceneaux 2008). But even these clever designs fail to appreciate the content of the advertisements and how the *content* versus the *effort* might make a difference.

Effort may in fact be the main reason that advertising and campaign visits by candidates have any effects at all. Much of what happens in campaigns might merely be activating people's latent political interests or reminding them that they are Democrats or Republicans. Alan Gerber and Don Green (2000) have shown that dropping leaflets and canvassing neighborhoods before local elections can increase turnout in those elections by anywhere from 5 to 12 percentage points. They even varied the message that canvassers and leaflets delivered with little change in the results. Regardless of whether they were reminding people of their civic duty or encouraging them to clean up the environment, the fact that someone or something stirred up political waters was enough to get more people to the polls.[2]

In get-out-the-vote (GOTV) television advertising experiments run on local cable television, Don Green and I have results that suggest the advertising message does matter. In 2003 we produced GOTV ads aimed at a general population, and managed to mildly (three points) stimulate turnout among people over forty. But in 2004 we partnered with Rock the Vote and showed their GOTV ads in randomly selected local cable systems around the country. Unlike our 2003 GOTV ads, the Rock the Vote ads are specifically aimed at young people with messages about being drafted or paying for college. The results were striking—the Rock the Vote ads increased turnout among 18–22-year-olds by about 3.5 percentage points and did not increase turnout for other age groups. Comparing the effects from 2003 and 2004, we conclude that the generic ads in 2003 mobilized older people but not younger people; and the ads aimed specifically at younger people in 2004 mobilized them but not older people. The content of the message in the advertisements influenced the effectiveness of the campaigns.

Does the actual content of presidential campaigns influence their effectiveness? We do not know the answer to this question because we rarely measure the content of presidential campaigns in systematic ways. On one hand, it is possible that the actual content of campaigns is irrelevant compared to the mere fact that they are happening. They may serve only as a very loud and expensive wake-up call reminding voters that an election is coming up, the economy is what it is, and they are members of whatever political party they like. On the other hand, presidential campaigns may actually help voters make decisions about who they will vote for and what issues are the most important in their decisions. The problem is, no one knows for sure, and the people who think they know for sure, professionals and candidates, have strong incentives to believe the latter is true.

For my purposes, I want to know what candidates are talking about in presidential elections and if and how that matters to voters. The link between the content of campaigns and the decisions of voters is underexplored and this work is a first step at connecting these two elements of presidential elections.

A central feature of this analysis of presidential campaigns is what exactly presidential candidates are talking about during elections. Knowing this gives some indication of the usefulness of the campaign typology (do candidates behave as the typology suggests?) and also directs the search for effects. This section of the book examines the content of modern presidential campaigns with

[2]Although the main finding of this piece is that personal contact works much better than impersonal contact.

an effort toward description, but also tests predictions about campaign content generated by the typology. The penultimate chapter of the book takes the observed measures of campaign content and uses them to assess campaign effects among voters.

Candidates' Messages and How to Measure Them

What are modern American presidential elections about? Off the top of one's head, memories of phrases such as "I shall go to Korea" or "Competence not Ideology" may come to mind, as well as slogans such as "Leadership that's Working" or "Nixon's the One." Some people may even remember songs like Irving Berlin's "Ike for President," the cartoon strip "Kennedy's for Me," or Lee Greenwood's "Proud to be an American." Certainly people recall the odd or bizarre moments, those the candidates hope are not their defining campaign moments, but that many consultants seem to think matter greatly—George Bush claiming that his "dog Millie knows more about foreign policy than those two bozos" or calling Al Gore "Ozone-Man" in 1992; how Michael Dukakis would feel about the death penalty if his wife were raped and murdered; or Jimmy Carter's famous description of the "lust in his heart" for women other than his wife. These are some of our anecdotal memories of modern American campaigns.

To this rich and varied assembly of memories, I add a systematic and rigorous analysis of the actual content of presidential campaigns, a description of the things candidates said while they were campaigning. The description comes from campaign advertisements, candidate stump speeches, and campaign coverage in the *New York Times*. I assemble these content data into a dataset called the Presidential Election Discourse Dataset (PEDD).

The decision to analyze the content of modern American presidential campaigns had many levels. Primarily, a choice had to be made about whether to sample from the ads, speeches, and campaign coverage or to analyze every ad and speech on record as well as every day of news coverage. As others have done (Geer 1998), I decided to do the latter, knowing it would take longer, but hoping it would provide a richer picture of exactly what these campaigns were about. The campaign content data in this chapter come from my reading of campaign stump speeches and news articles, and my viewing of campaign advertisements from the last fifty years of presidential campaigns in America.

Advertisements and Speeches

The Annenberg School of Communication and the Annenberg Public Policy Center at the University of Pennsylvania produced a CD-ROM in 1998 with the transcripts of speeches, television ads, and debates of twelve U.S. general election campaigns. The Annenberg/Pew Archive of Presidential Campaign Discourse includes the words of the two major party nominees in every election from 1952 to 1996, except for Barry Goldwater.[3] The collection on the Archive CD-ROM begins on September 1 prior to each general election and ends on the eve of Election Day, or Election Day itself if there were speeches. Included in the Archive are the texts of speeches, even if the same speeches were given day after day. Advertisements are also included even if they did not air with much frequency.[4] The speeches and advertisements in this collection exhaust the universe of speeches delivered and ads aired during these fifty years of campaigns (Jamieson 2005; Jamieson, Waldman, and Sherr 2000, 50). I code all the ads candidates made, but none of the ads made on their behalf by interest groups, nonprofit organizations, citizens groups, or parties (or ads made in Spanish).[5] If ads were made, but never aired, they are not included.[6]

For the 2000 election, the Stanford University Political Communications Lab and Stanford Mediaworks compiled an e-book, or CD-ROM, that included every public speech given by Bush and Gore delivered between June 1 and October 7. They then supplemented the e-book by posting a Web page that contained the campaign content from October 8 through Election Day. The collection also features television commercials.

Despite the fact that the Stanford Political Lab contains every public speech

[3]In an effort to code Goldwater's speeches, I traveled to the Goldwater Library at Arizona State University in Tempe. While the library is rich in information about Goldwater, it does not have presidential campaign speeches in its files, although it does have a box marked for them. In that box, I found Goldwater's Senate polling research and media coverage from the early 1960s.

[4]A possible criticism of this approach is that I do not have information about which ads were run, how frequently they were aired, and where. If you are interested in what candidate's messages to the public are made of, this information seems important. The relationship, however, between the importance or impact of an advertisement's message and the frequency with which or location in which it is aired, is not so clear. To illustrate this point, some of the most memorable campaign advertisements of the last fifty years were aired in particular places and with low frequency. Johnson's famous Daisy Spot ran only once; the Bush Revolving Door ad ran only a few times in the Midwest; and the Bush ad with the word "RATS" flashing across the screen was on air for only a day before it was pulled by the campaign. Even as candidates tailor their campaigns more and more to specific states (in 2000, no presidential candidate bought any national media time), there is evidence to suggest that actual messages they send are not that different, just arriving with different intensity. Geer reports that there are no significant regional or state differences in primary election ads across space (2007) and also that weighting his 1992 advertising data by West et alia's (1995) data on ad buys does not significantly alter the results in terms of the content of appeals made overall. Kenneth Goldstein's Wisconsin Advertising Project data for 2000 corroborate this finding.

[5]In the context of the 2004 election, this may seem problematic, but the high level of independent group (uncoordinated) and coordinated party ads aired in 2004 is not typical of prior campaigns.

[6]The total number of ads analyzed here differs from West (2005) because he coded only "Prominent" ads, specifically ads discussed in Jamieson, Waldman, and Sherr (2000), or covered in the news. This count differs from another good source of advertising content, the ad archive at the University of Oklahoma, which is incomplete for some years, while in others it includes ads that were made but never aired.

given by the candidates, there are many fewer speeches in this compilation than in the Annenberg collection for previous years. Several things may be going on that explain this. One is that the candidates actually gave fewer speeches in 2000 than in previous years. Another possibility is that what the Stanford Lab considered a "major speech" during the actual campaign period and what the Annenberg archivists found at the candidates' archives as "campaign speeches" are two different things. The Annenberg Archive contains every stump speech, and there is literally a speech almost every day. The Stanford e-book does not contain a speech a day, or anything close to that. This suggests to me that the Stanford compilation focused on major policy addresses, not the day-to-day proselytization of the electorate in which candidates are constantly involved.[7]

Newspaper Coverage

Newspaper coverage of modern presidential campaigns is easily obtainable through microfilm preservation of actual images of the papers, and coverage of campaigns in the papers per day is also ubiquitous. On any given day during a presidential campaign, there are between one and fifteen stories about the campaign in the front section of a national newspaper like the *New York Times*. Deciding which of these stories is important to a characterization of campaign content is an important task. Additionally, deciding which newspapers to include in the data set is also important.

Stephen Hess, in *The Washington Reporters* (1981), describes a series of concentric circles and likens them to groups of media organizations in America. The innermost circle is the closest to government and politics, not in proximity, but in the effort and professionalism with which they approach the task of covering politics and policy. These national inner-circle media outlets have dedicated reporters on political beats such as the White House, Congress, and the Supreme Court. Their reporters are seen as experts on the subjects of their beats—people like Cokie Roberts for National Public Radio on the Congress beat and Sam Donaldson for ABC news on the White House beat. In contrast to these inner-circle outlets are media organizations in the outer tiers of the circle; most local media are located here. These news agencies cannot afford to position a reporter at the White House all the time, so when news breaks from the briefing room in the West Wing, they rely on the inner-circle reporters to feed them the information. This is the classic role and purpose of a news organization like the Associated Press.

A few domestic newspapers are in the inner circle that Hess describes. In

---

[7]I do not feel that this biases the campaign content of 2000, mainly because the advertisements and news coverage remain consistent with previous years in terms of availability and coding. Further, C-SPAN has a collection of campaign speeches and advertisements on line at CSPAN.org and they report roughly the same number of ads and speeches in 2000 as the Stanford Lab. To my knowledge, no one systematically gathered speeches in 2004 and 2008, thus I analyze content from 1952 to 2000 in this chapter.

terms of campaign coverage, this means that they have reporters traveling with both candidates every day. The *New York Times* is in this category and I use it to gauge campaign activity not because it is thought of as "national" paper in some conventional way, but because its news organization has always had reporters with the candidates on the campaign trail—with both candidates—and over the years it has had some of the best political reporters in the country doing this reporting.[8] The *New York Times* has also maintained a consistent position as the country's most prominent newspaper for the five decades under study. Some argue that it serves as an agenda-setting source of other news organizations (Bartels 1996; Gans 1979; Wilhoit and Weaver 1991).

Since my ultimate interest is what candidates said or did on the campaign trail, the media coverage serves as a proxy for candidate-driven campaign rhetoric. Obviously, any story that details the candidate's day, where he or she went and what he or she said, would be included in this analysis. Typically, there are two stories like this every day during the campaign: one on the Republican candidate and one on the Democratic candidate. Because the news coverage is a proxy only for campaign-driven content, a wide range of campaign coverage is eliminated. For example, anything that is not based on reporting is eliminated, so opinion pieces and editorials are not included in the media coverage data set. Also disregarded are stories motivated by reporters or editors to educate readers—in-depth analysis pieces on important issues, sections that analyze whether advertisements are true or false, or "compare and contrast" pieces on the two candidates' positions. These kinds of stories are not driven by the previous day's campaign events but are the result of the editor wanting to do a feature article for readers. The final category of campaign story not included in this analysis is "horse race" or strategy coverage, as these stories are driven by media actors who want to attract readers, not by the candidates who want to attract voters. In their own campaign discourse, candidates rarely talk about who is ahead or the details of their strategic decisions.

Eliminating certain types of campaign stories from the newspaper content analysis is an attempt to reduce the content analysis to those stories that focus on what the candidates said and did on the campaign trail, to stories about candidate behavior. Another interesting, but essentially different project would be one that characterizes the content of all campaign coverage and assesses whether the news content itself, controlling for the things candidates say, affects people's vote choice. Other fruitful angles might include whether the tone of campaign coverage at all affects people's participation or decisions in elections. These other projects, though interesting, are decidedly different from the aim of this investigation, which is to detail the way candidate-driven campaign content makes its way into a vote choice.

I began the coding of campaign content six weeks prior to each election since

---

[8] I performed the same analysis on news coverage from the *Washington Post* and found no substantive differences in the content of the campaign coverage between the two papers.

1952, roughly after the conventions and Labor Day, at the proverbial kicking-off point for modern presidential campaigns. As table 4.1 reports, this starting point resulted in the accumulation of 895 advertisements, 2,517 speeches, and 956 articles about the campaigns.

There are no systematic relationships between the number of ads or speeches a candidate gives over time and party, predicted share of vote, eventual share of vote, or incumbency. Even time alone has not exhibited a systematic effect on the number of advertisements or speeches a candidate gives during presidential campaigns. There is, however, a decline in the number of candidate-driven campaign stories appearing in the front section of the *New York Times* over the period. Figures 4.1 and 4.2 depict the raw time trends.

Mixed in with coverage of Major League Baseball's World Series, campaign coverage holds a dominant place on the front page of the *New York Times* during most election years. Generally speaking, one article per day is devoted to each party candidate, and given journalistic norms and rules about fairness, the articles are often in mirrored places on opposite sides of a photo. Early coverage referenced cultural nuances of campaign events, such as what the candidates wore. This was particularly true if the wives of the candidates were traveling with them. As the century came to a close, however, first ladies began to get coverage in their own right, and not about their wardrobes.

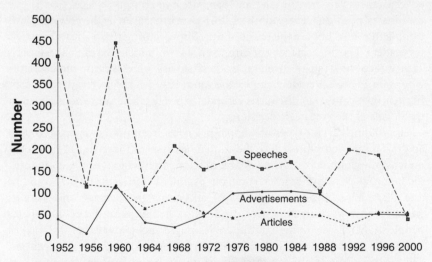

Figure 4.1 Number of Campaign Advertisements, Speeches, and Articles by Campaign Year
Scripts for advertisements and speeches provided by the Annenberg/Pew Archive of Presidential Discourse (1952–1996). Data for 1964 does not include Goldwater speeches, which are unavailable. Scripts for 2000 provided by Stanford Political Communication Lab. *New York Times* data coded by author.

TABLE 4.1
Campaign Ads, Stump Speeches, and *New York Times* Coverage
by Year and Candidate

Year/Candidate	Ads	Speeches	Articles
1952			
Eisenhower	33	231	75
Stevenson	11	186	69
1956			
Eisenhower	5	43	42
Stevenson	6	75	80
1960			
Nixon	23	136	56
Kennedy	98	312	60
1964			
Goldwater	9		40
Johnson	27	111	28
1968			
Nixon	27	58	43
Humphrey	31	153	48
1972			
Nixon	14	59	21
McGovern	36	98	37
1976			
Ford	74	128	20
Carter	28	55	26
1980			
Reagan	17	69	31
Carter	89	89	28
1984			
Reagan	47	108	27
Mondale	60	66	29
1988			
Bush	54	41	22
Dukakis	46	66	30
1992			
Bush	22	126	15
Clinton	32	76	14
1996			
Dole	22	78	32
Clinton	32	111	26
2000			
Bush	26	22	30
Gore	26	20	27
Total	**895**	**2517**	**956**

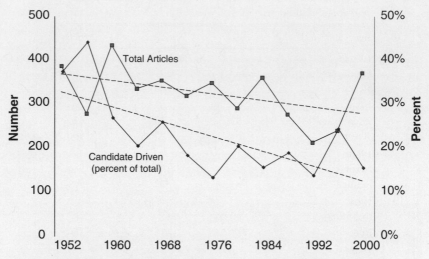

Figure 4.2 Percent of Candidate-Based Coverage Compared to All Stories about the Campaign
Data are from the *New York Times* A Section between September 1 and Election Day for each year. Candidate-Based coverage includes only stories about what the candidates said or did on the campaign trail. Opinion pieces, in-depth analyses, and horse-race coverage are included in the number of total articles, but not the number of candidate-based stories. Dashed lines are linear regression lines.

From a high of 144 articles in 1952 to a low of only 29 in 1992, a decline in the total number of articles about what candidates said or did on the campaign trail, per year, can be seen in the dashed line of figure 4.1. The drop mimics the decline in campaign coverage more generally (horse-race stories, in-depth issue analyses) over the period. A total of 4,197 stories about the campaign were run in the paper over this period, with the decline in coverage starting around 1980. By limiting the news analysis to stories that detailed the behavior of candidates only, 3,241 articles were eliminated. How much of the total campaign coverage is being eliminated? In other words, of all the coverage of presidential campaigns in the *New York Times*, how much of it is actually about what candidates did or said on the campaign trail and how much is about what editors and reporters want to write about? In 1972, 1976, 1992, and 2000, between 13 and 18 percent of *New York Times* articles about the campaign were based on candidate behavior, thus most of the coverage of the campaign in those years is not included in these data. In contrast to this is the coverage of the 1956 campaign, in which 44 percent of the stories were candidate-driven. You can see from figure 4.2 that there appears to be a decline over time in the number of stories based on what the candidates said or did as a proportion of all stories. Stories about the campaign in general are declining, but the proportion that are about what the candidates said and did on the campaign trail is declining at a greater rate.

Oddly, it is in 1960, the year of the first televised national debates and the highest number of campaign ads and speeches, in which coverage of actual campaign behavior decreases (given the period under investigation). In that year, coverage drops from levels of roughly 40 percent down to 27 percent. After 1960 the coverage of candidate behavior in campaigns bounces routinely between 18 and 27 percent, varying in a jigsaw pattern and taking a slight dip to its nadir in 1976.

The decline in candidate-driven coverage also imitates a decline in the overall tone of campaign advertisements as reported by Geer (1998) and a decline in the number of front-page stories in the *New York Times* that discuss policy issues (as opposed to strategic issues), as coded by Patterson (1993, 74). Concomitantly, Patterson reports a rise in what he calls "bad news" coverage of campaigns in *Time* and *Newsweek* magazines (1992, 20). Bad news coverage, according to Patterson, is coverage that is unflattering to a candidate, coverage that leads readers to have doubts about a candidate, and coverage that frames the candidate's behavior in a negative light. Bartels (2000, 25) reports declines in people's overall evaluations of the candidates over this same time period and slight declines in people's faith in elections (controlling for the faith in government).

Although in no way causal, these pieces of evidence paint a cynical picture of campaign news coverage and its potential effects on voters. As the number of stories about what the candidates actually do in campaigns goes down, and the tone of their campaigns gets worse, the stories that are printed in the news are mainly unflattering and focused on the strategy, not the substance, of the election.

The decline in candidate-driven news coverage of campaigns, however, is not by definition, a bad thing. Newspaper-driven coverage can be anything from very helpful in-depth issue analyses or ad-watches to not-so-helpful stories about strategy and who is ahead or behind in the polls. A low percentage of candidate-driven coverage does not have to mean the coverage of the campaign that year was poor. As reported in Gilens, Vavreck, and Cohen (2008), the overall coverage of presidential campaigns in the *New York Times* A-Section remains focused on policy, issues, and leadership—not horse-race coverage of who is ahead. Despite a tapering off at the end (1996 and 2000), most campaign coverage in the *New York Times* is not merely about who is winning or losing the election. Further, Bartels (2000, 32–34) notes that voters know at least as much, if not more, about candidates today than they did at any time in the previous thirty years.

Coding the Ads, Speeches, and News Coverage

The next important decision was how to measure what each advertisement, speech, or news story was about. One possibility was to use a computer program to search and count key words, something like Rod Hart did in *Campaign Talk* (2000), and many others have done using Lexis-Nexis. What you miss from this kind of analytic approach, however, is the context of the material you are coding—and often, in presidential campaigns, the context is critical. For example, a computer program would not have known that John F. Kennedy's discussions about American children performing poorly in mathematics was actually about the United States falling behind the Russians in terms of technology and progress. Similarly, merely knowing the number of times the word "nuclear" was mentioned in a campaign did not seem to be of much objective interest.[9] Further, some concepts are more difficult to understand than others and require more explanation, thus more words. Counting words associated with more complicated problems as being more important to a campaign's message did not seem to have much construct validity.

Without counting key words, how can the content of an ad or speech be measured? Many possibilities come to mind, including counting the number of paragraphs that mentioned important concepts or, following John Geer's (1998) lead, counting the number of "appeals" in each ad or speech. Counting the number of paragraphs with important key concepts seemed to fall prey to the same weakness as counting the number of times each word was mentioned—difficult or confusing concepts may be counted more frequently. Thus, I turned my attention to Geer's work on the content analyses of campaigns.

Geer content-analyzed advertisements from presidential campaign ads between 1952 and 1996. His unit of analysis was the "appeal." For example, one advertisement might contain many issue appeals and equally many trait appeals. In this method, an advertisement is not about only one thing. Through this method, Geer is able to capture the priorities of the candidate making the ad without losing information, as one would do if each advertisement were reduced to a single, dominant theme.

I adopt a coding scheme that is nearly identical to Geer's, except I do not code every appeal; I code only those that are not repetitively mentioned in relation to the same concept. For example, if a candidate is talking about "honesty" he or she might say something like this:

> Today I want to talk to you about honesty. Honesty is very important to the presidency. Honesty is something your president owes you. Ask yourself, has your current President been honest with this country?

In Geer's coding scheme, this text would consist of four appeals to honesty. In my coding of campaign content, this text contains one appeal to honesty. In this case, the same point is made without the first three sentences, thus, I find them

---

[9]A good example of the pitfalls of using search engines to do content analysis came when I experimented with one, asking it to search for the word "war." It returned an amazingly large number of hits, much to my surprise. As I investigated them, I learned that candidates use the word "war" to describe a lot of different things—cultural wars, a war for our future, war on poverty, war on drugs, war on values, etc. Relying on a search engine to tell me how many times a candidate spoke about war, in its intended foreign policy meaning, would have been a mistake.

redundant. I want to be clear that this is only because they do not add new information about honesty to the speech. It would be different if the candidate said this:

> Your president owes you honesty. Has my opponent been honest with you about taxes? No. Has he been honest about his private affairs? No. Has he been honest with you about our relations with Russia? No.

In this case, there are four appeals to honesty because each one is about a different concept—one is about the trait of honesty and its importance to the presidency, another is about economic policy, the next about personal conduct, and the last about foreign policy. Each one of these last three appeals would also be counted in the substantive category about which it is centered—the economy, personal conduct, and foreign policy. Another important coding point about the first example using honesty concerns repetition of themes that are not proximal to one another in the speech or ad. For example, if a candidate says:

> I'm going to cut taxes and balance the budget.

That statement gets two economic appeals. If it is followed by this sentence—

> Because that's the kind of economically minded president I am.

—the coding does not change; those two sentences together are two economic appeals (because no new information is added by the second sentence). However, if the candidate says these two sentences and goes on to describe the plight of a middle-class family in Detroit in some detail, then comes back to finish the story with these two sentences, I count them again. Clearly, this is not merely superfluous redundancy but purposeful redundancy. The candidate repeats these two sentences over and over again in the speech because they are important to him. Thus, I count them as many times as he says them. Repeating these two sentences seems conceptually different to me than adding the sentence, "That's the kind of economically minded president I will be" to the end of the first phrase, and my coding tries to account for this.

The actual coding of the campaign content contained a code sheet covering five major areas: traits, the economy, domestic policy, defense, and foreign policy. Within these five broad categories were nearly one hundred subcategories of coding. For example, within the traits category were things like honesty, leadership, experience, and characteristics such as hopeful and optimistic. Under the economy were separate categories for prosperity, inflation, unemployment, tax cuts, business tax cuts, and balancing the budget, among others. Domestic policies included everything from education and health care to science developments, infrastructure, and drugs. This was the category with the most subfields. Social, technological, agrarian, and developmental policies all had separate codes. Defense appeals had the fewest subcategories, including only spending, preparedness, and strength. Foreign policy appeals were also numerous, including things like nuclear weaponry, foreign trade, war, and peace.

Of immediate concern with content analyses is the reliability and validity of the coding. Before I began coding presidential advertisements, speeches, and news coverage, I obtained a set of midterm congressional and gubernatorial ads from 1998. I watched over one thousand of these ads in order to design a code sheet that would encompass most of the things candidates mention in their campaigns. I tested for interrater reliability using my code sheet on these midterm ads and using a subsample of twenty-five ads. The correlation among four coders ranged from .94 to .96.[10] I then moved to coding presidential ads, speeches, and news accounts, in which case two research assistants coded a party-stratified subsample of fifty ads (220 appeals) and fifty news articles (311 appeals). In this case, the research assistants and I agreed on the coding of the ads 88 percent of the time, and each article 87 percent of the time.[11] One final test was done in the middle of the analysis. I went back and recoded some of the ads and speeches that I read in the beginning phases of the content analysis to make sure I was not adjusting my coding as I "learned" how to do it better or faster. The across-time reliability of coding on the ads was 99 percent, and on the speeches it was 97 percent.

Finally, I coded only the spoken word and not the visual elements. It would be impossible to code the visual elements of speeches, despite the nuances provided in early news accounts of what the scene was like and what the candidates were wearing. Even with advertisements, the visual elements proved too complicated in terms of reliability to warrant any sort of rigorous collection. I think, however, that the visual aspects of advertisements, campaign speeches, and news accounts are very important and encourage future scholars to pursue this line of inquiry directly.

Since the coding of campaign content is central to my analysis and it is likely to be a focal point for many readers, here is an example of an ad to illustrate how the coding scheme works. In 1984 Ronald Reagan ran the following advertisement:

Ronald Reagan: In 1980 we said we would reduce inflation and we have. We said we would create new jobs, lower taxes, rebuild our defenses, and we have. But in the next four years we must do more. We must help those who haven't shared fully in the recovery. We must build a lasting peace and create millions of new jobs. We pledge cities of promise and a country of opportunity and pride.

Announcer: President Reagan. Leadership that's working.

[10]These measures of reliability are done using what results as the top three content categories of an ad or speech. If two coders match on all three categories for all the ads they are coding, their interrater reliability is 100 percent.

[11]Cohen's Kappa is a conservative test for intercoder reliability that accounts for agreement by chance (see Lombard, Snyder-Duch, and Bracken 2002, for complete discussion of interrater reliability procedures and measures). In both cases, the null hypothesis of independence can be rejected with confidence (Cohen's Kappa $= .72$, $Z = 9.0$ for ads; and Kappa $= .82$, $Z = 9.5$ for news).

There is no doubt that the main theme of this ad is economic and foreign-policy successes during the previous four years, and the likelihood that those successes would continue for four more years. Here is how my coding scheme applies to this ad:

> *Ronald Reagan:* In 1980 we said we would reduce inflation (**1 Inflation**) and we have. We said we would create new jobs (**1 Jobs/Unemployment**), lower taxes (**1 Personal Taxes**), rebuild our defenses (**1 Defense Strength**), and we have. But in the next four years we must do more (**1 Future/Hope**). We must help those who haven't shared fully in the recovery (**1 General Economy**). We must build a lasting peace (**1 Peace**) and create millions of new jobs (**1 Jobs/Unemployment**). We pledge cities of promise and a country of opportunity (**1 Future/Hope**) and pride (**1 Pride**).

> *Announcer:* President Reagan. Leadership that's working (**1 Leadership**).

This ad is straightforward, almost every sentence an appeal to a new concept. The only exception is the last sentence of Reagan's text, in which he says, "We pledge cities of promise and a country of opportunity and pride." Here is an excellent example of repetitiveness that does not add anything new conceptually to the content. The phrase "cities of promise and a country of opportunity" would have the same meaning if it just said "cities of promise." "Promise" and "opportunity" describe the same appeal in my coding—a gesture toward the future and how good it will be. It is not until Reagan adds, "and pride" to the end of the phrase that he introduces a new concept to the sentence. Thus that final sentence adds an additional appeal in the trait category of "Future/Hope" (but not two additional appeals) and one appeal in the trait category of "Pride." Thus, this ad has five economic appeals, one foreign policy appeal to peace, one defense appeal, and three trait appeals.[12]

The Content of Modern Campaigns

What are candidates talking about in modern presidential elections? When candidates put forward their own message in ads and speeches, they talk mainly about domestic policy; the news coverage of their campaigns, however, is about something else—predominantly foreign policy. As I show in table 4.2, not only are there differences in terms of media coverage, but candidates use advertising to deliver messages different from those delivered in speeches, perhaps in an effort to attract attention from a deadline-driven media.

---

[12]This coding scheme taps into the content of advertisements relatively well. In order to assess the validity of these measures, I compared my findings to those of Geer. In terms of the dominant theme of modern campaigns, my analysis matches Geer's analysis in 90 percent of the cases. Thus, I have confidence that my method is extracting the content of campaigns in a tractable and reasonable manner.

TABLE 4.2
Content of Campaign Ads, Speeches, and News Coverage

	Advertisements	Speeches	News Coverage
Traits	21.52	8.65	23.61
Economy	28.0	27.48	19.41
Domestic Policy	**29.73**	**39.52**	20.21
Defense	3.83	3.33	4.58
Foreign Policy	16.72	21.02	**32.17**

Note: Data are content analyses of ads, speeches, and news stories from presidential campaigns for the period 1952–2000. Unit of observation is the appeal. Modal categories by column are in bold. See table 4.1 for information on numbers of cases in total and broken out by candidate and year.

Nearly 22 percent of candidates' advertisements are predominantly about candidate traits or themes (either theirs or their opponents'), while a little more than 8.5 percent of their speeches are predominantly about these things.[13] Candidates use their ads to suggest that their opponent is weak or inexperienced in a way that they cannot do in a speech. One thing that distinguishes a speech from an ad is that in the latter, the campaign can have someone else do the talking—the candidate does not have to use his or her own voice—making it much easier to attack the opponent's traits or to boast about one's own good qualities (Adasciewicz, Rivlin, and Stranger 1997). In a speech where, by definition, the candidate is talking in his own voice, these things may seem less appropriate to candidates. For example, think about Reagan's 1984 campaign slogan, the double entendre, "Leadership that's Working." This phrase is uttered by a voice-over actor in almost every advertisement that Reagan makes, but Reagan himself never says it in any of his speeches. What is also clear from table 4.2 is that in order to talk more about traits in the advertisements, candidates talk less about domestic and foreign policy.

The Media Disconnect

The news coverage of campaigns does not appear to mimic either the advertisements or the candidate speeches directly. In relation to what the candidates are actually talking about, there is more news coverage of traits and foreign policy, and less news coverage of the economy and domestic policy.

Foreign policy and candidate traits are exactly the kinds of topics that journalists and editors can dramatize and sensationalize. Foreign policy easily fits into this mold as candidates are often talking about war, hostages, torture,

[13]Geer's advertising content analysis shows similar results.

terrorism, or the threat of nuclear disaster. The stakes are tremendously high. Coverage of candidate traits also allows reporters to create drama and sensation where there may in fact be very little. Was it the press in 1987 or a Democratic opponent who first dubbed George H. W. Bush a "wimp"?[14] And, in 1992, which article seems more likely to sell newspapers, the one about Clinton's ideas on Americorp or about the revelation that he wears briefs not boxers? Many media critics have documented these trends in American journalism (Fallows 1996; Kovach and Rosenstiel 1999). In *Breaking the News: How the Media Undermine Democracy*, James Fallows writes:

> Step by step, mainstream journalism has fallen into the habit of portraying public life in America as a race to the bottom, in which one group of conniving, insincere politicians ceaselessly tries to outmaneuver another (1996, 7).

Fallows's ideas connect back to Patterson's (1993) argument about good and bad news frames or strategy versus policy frames. Other frames are imaginable that have just as many consequences for public life, and Fallows, in the above statement, is suggesting that reporters have gotten into a habit of framing news stories about politics in a particular way—one that emphasizes candidates' traits at the expense of emphasizing their policy differences.

Breaking down the campaign communication by year gives a better sense of how the media cover campaigns and how candidates use their campaigns. As table 4.3 shows, there is a noteworthy trend that emerges over time.

In the early part of the period, the news coverage of campaigns is about foreign policy, even when neither candidate is discussing foreign policy dominantly—1968, 1972, and 1984. These first two years (1968 and 1972) are years in which the United States was involved in a foreign war, thus maybe it makes sense that the media would cover the campaign within this framework even though the candidates were not talking about it as much as they were talking about other things. It could also be true that the conflict and drama associated with Vietnam, and the fear Americans had about the resolution of the war, allowed the press to take advantage of the situation—playing on readers' anxiety to sell papers.

What I find most compelling about these data is that after the Cold War essentially ends, beginning in 1988, the news coverage of campaigns is no longer about foreign policy, but instead about candidate traits—also something on which neither candidate is focusing. This switch from foreign policy to trait coverage leads me to conclude that the media coverage of foreign policy in the early period was motivated, at least in substantial part, by a desire to generate

[14]It was *Newsweek* magazine that first labeled Bush a "wimp" on October 19, 1987, in an article titled: "Bush Battles the Wimp Factor" with the accompanying photo on the cover. A week after that, Al Haig, also a candidate for the Republican nomination, substituted the word "whimp" for "whimper" in a debate accusation directed at Bush, and subsequently, there were 549 stories associating Bush with the word "wimp" in major papers from October 26 until Election Day 1988.

TABLE 4.3
Dominant Subjects of Campaign Advertisements, Speeches, and News Coverage by Year

	Advertisements	Speeches	News
1952	Economy	Foreign Policy	Foreign Policy
1956	Traits	Foreign Policy	Foreign Policy
1960	Domestic Policy	Foreign Policy	Foreign Policy
1964	Foreign Policy	Economy	Foreign Policy
1968	Domestic Policy	Domestic Policy	Foreign Policy
1972	Economy	Domestic Policy	Foreign Policy
1976	Traits	Economy	Economy
1980	Foreign Policy	Domestic Policy	Foreign Policy
1984	Economy	Domestic Policy	Foreign Policy
1988	Economy	Domestic Policy	Traits
1992	Economy	Domestic Policy	Traits
1996	Domestic Policy	Domestic Policy	Traits
2000	Domestic Policy	Domestic Policy	Traits

Note: Dominant subjects are those major topic areas that received a plurality of appeals in a given year.

an interesting drama. Once people were no longer scared of the Russians and we were not fighting major wars against communists, the press found a new area in which to create compelling campaign dramas—and as Fallows suggests, candidate traits was the winner. Trait coverage includes stories about candidates accusing one another of negative campaigning or of dirty attacks; it gives reporters the freedom to investigate allegations of past draft dodging, marital infidelities, or drug use. In the absence of war, these salacious tidbits are likely to sell papers and increase readership.

This may be too cynical a view. The media may not be reporting on the most dominant issue discussed in elections, but may in fact be reporting on what one of the candidates is talking about, even though he may be doing so less frequently than the other candidate. The media coverage in table 4.3 might reflect the discourse of one of the candidates, but not both. I present the content data broken out by candidate in table 4.4.

As table 4.4 shows, this is sometimes the case, as Nixon and Mondale both talked about foreign policy in 1972 and 1984, respectively, making its presence in the news less of a mystery. In 2000, however, only Bush was talking about traits with any frequency. This leads to a question about why the news media in

TABLE 4.4
Dominant Subjects of Campaign Advertisements, Speeches, and News Coverage by
Candidate and Year

Year/Candidate	Ads	Speeches	News
1952			
Eisenhower	Economy	Economy	Foreign
Stevenson	Foreign	Foreign	Foreign
1956			
Eisenhower	Traits	Economy	Foreign
Stevenson	Domestic	Domestic	Foreign
1960			
Nixon	Foreign	Foreign	Foreign
Kennedy	Domestic	Domestic	Foreign
1964			
Goldwater	Foreign	Not Available	Foreign
Johnson	Domestic	Economy	Foreign
1968			
Nixon	Domestic	Domestic	Foreign
Humphrey	Domestic	Domestic	Traits
1972			
Nixon	Domestic/Foreign	Domestic/Foreign	Economy
McGovern	Economy	Economy	Foreign
1976			
Ford	Traits	Economy	Economy
Carter	Traits	Economy	Traits/Economy
1980			
Reagan	Economy	Economy	Economy
Carter	Foreign	Domestic	Foreign
1984			
Reagan	Economy	Economy	Foreign
Mondale	Foreign	Domestic	Foreign
1988			
Bush	Economy	Domestic	Traits
Dukakis	Domestic	Domestic	Traits
1992			
Bush	Economy	Economy	Traits
Clinton	Economy	Domestic	Traits
1996			
Dole	Economy	Economy	Traits
Clinton	Domestic	Domestic	Domestic
2000			
Bush	Domestic	Traits/Domestic	Domestic
Gore	Domestic	Domestic	Traits

Note: Dominant subjects are those major topic areas that received a plurality of appeals.

1988 and beyond spent most of their time talking about the candidates' traits when only one of the eight candidates who ran during that time period talked predominantly about traits. The media sometimes frame their reporting around things that neither one of the candidates is discussing, and this is troubling if most voters experience the presidential campaign through the media. It is especially troubling if people believe the media are reflecting the campaign with high fidelity.

In many cases it appears as though reporters have one frame in mind and cover both candidates within the same frame. In seven of the thirteen elections (1952 through 1964 and 1984 through 1992), the main issue of news coverage was the same for both candidates. In half those cases (1952, 1960, 1964, 1984), at least one of the candidates was talking predominantly about what the news was covering, but in the other half of the cases, neither candidate was talking about the topic of media coverage. Further, in 62 percent of the twenty-six cases, the dominant topic of media coverage was not the same as the dominant topic of either the candidate's ads or speeches. For example, in 1988 neither Bush nor Clinton talked about their traits more than anything else, but the media coverage of their campaigns was focused on candidate characteristics, not policy.

A multinomial logit analysis estimating the extent to which the dominant topic of ad or speech content drives the dominant topic of news content reveals no significant relationships between the news coverage and what candidates say in their ads or speeches, controlling for the party of the candidate.[15]

Despite the lack of media connectedness to their campaigns, candidates are fairly good at delivering a central message and staying on target. Seventeen of the twenty-six candidates who ran for president from 1952 to 2000 stressed the same issues in their advertisements and their speeches. In most cases, competing candidates focused on different issues. Still, in four elections—1968, 1976, 1992, and 2000—competing candidates talked mainly about similar topics. In 1968 both Nixon and Humphrey talked about domestic politics (albeit somewhat different ideas about domestic policies). In 1976 both candidates talked about the economy in speeches, and characteristics in ads. In 1992 it was the economy and domestic policy, and in 2000, both Bush and Gore talked mainly about education and health care. For the remainder of campaign years, candidates campaigned on different topics—defining their messages almost as if the other candidate was not in the race. All of this may be for naught, though, since media coverage of campaigns only loosely resembles actual campaign discourse.

These findings beg the question of whether the news media ought to be reporting on what they think is important in the given political climate or on what the candidates actually say. A mirror model of news-making would suggest the latter. Seeing the media as responsible for putting objective events in

---

[15]Standard errors are clustered around election year. Tests for significance performed at the 95-percent confidence level. Content variables are coded to reflect the dominant subject of ads, speeches, and news.

context would be consistent with the former. Still another possibility is that the media frame their campaign stories based on what the public thinks is the most important issue at the time, regardless of whether the candidates talk about it or the journalists think it is important. Data from Gallup on the nation's most important problem sheds some light on the last possibility (see table 3.1). In the 1960s and 1970s, Americans indeed thought foreign policy was the nation's most important problem. I was sure to use surveys prior to the start of the election campaign so that causality could be somewhat isolated. In elections after 1972, the economy becomes more important to voters than foreign policy— and yet, the news coverage does not change to an economic frame, but instead to a traits-based framework. This seemingly rules out public opinion as the driving force behind the news frame of campaigns.[16]

Exploring the overreporting of traits and foreign policy in more detail, I show in figure 4.3 that candidates are not talking about these topics as much as reporters are writing about them.

Figure 4.3 presents four graphs that describe the relationship between ad and speech content, and news reports. The horizontal axis presents the percentage of ad or speech content for a given candidate in a given year that is dedicated to either traits or foreign policy. The vertical axis presents the percentage of campaign stories about that same candidate in the same year about the relevant topic. As is evident, candidates do not need to spend much time talking about traits, especially in their speeches, to receive news coverage about traits. The situation is even worse for foreign policy. In some cases, candidates are spending less than 15 percent of their speeches discussing foreign policy, and the news reports about their campaigns are more than 50 percent about foreign policy. There is literally no relationship between the amount of time candidates spend talking about traits in their ads and the amount of news space dedicated to discussing their traits.

Figure 4.4 presents the same analysis for other issues—domestic and economic policies. While the trend lines remain positive, the difference in the distribution of data is noticeable. For domestic and economic policies, some candidates are being overcovered and some undercovered.

For traits and foreign policy, nearly all the candidates are being overcovered on these topics; in other words, the media reporting on the topics is not balanced, and this is not a by-product of candidate behavior since candidates spend

[16]Larry Bartels points out in response to this evidence that even if voters cared about traits, they would probably not offer them up as answers to a question about the nation's most important problem. This is a fair point, however, the Gallup data show people offering answers about traits, characteristics, and values with some regularity. The following topics received just under 16 percent of the answers to one of the most recent Gallup polls (November 14, 2007) on the question about the nation's most important problem: dishonest/integrity, unifying the country, abusing power, poor leadership, corruption, the way we raise our children, breakdown of family values, lack of respect for one another, or ethical/moral/religious decline.

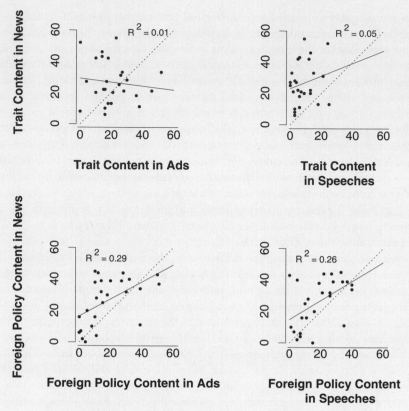

Figure 4.3 Fidelity between Candidate Content and News Coverage: Traits and Foreign Policy

News content data are from the *New York Times* A Section between September 1 and Election Day for each year. Candidate content from ads and speeches cover same period. Forty-five-degree lines represent perfect fidelity. Fitted lines are linear regression lines. N = 26 candidates from 1952 to 2000.

much more time discussing the economy and domestic policy than they do traits and foreign policy. The data demonstrate clearly that the media systematically overreport on traits and foreign policy and underreport on other issues.

Reporters, faced with quickly approaching deadlines and boring candidates who repeat themselves day after day, must come up with an easy way to write about the day's campaign events and look good to their editors or producers. Helping to sell newspapers or gain television viewers is one way for a reporter to gain credibility with the bosses, thus, stories about campaigns get reduced to a ready-made, reader-appealing controversy.

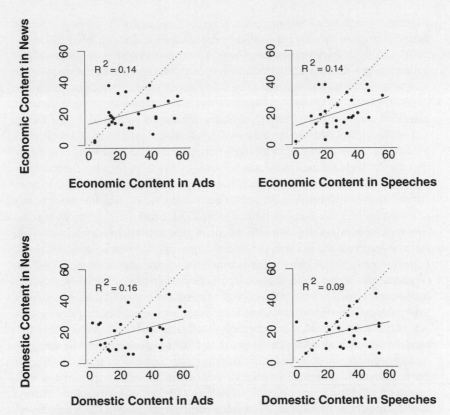

**Figure 4.4 Fidelity between Candidate Content and News Coverage:
Economy and Domestic Policy**
News content data are from the *New York Times* A Section between September
1 and Election Day for each year. Candidate content from ads and speeches
cover same period. Forty-five-degree lines represent perfect fidelity. Fitted
lines are linear regression lines. N = 26 candidates from 1952 to 2000.

Most citizens probably experience campaigns through the news, thus the
media have tremendous power to shape the manner in which people conceive
political choices. Candidates, at least in the period under discussion, are left with
little ammunition against the media's deconstruction of their campaigns. Perhaps one of the reasons candidates strive to get free media time for their advertisements is so they can actually frame the news story about their own campaign.

The media may be a business driven by the bottom line, which is why cries
for reforms of the sensational and salacious casting of news stories are ill effective.[17] But, media reforms that encourage reporters to stick closer to the actual

[17]After all, very few people choose to watch PBS or BBC even though they have the choice.

content of campaigns may have merit. It is one thing to ask the media to change behavior because they are producing a type of content that some feel is bad for public civility. It is quite another to learn that the news stories about presidential campaigns do not mimic the behavior of candidates on the campaign trail very well at all. Much of the public cynicism about politics, which is ceaselessly attributed to the unappealing characteristics of politicians and government institutions, may well be driven by the representation of politics in the media.

The disconnect between media coverage of campaigns and the rhetoric candidates use in their campaigns sets up a natural test of whether voters are influenced more by what the candidates are saying directly or by what the media is reporting. The answer to this question will have implications for the theory of campaigns—if voters are most influenced by the news, and the news is not affected much by the composition of campaigns, candidates' fortunes may be largely in the hands of a revenue-driven media that wants to maximize sales. This scenario leaves candidates with very little control over the outcomes of elections.

In the contest over influencing voters between the media content and the candidate discourse, there is reason to believe that the candidate-sponsored content will win. Remember that one of the measures of candidate discourse is paid political advertising, and there is certainly no shortage of that during this period. In fact, since voters may be incidentally exposed to advertising, as a by-product of watching television shows they like, it is possible that the ads may reach a segment of the population that the news media does not—those who are only casually interested in politics. Because of this, the effects of ads may trump the effects of news, especially if Zaller's (1992) notion of attitude change applies, and those most likely to be influenced are those with the lowest levels of previously stored political information.

I turn now to testing these ideas. I begin the next chapter looking at advertisements and speeches to explore whether predicted clarifying candidates talk more about the economy than anything else and more about it than their opponents—and whether predicted insurgent candidates are mainly talking about something else on which they have an exclusive advantage. In the following chapter, I return to the question of competition between candidate and news content in the campaign environment.

Chapter Five

THE MESSAGE MATTERS: CANDIDATE-LEVEL
TESTS OF THE THEORY

DOES MY THEORY OF campaign behavior explain the actual behavior of candidates in campaigns over the last fifty years? I begin the presentation of evidence on this matter in table 5.1, which uses the content analyses of ads and speeches to list candidates by predicted campaign type along with the issues each talked about most often in their campaign.

Before examining table 5.1, it will be helpful to discuss how best to evaluate the evidence. What does it mean to behave as the theory predicts? For clarifying candidates this means focusing predominantly on the economy, either in ads or speeches. The clarifying candidate wants to dominate the discussion of the economy, but also has the luxury of being able to discuss other things. The clarifying candidate may even want to discuss the insurgent issue if the insurgent candidate has not picked the issue carefully. For example, if the insurgent candidate did not pick an issue that exploits the clarifying candidate's constraints (note that in table 5.1 this is *not* a criteria for theoretical compliance), then it may make sense for the clarifying candidate to talk about the insurgent issue in order to neutralize the insurgent candidate's claims and garner some of the benefits from this issue's growing importance.

For insurgent candidates, following the theory's predictions means focusing principally on something other than the economy in ads or speeches (the focus of each need not be the same).

As table 5.1 shows, eight of the thirteen clarifying candidates focused either their ads or their speeches on the economy, and ten of the thirteen insurgent candidates highlighted something other than the economy in their speeches or ads. As a rough cut at the first part of the campaign typology, candidates are behaving as the typology predicts. But are those who stray from the typology's prescriptions losing elections? In fact, of the five clarifying candidates who did not focus on the economy, only two of them (Nixon in 1972 and Clinton in 1996) won their elections—and in these two years, the insurgent candidates (McGovern and Dole) may in the end have helped by stressing the economy instead of some other issue, thereby increasing votes for the clarifying candidates. The other three clarifying candidates who did not stress the economy (Nixon in 1960, Humphrey in 1968, and Gore in 2000) were all vice presidents, perhaps hoping to break out of the shadow of a strong president by downplaying the

TABLE 5.1
Dominant Subjects of Campaign Ads and Speeches by Campaign Type

	Clarifying	Insurgent
1952	*Eisenhower*	**Stevenson**
Ads	Economy	Foreign
Speeches	Economy	Foreign
1956	*Eisenhower*	**Stevenson**
Ads	Traits	Domestic
Speeches	Economy	Domestic
1960	**Nixon**	*Kennedy*
Ads	Foreign	Domestic
Speeches	Foreign	Domestic
1964	*Johnson*	**Goldwater**
Ads	Domestic	Foreign
Speeches	Economy	NA
1968	**Humphrey**	*Nixon*
Ads	Domestic	Domestic
Speeches	Domestic	Domestic
1972	*Nixon*	**McGovern**
Ads	Domestic/Foreign	Economy
Speeches	Domestic/Foreign	Economy
1976	**Ford**	*Carter*
Ads	Traits	Traits
Speeches	Economy	Economy
1980	*Reagan*	**Carter**
Ads	Economy	Foreign
Speeches	Economy	Domestic
1984	*Reagan*	**Mondale**
Ads	Economy	Foreign
Speeches	Economy	Domestic
1988	*Bush*	**Dukakis**
Ads	Economy	Domestic
Speeches	Domestic	Domestic
1992	*Clinton*	**Bush**
Ads	Economy	Economy
Speeches	Domestic	Economy
1996	*Clinton*	**Dole**
Ads	Domestic	Economy
Speeches	Domestic	Economy
2000	**Gore**	*Bush*
Ads	Domestic	Domestic
Speeches	Domestic	Traits/Domestic

Note: Winners in italics. Shaded cells mark theoretically correct behavior.

administration's successes. These three elections are also the closest elections in the last fifty years.

In 1960 Nixon lost with 49.9 percent of the two-party popular vote; in 1968 Humphrey lost with 49.6 percent; and in 2000, Gore lost the Electoral College vote, although he won 50.3 percent of the two-party popular vote.[1] Would these candidates have won if they had discussed the economy and focused on their administration's efforts in cultivating strong economic conditions? We can try to construct answers to this question by learning whether candidates who talk about the economy increase its importance to voters or clarify their responsibility for it to voters—and whether these things increase their vote share. That is the aim of chapter 6.

For now, what seems clear is that if clarifying candidates' treatment of the economy in their campaigns matters at all, it matters at the margins, which means that in some cases it could be critical. To buttress the previous statement, how many clarifying candidates who talked about the economy lost elections? Only one, Ford. And this is the next closest election in fifty years with Ford losing after earning 48.9 percent of the two-party vote.

An analysis of whether following the theory's prescriptions is related to winning elections, done at the candidate level, shows that candidates who violate the prescriptions win elections only 25 percent of the time compared to those who follow the prescriptions—who win elections 61 percent of the time. The null hypothesis of independence between these two variables can be rejected, even considering that the outcome variable is not independent across candidates. As you can see in table 5.2 (on the next page), following the theory's prescriptions is systematically related to winning elections.

In table 5.2 I define following the theory in terms of the main components only. This table uses the "relaxed" definition of compliance: a clarifying candidate is in compliance with the theory if he talks predominantly about the economy in either ads or speeches and an insurgent candidate is in compliance if he talks predominantly about something other than the economy in ads or speeches. In the next section, I tighten the definition of compliance to include the theory's corollaries as discussed in chapter 3.

Clarifying Campaigns: Dominating Economic Discussion

Of the thirteen elections in this analysis, a clarifying candidate won nine of them. These cases are not the most interesting to explore, since, by definition, these candidates are expected to win based on a good economy, and many do.

[1] Some people may disagree with my categorization of Gore as an election loser since he won the popular vote but lost the Electoral College vote based on decisions that some may say compromised the counting of all ballots in Florida. I am sensitive to this line of thought and try to do very little with this particular case as a consequence.

TABLE 5.2
Theoretical Predictions and Election Outcomes

	Follows Theory	Violates Theory	Total
Loses	38.88	75.00	50.00
	(7)	(6)	(13)
Wins	61.11	25.00	50.00
	(11)	(2)	(13)
	100	**100**	**100**
	(18)	**(8)**	**(26)**

Notes: Candidates are the unit of observation. Period covers 1952–2000.
Chi Square = 4.3, p = 0.04.
Fisher's Exact = .10.

There is, however, the compelling finding presented earlier: with impressive regularity, clarifying candidates who do not talk about the economy often lose elections. Of the thirteen clarifying candidates, eight talked about the economy more than anything else in their campaigns and talked about it more than their opponents. These eight candidates met the main component of the theory (talking about the economy more than anything else in their *own* campaigns) *and* they met the more nuanced theoretical corollary—dominating their opponent in terms of economic discourse. Of these eight clarifying candidates, only Ford is unsuccessful after running a clarifying campaign that meets the theory's mandates (he talked about the economy and talked about it more than Carter, but he lost). Five of the thirteen clarifying candidates did not talk about the economy more than anything else in their campaigns, nor did they talk about it more than their opponents (Nixon in 1960 and 1972, Humphrey, Clinton in 1996, and Gore). Three of these candidates (the three nonincumbents) lost their elections. Although they did not run clarifying campaigns that satisfy the theoretical definition, Nixon (1972) and Clinton (1996) won their elections.

It comes as no surprise that both Nixon (1972) and Clinton (1996) focused their elections on domestic-policy items, and for Nixon, foreign policy. These candidates ran classically defined retrospective campaigns in which they reminded voters of all the good things they had done. In contrast, in 1960, Nixon was immediately put on the defensive by Kennedy, who accused the Republican administration of presiding over a slump in American competitiveness with the Russians. The same thing happened to Humphrey in 1968, who reacted to Nixon's accusations about law and order. Neither candidate was able to recover his own message in the campaign, instead they were constantly reacting to what their opponent said about them or their administration's recent tenure in office.

TABLE 5.3
The Behavior of Clarifying Candidates and Their Electoral Success

	Clarifying Candidate	Won Election?
Behave as Campaign Typology Predicts:	Eisenhower 52	YES
	Eisenhower 56	YES
Talks about economy more than anything	Johnson 64	YES
else in their campaign	Reagan 80	YES
	Reagan 84	YES
Talks about economy more than their	Bush 88	YES
opponent	Clinton 92	YES
	Ford 76	NO
Does Not Behave as Campaign Typology Predicts:	Nixon 72*	YES
	Clinton 96	YES
	Nixon 60	NO
	Humphrey 68	NO
	Gore 00	NO

*Although classified as not following the theory's mandate, almost half of Nixon's newspaper coverage in 1972 was on the economy and he got more economic coverage than McGovern.

Note: Data on candidate behavior are based on content analyses of campaign ads and speeches.

Finally, Gore's campaign focused on domestic policy, neither as a reaction to his opponent's criticisms nor as a retrospective cue. Gore's focus on education seems to be a deliberate choice—perhaps driven by a desire to distance himself from the problems of the Clinton administration. I present a description of the candidates' actual behavior and the actual election outcome for clarifying candidates in table 5.3.

INSURGENT CAMPAIGNS: ISSUE SELECTION MATTERS

The insurgent candidates are a more interesting group of candidates to analyze since the task in front of them is a greater challenge. Not benefiting from the state of the nation's economy, they must find some other issue on which to refocus the national electorate. Wisely choosing this issue (or theme) is critical to their success, and they must bear in mind that the issue should be one on which they are closer to most voters than their opponent and on which their opponent is committed to an unpopular position.

In table 5.4, I present each insurgent candidate, the outcome of the election, and the answers to two simple questions: First, did the insurgent candidate talk

TABLE 5.4
The Behavior of Insurgent Candidates and Electoral Success

Candidate	Winner?	Satisfies Main Theory *Focus on something other than economy?*	Satisfies Both Corollaries *Insurgent closer to most voters on this issue?* *Opponent constrained to unpopular position?*
1952 Stevenson	NO	Yes Ending war and communism	No Ike can end the war and vows to do so
1956 Stevenson	NO	Yes Foreign policy is bankrupt	No Ike ended the war and kept us out of Hungarian and Suez crises
1964 Goldwater	NO	Yes Nuclear-weapon use	No More than half of all Americans think nuclear war will kill them (Gallup 1963)
1972 McGovern	NO	No Tax reforms	No Economy favors Nixon
1980 Carter	NO	Yes Threat of nuclear war/energy	No Carter failed at SALT II
1984 Mondale	NO	Yes Nuclear arms control	No Reagan to attend force reduction talks in Geneva and Vienna during summer of 1984

1988 Dukakis	NO	Yes Domestic policies/experience	No Bush demonstrates Dukakis's failures on drugs and education in MA
1992 Bush	NO	No Tax cuts	No Economy favors Clinton
1996 Dole	NO	No Tax cuts	No Economy favors Clinton
1960 Kennedy	YES	Yes New Frontier/Missile Gap	Yes Nixon cannot prove gap does not exist; presided over slump in productivity vis-à-vis Russians
1968 Nixon	YES	Yes Law and order	Yes Crime issue really primes race and Nixon closer to voters on desegregation than Humphrey (Gallup 1967)
1976 Carter	YES	Yes Washington outsider	Yes Ford appointed to VP and to President; Pardoned Nixon
2000 Bush	YES	Yes Common ground/uniter/education	Yes Gore part of divisive Clinton team

Note: Topics listed in column 3 (Satisfies Main Theory) are based upon content analyses of ads and speeches made by insurgent candidates. The judgments made in column 4 (Satisfies Both Corollaries) are more subjective, but where possible, I have noted citations to polls or attempted to present factual information that shows why this insurgent issue was a poor/wise choice.

mainly about something other than the economy? The answers to this question are based on the content analysis of ads and speeches described in the previous chapter. Second, did the insurgent candidate choose an issue on which he was closer to most voters than his opponent was? And was his opponent constrained to an unpopular position on this issue? The last more nuanced two questions are necessary conditions for making a wise insurgent-issue choice, since it does not help a candidate to make an election about an issue on which he or she does not benefit. If the opponent is not committed to the unpopular position, he or she can simply adopt the same position as the insurgent candidate and split the spoils.

In order to make judgments about whether insurgent candidates met these two corollaries of the theory, a fair amount of judgment comes into play. Wherever possible, I justify my judgments with the most obvious facts or provide citations to public-opinion polls from the time. The table is meant to be parsimonious—more detailed discussions of each case and the reasons for my judgments follow in the next section.

As table 5.4 makes clear, many insurgent candidates are drawn in by the popularity of foreign policy as one of the country's most important problems even though opinion on this issue is divided and malleable. Many insurgent candidates may figure that among the people who are likely to vote for them in the first place, opinion on foreign policy may not be divided thereby making this seem like a good choice for an insurgent issue at first blush. The insurgent candidates who focused on foreign policy did not win elections—it is not a lopsided enough issue.

Of the thirteen insurgent candidates who ran for president, only four of them won their elections. These numbers underscore the difficulty of running an insurgent campaign successfully. Of the thirteen candidates, only three of them (mistakenly) decided to run on the economy—even though it was not necessarily a benefit to them (McGovern, Bush in 1992, and Dole in 1996). Here is an example of what an insurgent talking about the economy might say. McGovern talked forcefully about closing tax loopholes that benefit the rich:

> I have demanded a program to close $22 billion in tax loopholes. It will not take one extra cent from any American whose income comes from wages or salaries, or from investments that are already fairly taxed. None of you will pay more—but corporations and the wealthy will finally pay what they owe to their country. . . . Richard Nixon also has a plan for your taxes. It is a secret plan—the same kind of plan he promised for peace in Vietnam four years ago. And I think this time the secret plan is not to reduce your taxes but to raise them. (September 25, 1972)

While credit should be handed to McGovern for recognizing that the War in Vietnam was not going to be an issue that could unite people on his behalf, his choice of economic policy was not a winning substitute.

In 1992 George H. W. Bush's campaign was dominated by explanations of why the economy was growing so slowly and how ending the Cold War slowed economic growth. He repeatedly painted Bill Clinton as a "tax and spend liberal," and an old-school "New Deal Liberal" who would surely raise taxes. In his Agenda for American Renewal, released relatively early in the campaign, Bush called for a period of massive economic growth:

> My agenda offers the promise of a renewed America, an America with a $10 trillion economy by early in the next century. With that kind of dynamic growth we can address our problems here at home and guarantee that America will remain not just a military superpower but an export superpower and an economic superpower. (September 12, 1992)

The problem with defending a stagnant economy is that Bush looks and sounds like he thinks it is a good thing. Bush essentially spent most of his time during the 1992 campaign reminding voters that the economy was actually not moving very quickly, despite the fact that the recession was over and indicators were headed in positive directions. Bush further hurt his chances by choosing to label Clinton as a New Deal Democrat. Clinton, whose campaign called him "A New Kind of Democrat," and who had been instrumental in developing the Democratic Leadership Council, was moving away from New Deal programs like welfare. Bush's strategy here is a clear violation of the theory's explanation of winning insurgent campaigns—insurgent candidates have to focus on issues on which their opponents are *committed* to unpopular positions. Clinton was not a committed New Dealer, and in fact, he was a committed new kind of Democrat.

Bob Dole focused on a 15-percent across-the-board tax cut for all Americans in 1996. He reminded voters about Clinton's 1993 tax increase, the "largest tax increase in America history," he said. And he explained systematically how he could cut taxes and balance the budget:

> If elected, Jack Kemp and I will cut tax rates by 15 percent for every American taxpayer, and middle- and lower-income taxpaying families will receive a $500 tax credit for every child under the age of 18. We will also cut the capital gains tax rate in half, there—thereby creating more jobs and more opportunities for Americans everywhere. And that's just phase one. Our goal in phase two is to end the IRS as we know it and make our entire tax system fairer, flatter, and simpler. By saving only five to six cents on the dollar in other areas of the federal budget, we will still save $576 billion over the next six years—more than enough to pay for my tax relief proposals. These savings, combined with the sale of some government assets like the broadcast spectrum, and the economic growth that will result from my program of tax reduction, would complete the job and balance the budget by the year 2002. (September 7, 1996)

These insurgent candidates who focused on the economy chose to talk about taxes in years when voters were feeling good about the economy and they were going to reward the other candidate for this good mood. All three of the insurgent candidates who focused their campaigns on the economy lost their elections.

Of the remaining ten insurgent candidates, six of them lost, despite running on an issue other than the economy. To better understand why their choices did not lead to electoral success, the corollaries of the campaign typology must be evaluated. Were these candidates closer to most voters on the insurgent issue than their opponents were? Was the clarifying candidate somehow constrained or committed on this issue by an unpopular position or unflattering characteristic? Unfortunately, the answers to these questions are often a resounding no.

Stevenson 1952 and 1956: Second Time Same as the First

In 1952 and 1956 Stevenson chose foreign policy as his insurgent issue. Specifically, in 1952 he focused on the war in Korea and the spread of communism around the globe. In the face of widespread paranoia about communism and nuclear war, this may have seemed like a winning choice. Stevenson eloquently worried about what happens to art, poetry, and happiness in general when communism is allowed to run rampant:

> In the Soviet Union we see the totalitarian state in its gloomy reality. The first casualty of the Communist regime is the free mind; and, once the free mind disappears, all else must follow. Thus in Soviet Russia today the last trace of freedom has been extinguished. Not only history and economics and politics, but science and art and music are enslaved by the regime. The unorthodox experiment, the unacceptable melody, the extreme painting, become evidences of disloyalty. Unorthodoxy is treason to the state. (October 8, 1952)

Implicit in these statements is the suggestion that Eisenhower allowed communism to grow or that he was "soft" on communism. Sometimes, Stevenson helped voters draw the inference more explicitly:

> This man [Eisenhower] had stood out against American isolationism, had supported the Marshall Plan for aiding Europe, and had defended General Marshall as a great patriot. But now he puts his arm around Senator Jenner, who called General Marshall a willing front man for traitors, and here in Milwaukee, we are told, he deleted a defense of General Marshall from his text when Senator McCarthy requested it. (October 8, 1952)

Connecting Eisenhower to McCarthy (in McCarthy's home state) was a brave move by Stevenson, who clearly hoped to capitalize on the country's growing dissatisfaction with the senator and his methods. He attempted to paint Ike as a puppet of McCarthy, someone willing to throw his colleagues under the bus if asked to do so by a megalomaniac like McCarthy. This was a hard sell for Stevenson. Eisenhower's military record, his proud, matter-of-fact mannerism, and his straight-talking style all suggest that he was not a man who bowed down to tyrants like Joseph McCarthy, nor was he a man who sympathized with communists. If anything, the innuendos that Stevenson delivered on this refrain likely only led to further dissatisfaction with him by voters, who by 1952 were getting tired of baseless accusations without substantiation.

In 1956 Stevenson played the same familiar tune, stating that Eisenhower's foreign policy was "bankrupt" and that he had no vision for America's role in the world:

> We must have a foreign policy that is firm, consistent, and also comprehensible. We must stop bluffing our enemies, boasting to our friends, and misleading our people here at home. . . . We cannot stop this dangerous drift in foreign affairs by pretending that all is well while Communist influence is spreading everywhere, while North Africa is in rebellion, while the guns are loaded in the Formosa Strait, and when the Russians have a foothold in the Middle East for the first time, when the Suez lifeline of Western Europe is in peril for the first time, when Arab nationalism is rampant and Communism its ostensible protector. (September 23, 1956)

Again, it is easy to appreciate Stevenson's belief that the fear of communism was the right issue for the time. It just was not the right issue with which to beat incumbent President Eisenhower. By 1956 most Americans wanted to stay out of world politics (Farber 1994). Americans wanted to have the benefit of their cars, their refrigerator-freezers, their air conditioners, and they enjoyed the general sense of prosperity that seemed to accompany the Eisenhower years. In 1956 more Americans held white-collar jobs than blue-collar jobs, and for the first time in the nation's history, more people worked in the service industry than in production. The technological innovations and the progress of the period played out in front of the backdrop of the Cold War, and although Americans' fears of a theoretical Communist takeover were bona fide, their lives were pretty good in reality, and getting better.

At first glance, Stevenson's choices may seem like good insurgent issues. After all, nearly all Americans preferred less communism around the globe to more; and a rich foreign policy is better than a bankrupt one. But the question remains, does Eisenhower have anything to do with promoting (or not stopping) the spread of communism and does he really lack a world vision for the United States? Both of these seem like a hard sell for a popular and successful war general. Even more important is the fact that Eisenhower was not constrained in any way by being a communist sympathizer at any point in his history. He fought and won a world war against repressive regimes—if anything, Americans identified him as tough on communism. But Stevenson's claims in 1952 were born of the Korean War; could Ike end *that* war?

This is essentially what Stevenson was asking Americans to consider. Eisenhower is certainly not committed or constrained by anything in his past that might have led him to behave in ways that would prolong the war, making this choice of insurgent issue risky. In fact, on October 24, 1952, in Detroit, Michigan, Eisenhower did exactly what an unconstrained clarifying candidate should do—he moved in on Stevenson's insurgent issue, which was likely becoming more important to voters, and declared: "I will go to Korea. I will end the war." In a single campaign moment, Eisenhower neutralized Stevenson's insurgent issue. Ike was not constrained in any way to an unpopular position on the war in Korea or to the spread of communism. And his candidate characteristics worked against Stevenson's attempts to portray Eisenhower as soft on communism.

In 1956 Stevenson's claims that Ike had a bankrupt foreign policy were neutralized in much the same manner. Eisenhower ended the Korean War, as he said he would. And coincidentally, in the final days of the campaign, the world cooperated and provided Eisenhower with opportunities to show his foreign-policy strengths. In Budapest, revolutionaries were suppressed by Russian tanks; and the British, French, and Israelis invaded Egypt to reclaim the Suez Canal from General Abdel Nasser. Stevenson was immediately critical of how Eisenhower handled these world crises. He argued that Eisenhower had told Americans that the world was at peace, when in reality there was conflict everywhere. He accused the president of golfing too much and paying too little attention to foreign-policy matters. As for the Middle Eastern invasion, he claimed that Eisenhower, only days before the seizure, claimed there was "good news" about progress in the region. But the facts remained that Eisenhower had avoided an interaction with the Russians over the Budapest uprising and had joined with the Russians and the United Nations in stabilizing the rocky Middle East. If Ike's foreign policy was bankrupt, it was doing a good job of keeping the United States out of military conflicts with its major enemies. Similar to 1952, by handling these crises with aplomb, Eisenhower was able to neutralize Stevenson's insurgent issue for the second time.

Goldwater 1964: Just Enough Power to Get the Job Done

In his nominating-convention acceptance speech, Barry Goldwater said, "I would remind you that extremism in defense of liberty is no vice. And let me remind you also that moderation in the pursuit of justice is no virtue." And when Republicans held up signs that read Goldwater's slogan: "In your heart you know he's right!" Democrats countered with their own signs reading: "Yeah—extreme right!" And so went the Goldwater campaign of 1964. When the election was over, Goldwater revisited his candidacy, and speaking about the convention speech, he lamented, "If I had a pint of brains I should have known in San Francisco that I had won the nomination but lost the election right there" (Goodwin 2002).

Goldwater was an ideologue, a "shoot from the hip" speaker, and a candidate with a record in the U.S. Senate that would back up any claims from his opponent about his radical policy positions. Goldwater voted against the 1964 Civil Rights Act, wanted to break off relations with Russia, wanted out of U.N., and advocated the use of "low-yield nuclear bombs" to fight the communists. In responding to a question about containing the War in Vietnam, Goldwater said he would like to "lob one [a nuclear bomb] into the men's room of the Kremlin and make sure I hit it." He thought Americans were afraid of the word "nuclear"—unrealistically afraid—and that it was his job to disabuse them of their misgivings about mushroom clouds and fallout. Most of the time, Goldwater argued, nuclear firepower is "just enough power" to get the job done (Boller 1996).

Goldwater's own statements about the use of nuclear weapons and breaking off relations with the Russians made Johnson's advertisement the Daisy Spot provocative. Ultimately repudiated by Johnson and only aired once, this commercial begins with a little girl picking the petals off a daisy in the familiar "he loves me, he loves me not" manner. As she miscounts, the camera zooms in on her eye and a reverse countdown to a missile launch is heard in the background. The little girl's eye turns into a mushroom cloud as Johnson's voice is heard:

> These are the stakes: To make a world in which all of God's children can live, or to go into the darkness. We must either love each other, or we must die.

Finally a voice-over announcer says, "Vote for President Johnson on November 3rd. The stakes are too high for you to stay home."

Although the ad itself never mentions Goldwater by name, Goldwater's own statements about the use of nuclear weapons and Johnson's discussion of it during the campaign help the viewer understand or infer that this ad is about what might happen to our children if Goldwater is elected. The ad played on people's fear of nuclear weapons, the same fear that Goldwater was hoping to ameliorate.

In truth, Gallup reports that many Americans were afraid of nuclear weapons and their use, making this a poor choice for an insurgent campaign issue. On February 7, 1963, Gallup asked Americans whether they thought the hydrogen bomb would be used against the United States in the next world war. Sixty percent of Americans said yes. In March of 1963, Gallup asked people if they thought they would live through a nuclear war. One out of every two people said their chances of doing so were unlikely. In the same poll, 51 percent of Americans said they did not believe we would ever have a nuclear test-ban treaty with the Soviet Union, and, that if we did, two-thirds of Americans believed the Soviets would not hold up their end of the deal. Half of the people living in America in 1963 were convinced nuclear war was on the horizon and that it would kill them. Goldwater's desire to disabuse Americans of their fear of the word "nuclear" was timely, but unlikely.

Goldwater simply was not closer to most voters on this issue. Even though he may have successfully reset the electoral agenda onto this issue, he did not benefit from the effort. In October of 1964, only a few weeks before the election, the National Election Study reported that 63 percent of Americans had no confidence in or were not sure about Goldwater's abilities to handle nuclear weapons—too bad for him that he had refocused the entire election onto this dimension.

Carter 1980 and Mondale 1984: War through Strength

Amid high inflation, high unemployment, and stagnant growth, Carter in 1980 chose the control of nuclear weapons as his insurgent issue. It was likely this statement, which Reagan made in his convention acceptance speech, that gave the Carter campaign enough grist for their mill:

> Of all the objectives we seek, first and foremost is the establishment of lasting world peace. We must always stand ready to negotiate in good faith, ready to pursue any reasonable avenue that holds forth the promise of lessening tensions and furthering the prospects of peace. But let our friends and those who may wish us ill take note: the United States has an obligation to its citizens and to the people of the world never to let those who would destroy freedom dictate the future course of human life on this planet. I would regard my election as proof that we have renewed our resolve to preserve world peace and freedom. This nation will once again be strong enough to do that. (July 7, 1980)

Carter told audiences across the country that if elected, Reagan would be the first president since Truman to actively cultivate growth in the number of nuclear weapons. He insinuated that Reagan was a warmonger, anxious to show America's foreign strength by actively demonstrating her might. Carter said:

> Our greatest commitment, ever since Harry Truman was in office, by Presidents, Democratic and Republican, has been to control nuclear war, prevent the spread of nuclear weapons to radical nations like Libya and Iraq and others, to have a careful, balanced, verifiable control of nuclear arms. It's the greatest overriding issue of this campaign. The greatest legacy we can leave our children is a nation more peaceful, more dedicated to the pursuit of peace. The election of 1980 is really a choice not just between two candidates or even two parties but a choice between two futures. (November 3, 1980)

As an insurgent candidate, Carter was somewhat similar to Stevenson. Did Reagan say he wanted to build more nuclear weapons? Or did he just say he wanted to achieve "peace through strength"? Carter made strength and nuclear arms synonymous, when in truth, and even in Reagan's construction, they were not. Much like Eisenhower, when Reagan sensed that Carter's accusations were gaining traction, he neutralized them by declaring that arms reduction was a priority in his campaign. Reagan retorted:

> I would assign a high priority to strategic arms reduction. I have repeatedly said in this campaign that I will sit down with the Soviet Union for as long as it takes to negotiate a balanced and equitable arms limitation agreement, designed to improve the prospects for peace. (October 19, 1980)

Going even further, Reagan turned the issue around on Carter, quoting John Glenn, who spoke against Carter's Strategic Arms Limitation Treaty II. Glenn said that he did not appreciate being characterized as a warmonger simply because he was against this arms-control treaty (along with many other senators). Since Carter's attempt at strategic arms negotiations was never ratified, Reagan painted Carter as a foreign-policy failure and promised that if elected he would begin immediate preparation for negotiations on a SALT III treaty. "My goal is to begin arms reductions," Reagan said in a televised national speech on a strategy for peace in the 1980s. Reagan neutralized Carter's insurgent issue by adopting the same positions that Carter had. Since he was not constrained in any real way by being an advocate for nuclear proliferation (despite other similarities he did not have Goldwater's record on the topic), Reagan was able to reasonably move over and share the voters who cared about this issue with Carter.

As if he had not seen the 1980 election, Walter Mondale chose to exploit the exact same issues in 1984 when he ran against Ronald Reagan. Reagan was a hawk, Mondale claimed, and he was going to get us into nuclear war:

> America must always be strong. But in a world with fifty-thousand nuclear weapons, a president must use our strength to work for peace, and reduce the risk of nuclear war. That isn't just an important issue. It is the issue. Mr. Reagan doesn't understand that. He joked about bombing the Russians and starting World War III. It's time we had a president who understands that nuclear war is no laughing matter. Mr. Reagan called supporters of a mutual, verifiable nuclear freeze "jackasses" and "dupes of Moscow." It's time we had a president who is a freeze supporter. (September 3, 1984)

Much as he did in 1980, Reagan demonstrated that despite not achieving nuclear-arms limitations with the Soviets in the previous four years, he was trying. On January 16, 1984, he gave a speech outlining his proposals for arms reductions. In it, he made the following suggestions, which he repeated in many campaign speeches:

> Our second task must be to find ways to reduce the vast stockpiles of armaments in the world. I am committed to redoubling our negotiating efforts to achieve real results: in Geneva, a complete ban on chemical weapons; in Vienna, real reductions to lower and equal levels in Soviet and American Warsaw Pact and NATO conventional forces; in Stockholm, concrete practical measures to enhance mutual confidence, to reduce the risk of war, and to reaffirm commitments concerning nonuse of force; in the field of nuclear testing, improvements in verification essential to ensure compliance with the threshold test ban and peaceful nuclear explosions agreements; and in the field of nonproliferation, close cooperation to strengthen the international institutions and practices aimed at halting the spread of nuclear weapons, together with redoubled efforts to meet the legitimate expectations of all nations that the Soviet Union and the United States will substantially reduce their own nuclear arsenals. (September 24, 1984)

Working in concert with statements like this was the image of American pride and strength that Reagan's campaign exuded. His famous "It's Morning Again in America" advertisement used flags and farmers while a dizzying array of

booming economic statistics melted off of the announcer's voice. "Are you better off today than you were only four short years ago?" the voice-over rippled
hauntingly throughout the campaign. Most Americans had to answer "yes" to
Reagan's rhetorical question. We were still at peace and the economy was growing. Reagan had neutralized the arms-control issue again.

Dukakis 1988: An Unfocused American Dream

There may be more written on the 1988 election campaign than any other campaign in history. This campaign was attack oriented, it was negative, it contained race baiting; some people think Bush's ads were clever, others think they
were dishonest, and others claim they were all about race. Through it all, however, Michael Dukakis was an optimist. His campaign centered around domestic-policy themes—particularly, education and health care. With the Cold War
essentially over, a new drama had begun.

Dukakis spoke often about creating "opportunity for every American citizen"
and providing "good jobs at good wages" for everyone who wanted to work. He
said he would "bring prosperity home to the American people." His was a campaign about getting things done—about government working well to help
people achieve goals. No single issue leaps out as the one thing Dukakis discussed—and perhaps this was part of the problem—and his message, although
wholly inspirational, lacked focus. It had breadth but little connection. After
reading his speeches and talking to him as I wrote this book, however, I am convinced that the glue that held his ideas together was the notion that government
could work: it could do good things for people. Dukakis's energy certainly encouraged people to believe him, and his rhetoric backed it up:

> I want to be the president who stands up for the families of this country. I want to
> build an America where our kids can afford a new home; where our parents can get
> decent health care and enjoy a secure retirement; and where every American family is
> a full shareholder in the American dream.

Dukakis was unable to refocus the electoral agenda onto his insurgent issue
because of the unconnectedness of his messages. If voters did pick up on the
"government that works" theme, they were loudly and ubiquitously reminded
of all of Dukakis's failures as a manager and governor of Massachusetts. It
turned out, according to the Bush campaign, that government in Massachusetts
did not work that well at all.

Bush claimed that under Dukakis's stewardship Boston Harbor became the
"dirtiest harbor in America," children in schools were denied the opportunity
to say the Pledge of Allegiance, education in Massachusetts sank to the bottom
of all states, the state pension fund was raided to the tune of 27 million dollars,
and furloughed prisoners committed heinous crimes.

The Revolving Door ad, made by the Bush campaign, followed closely on the heels of an ad made by an independent group about a man named William Horton, who was involved in a murder while on furlough from state prison. This was, according to the ad, the fault of the Dukakis crime policy—which, consistent with Bush's theme, was much too liberal. These two campaign ads (and the entire 1988 campaign) have been analyzed and reanalyzed by journalists, pundits, and political scientists for twenty years now (for one complete treatment, see Mendelberg 2001). Whether one is convinced by Mendelberg's argument that the Revolving Door ad was made to prime racial resentment among whites in an implicit manner through the images in the ads, or the host of other scholars who argue that the impact of the ad in *real time*, that is during 1988, was to focus on Dukakis's failed crime policy (Farah and Klien 1989; Hershey 1989; Anderson 1995; Hagen 1995), one thing was made clear by Dukakis's response to these advertisements: not striking back immediately and intensely further reinforced the notion that Dukakis's campaign lacked a message.

The Bush campaign further capitalized on the Dukakis campaign slogan, "The best American is yet to come!" by reminding voters:

> And now he [Dukakis] wants to do for America what he's done for Massachusetts. America can't afford that risk.

If it was Dukakis's goal to convince voters that the best America was yet to come and that government could help them realize it, Bush did not so much neutralize the issue as he demonstrated that Dukakis could not *do* what he was promising. Further, Bush was not constrained by prior commitments or characteristics that made him weak on education or health care. In fact, he went on to label himself the "education president."

INSURGENT CANDIDATES MAKING WISE CHOICES

Of the thirteen insurgent candidates, four eventually win their elections (Kennedy, Nixon in 1968, Carter in 1976, and Bush in 2000). These are the most interesting cases to explore, as they help to illustrate why the slightest change in the way an issue is framed can make a difference, and why some issues have traction at certain times when they do not at other times. Most important, these cases show how exploiting an opponent's weaknesses, weaknesses to which they are permanently attached, is effective. It is these candidates who are able to overcome the structural conditions and the powerful economic context of their elections.

Kennedy 1960: High Hopes

John F. Kennedy ran a classic insurgent campaign in 1960. What is striking about his candidacy is that his ultimate focus was on the same underlying issue into which Stevenson twice tried to tap. Kennedy, however, gives fear of the communists a slight twist and pins Nixon into a corner he cannot back out of.

Kennedy talked about a "New Frontier":

[W]e stand today on the edge of a new frontier—the frontier of the 1960s—a frontier of unknown opportunities and perils—a frontier of unfulfilled hopes and threats. . . . Beyond that frontier are uncharted areas of science and space, unsolved problems of peace and war, unconquered pockets of ignorance and prejudice, unanswered questions of poverty and surplus. . . . For the harsh facts of the matter are that we stand on this frontier at a turning point in history. We must prove all over again whether this nation—or any nation so conceived—can long endure; whether our society—with its freedom of choice, its breadth of opportunity, its range of alternatives—can compete with the single-minded advance of the Communist system. Can a nation organized and governed such as ours endure? That is the real question. Have we the nerve and the will? Can we carry through in an age where we will witness not only new breakthroughs in weapons of destruction, but also a race for mastery of the sky and the rain, the ocean and the tides, the far side of space and the inside of men's minds? Are we up to the task? Are we equal to the challenge? Are we willing to match the Russian sacrifice of the present for the future? Or must we sacrifice our future in order to enjoy the present? That is the question of the New Frontier. (July 15, 1960)

Instead of highlighting fear of communist expansion as reason to elect a strong military leader or a seasoned negotiator, Kennedy used this fear to pit American against Russian in an all-out showdown for the future of everything. Who will explore space? Who will understand the oceans? Who will better educate their children? Ultimately, who will win this war between nations? Capitalizing on the Soviets as enemy number one, Kennedy was able to rally voters to "his" side, the "American" side. Want better schools? Maybe people did not, but once they heard that Russian schoolchildren could outperform American kids in math, they changed their minds. Want to explore space? A lot of people did not, but when reminded that the Russians beat us to the moon (*Luna 2* landed on the moon on September 14, 1959) a lot of people changed their minds about space exploration. Kennedy reminded voters that the first emblem on the moon was a Soviet symbol, not an American one (*Luna 2* scattered Soviet "pennants" around the Moon on impact). The first satellite in space was theirs, not ours. He told them that "the first canine passengers to outer space who safely returned were named Strelka and Belka, not Rover or Fido, or even Checkers" (September 7, 1960). Kennedy managed to work the idea of the New Frontier into every aspect of his campaign. Whether it was domestic policy or foreign policy, it always came back to how we were going to do better than the Russians.

The single issue that stood out was the "missile gap," the alleged fact that the Soviets had outproduced the Americans in missiles. Kennedy had quotes from all sorts of military generals:—"We are in mortal danger. The missile lag portends serious trouble" (Lt. Gen. James Gavin 1960) and "We are now threatened with a missile gap that leaves us in a position of potentially grave danger" (General Maxwell Taylor 1959).[2] The Russians had more missiles, more and better scientists, had beat us to the moon, and Kennedy even argued that their economy was doing better than America's in what he called the "economic gap."

How did Nixon respond to Kennedy's claims about the mediocrity of everything American? In Kennedy's hometown of Boston, Massachusetts, Nixon said, "The American people believe in measuring promises against the solid performance, and they are going to vote for real performance and not unreal problems." Nixon claimed Kennedy was a dreamer whose visions amounted to nothing more than a return to pre-1952 Democratic policies. But in so doing, he adopted Kennedy's language. Almost from the very beginning, Nixon was letting the Kennedy campaign set the agenda and define the terms of debate, literally. In a televised national speech on September 29, 1960, Nixon countered Kennedy:

> High hopes? Yes. High spirits, lofty expressions—these are great. We [Republicans] have them, too. They are all commendable, but they are a poor substitute for solid performance, and on performance they [Democratic Congress] haven't produced and they can't produce and won't. Why? Because they would go back, go back to policies that we left in 1953. You've heard about these new frontiers. We all travel to new frontiers.

But when Nixon told voters to weigh solid performance over unreal promises, Kennedy took him up on that charge and began detailing the record Nixon had accumulated and that constrained him in this campaign.

> [A]nd I think that we can compare very satisfactorily not only Mr. Nixon, but the Republican party's record of their performance against the promises of this campaign, for the Republican party, the same party which gave us the missile gap, and the economic gap, have also given us a performance gap, and that is the gap which will bring about the rejection of the Republican party this November.

Kennedy goes on to explain that Nixon's campaign promise of a new housing program is empty because Nixon voted against the Housing Act of 1949 when he was in Congress; and as vice president, he cast the deciding "no" vote on a bill that would have decreased interest on GI home loans. Nixon promises to keep the cost of living down? Unlikely, said Kennedy, as in the previous eight years Nixon had supported policies that had increased the cost of medical care by 32 percent, rent by 20 percent, household management by 23 percent, and he had signed off on adding $3 billion of interest to the debt. Nixon promised health care for seniors and improvements to social security? Not likely, Kennedy responded. He directed the opposition to a bill that would have helped seniors get medical care; and worse yet, when the roll-call vote was read in the chamber, Kennedy told voters that Nixon had smiled at its defeat (Boller 1996).

[2] Quoted by Kennedy on October 18, 1960, Miami Beach, Florida.

There was no end to Kennedy's ability to find Nixon, on the record, undoing something he had just promised to do. This constrained Nixon's chances to neutralize Kennedy's issues—he could not do it, since Kennedy had already demonstrated to voters where Nixon really stood on most important matters. The choice of a package of promises called the "New Frontier" and particularly the scary Missile Gap were great insurgent issues. Not only was Kennedy's position on beating the Russians a patriotic one for nearly all Americans, Nixon could not come up with any evidence that these "gaps" did not exist. He was a part of the administration that let America fall behind the Russians in education, in missile production, and in space exploration, and there was nothing he could do to counter that.[3]

Even though this election took place in an unstable economy, slightly benefiting Nixon, but not by much, and Kennedy ran a tremendous insurgent campaign, it was still the second closest election in history with a vote margin of two-tenths of a percent. Nixon lost by only 114,673 votes or 84 Electoral College votes. Even the best insurgent campaigns result in only modest victories for insurgent candidates.

Nixon 1968: Freedom from Fear or Racial Appeal?

In 1968, despite the good economy, people were scared. What were they scared of? Quite simply, one another. The nonviolent-turned-violent protests by civil rights activists, free speech advocates, and students led to a state in which Americans felt they needed protection, one from the other, more than ever. Civil rights were never more important in an election than they were in 1968.

Americans' sense of fear in this period was spurred on by large-scale riots in major cities like Newark and Detroit. Young African American men, who were being let go from industrial jobs due to the onset of automation of the assembly line, clashed with the mainly white ethnic police officers maintaining order in the cities. Often, a simple misunderstanding (like a taxi driver pulling around a double-parked police cruiser in Newark) sparked multiple days of rioting, leading to hundreds of deaths and nearly ten thousand arrests. In addition to big-city riots in Northern cities, there were clashes over segregation in the South, particularly on college campuses, which were becoming symbolic of protest and violence. The Orangeburg Massacre resulted in the deaths of three college students from South Carolina State College, who were rallying around a bonfire on the campus. The students were protesting a whites-only bowling alley in town, and after a couple of days police came to extinguish the fire. One officer fired his pistol into the air to clear the crowd in an attempt to restore order to the situation. Other officers responded by firing their weapons into the crowd, resulting in multiple deaths.

[3] It was not until the election was over that Kennedy learned the Russians had only four intercontinental ballistic missiles, many fewer than the United States (*Los Angeles Times*, February 24, 2001).

As if the brutality in big cities and on college campuses were not enough, there was also the War in Vietnam. In 1968 American opinion started to turn against the war as images of executions and civilian deaths entered American culture. The Tet Offensive, the Battle of Saigon, and the My Lai massacre happened before the year was half over. Twenty-four thousand troops were committed to fight in a second tour in Vietnam, involuntarily.

Perhaps the most powerful demonstrations of violence during this year, however, came in the assassinations of Martin Luther King Jr. and Robert F. Kennedy. King was shot on April 4 in Memphis, Tennessee, after a powerful speech about hope and progress, and Kennedy was shot two months and a day later in Los Angeles, leaving a hotel after declaring victory in the California Democratic primary. When it was announced that King had died, riots broke out in sixty cities around the nation.

Both King and Kennedy held Americans' imaginations—their language and rhetoric centered around hope, the future, and the possibility of better times. The fact that both men died horribly, at the hand of another, was symbolic of the disorder and chaos of the time. The possibility of violence was everywhere, and when realized, it was destroying even the most hopeful of Americans.

Nixon capitalized on this unrest and the high level of crime in his 1968 campaign. Running for the fourth time on a presidential ticket, he focused his campaign on something entirely different from what he had ever spoken about before: order, hope, and progress. His theme was reassuring to voters; he acknowledged their fear and told them it was okay to be afraid, but that more police, more order was not the right solution. In other words, Johnson's solution of pouring more government money into more police was not going to help. Nixon argued that order without hope blocks progress, and he wanted order and progress, so he would provide Americans with the hope that in the future, they could be free from fear:

> I want to tell you my views. I say that when crime has been going up nine times as fast as population; I say that when over a hundred cities have experienced riots and burnings in various parts of those cities; I say that when the city of Washington, D.C., which should be an example of respect for law around the world, becomes so unsafe that Charlie Jonas' secretary . . . can't work after dark and go home because of fear of what could happen because of crime there; I say to you that when we find that kind of a situation in America, it is time for new men and new policies that will stop the rise in crime and also establish respect for law all over this nation. I pledge that kind of leadership. It will be fair; we will have justice with order. But let us never forget that without order you cannot have progress. (September 12, 1968)

But what does it mean in 1968, a year in which the country witnessed police clashing with Southerners over civil rights, for Nixon to have said he wanted to establish "respect for law all over this nation"? Whose law and whose justice was Nixon talking about? Nixon's choice of an insurgent issue may have been more complicated than it first seems. Some analysts of this election argue that Nixon's issue resonated so well with voters because it contained, as Mendelberg (2001) describes, an "implicit appeal to race." This embedded appeal triggered racial antipathy among whites that manifested itself in support for Nixon. It suggested that the unspoken appeal to race would allow voters to express latent preferences for *less* equality without explicitly or consciously stating that position. This is valuable because many people would have found it difficult to express overtly segregationist positions in 1968. If true, the implicit connection to race is also important in understanding this election because Humphrey did not reveal Nixon's issue as secretly race-based (which Mendelberg argues would have neutralized it).

In 1968 Humphrey only tangentially discussed race during the campaign. Humphrey was vulnerable on this issue, not because crime had gone up under his watch, but because he was committed, beyond any doubt, to advancing civil rights. The 1968 election, and its interpretation in the secondary literature, is much more complicated than it first seems. The implicit racial appeals worked well in this case because *no one exposed them for what they were*; this is critical, according to Mendelberg's theory. Although Humphrey talked about the "other side" of this issue, he never came out and explicitly told people that Nixon's campaign was appealing to their sense of white pride or racism. Humphrey said:

> The choice is simply this: shall we—as a nation—move forward toward one society of opportunity and justice or shall we abandon this commitment out of fear and prejudice and move instead toward a fractured and separated society—black against white, rich against poor, comfortable against left-out?
>
> The decision we make this year will, in fact, answer this question for ourselves, for our children, and for all those who have believed and sacrificed in the building of this nation.
>
> It is my belief that the modern movement for human rights in America is one continuous struggle, that it is still going on, and that for us to survive as a free nation, it must continue.
>
> For about a quarter of a century our nation has been making steady progress toward equal treatment under law and social opportunity for all Americans. In the last decade, it has been rapid progress.
>
> Think how far we have come in the past generation in civil rights alone: the wartime FEPC; the desegregation of the armed services; the adoption of a strong civil rights plank at the 1948 Democratic Convention; the Truman civil rights program; the 1954 Supreme Court decision outlawing legal segregation; the Montgomery bus boycott; the 1957 and 1960 Civil Rights Acts; the sit-ins movement; the freedom rides; the Voters' Rights Act; the Voting Rights Act of 1965; the Civil Rights Act of 1968.
>
> There has been historic progress in lifting the level of health, of education, of housing for every American. Not enough progress, but nonetheless historic progress. . . .
>
> Until now, we have been moving steadily forward—making progress under law together, Republicans and Democrats, black and white, rich and poor. The North

united with a growing part of the South—in fact, slowly and steadily all Americans increasingly pulling together.

But now in 1968 there comes a crossroads: a dangerous election, a hazardous national choice.

Opponents and some who were once supporters of the movement for equal rights and social opportunity now disdainfully write it off. Some Americans of all races, creeds and colors look upon that movement as finished—maybe even as a failure. (September 8, 1968)

Humphrey's retort was subtle—a "much has been done but more needs to be done" argument. He alleged that under Nixon, the country may have been separated, white from black, but he did not go on to explain why or how—and as Mendelberg claims is needed, Humphrey did not go on to bluntly explain that Nixon was "playing the race card."

At one of the most disorderly times in recent history, Nixon found two insurgent issues that met all the criteria and that worked together in symbiosis. Maybe he was being strategic, as Mendelberg and others describe; or maybe the link between crime and race was so strong in the minds of Americans that any mention of urban unrest would have primed people's racial predilections, *regardless of Nixon's intent.*

Both crime and race were salient issues in 1968, and Nixon was closer to most voters than Humphrey on important aspects of both of them. On February 28, 1968, Gallup issued a press release titled, "Crime Tops All Domestic Worries for First Time in Polling History." The report quotes an elderly California woman who said, "It's a different world we are living in. I don't even dare step out on my porch at night" as typical sentiment among Americans. Nearly 30 percent of Americans were afraid to go out alone in their own neighborhoods at night, and among women or those living in large cities, the number was 40 percent. By October 1968, nearly half the country's women were afraid to walk alone within a mile of the neighborhood in which they lived. These sentiments were felt most severely in the Midwest.

Nixon held the advantage on race relations as well, so if the crime issue triggered that response for voters, Nixon would also benefit vis-à-vis Humphrey. The closest polling on desegregation from the period was done in 1969, just after the Nixon administration announced abandonment of the school desegregation deadlines set by the Johnson administration. Gallup reported in July of 1969 that "twice as many" Americans thought school desegregation was moving "too fast" as compared to "not fast enough." They quoted a young housewife, who said, "People can't accept integration too quickly. If it's pushed, trouble breaks out." Another man said, "A gradual approach [to desegregation] will keep things from getting out of hand." These last two comments show the connection in people's minds between race relations and crime. Whether purposefully or not, Nixon, by talking about crime reduction was also signaling to voters that he would slow systematic efforts at integration.

Nixon was not the only person in the 1968 presidential race with this set of policy positions. No discussion of the 1968 campaign would be complete without mention of George Wallace, the former (and future) governor of Alabama. Wallace ran on the American Independent Party ticket and received nearly 1 million votes. He won forty-six Electoral College votes and carried five Southern states. Wallace ran a law-and-order campaign, similar to Nixon's, although there was nothing implicit about its ties to race. Wallace was a segregationist and did not apologize for it. He criticized pointy-headed intellectuals and federal encroachment on states' rights as he attempted to court blue-collar voters. Wallace's rhetoric became more and more extreme as the campaign wore on. He shouted back at one campaign stop suggesting that there were a few four-letter words that hippies did not know, for example, "work" and "soap." He later told campaign supporters that they were building a bridge over the Potomac River for all the "white liberals fleeing to Virginia." Statements like this reminded people of Wallace's most famous speech, his first inaugural address in 1962, in which he uttered the now infamous phrase, "I say segregation now, segregation tomorrow, segregation forever." In the end, it was the white Southerners who kept him from being governor in 1958 (when he was moderate on race) and elected him governor in 1962 (after he embraced segregation to win their votes) who mainly voted for him in this presidential election. His message, though similar to Nixon's, was much more explicitly racial—and as Mendelberg suggests, the explicit nature of the appeal probably worked against him.

The twist that Nixon appreciated and Wallace did not was that the segregation issue could be masked in the cloak of law and order. Nixon got all the benefit of running on race without any of the backlash. People were able to rally around Nixon without concern over what others thought of their opinions. Another twist is that Nixon did not have to worry about Humphrey changing his position and stealing this issue away—Humphrey, in a million years, would never have denounced civil rights; and in its more clever construction, it is hard to be *for* urban unrest and disorder.

Carter 1976: Outside and Honest

Jimmy Carter saw an opportunity in 1976 to exploit a characteristic of Gerald Ford that he knew was immutable—the fact that Ford had been in government for a long time and was part of the group of politicians that created cynicism in America about politics—and that meant Ford could not be part of the solution. How could the man who pardoned Richard Nixon heal the country's wounds from Watergate and Vietnam? Carter said:

There has never been an American election quite like this one. We have had economic problems before. We have had poor leadership before. But never before have we had such widespread lack of trust in our government. Because of a war our people did not want, because of scandals our people did not want, because of economic mismanagement our people did not want, millions of Americans have lost faith in our government.

We feel we have lost control of our own government, that it has become our master instead of our servant, that we are being ruled by special interests, and by politicians who don't care about us. To a tragic extent, that is exactly what has happened.

That is what this campaign is all about. We as Democrats must give our people faith in our government again by giving our people control over our government again.

Government by the people—that is the issue this year. Once the people rule again, we can solve our economic problems. Once the people rule again, we can have a fair tax system. Once the people rule again, we can reorganize our government and make it work with competence and compassion. Once the people rule again, we can have a foreign policy to make us proud again.

It all depends on the people.

This is why we are going to win. Because we have gone to the people. Because we have listened to the people and learned from the people. Because we take our strength and our hope and our courage from the people. Because we owe the special interests nothing. Because we owe the people everything. (September 15, 1976)

In response to Carter, Ford tried to convince people that things were much better in America in 1976 than they were in 1974 when he became president. Maybe he reminded people too well of 1974, repeatedly campaigning, "as I said in 1974, 'Our long national nightmare is over.'" People may have focused on the "national nightmare" part and not the "over" part. Despite what Ford wanted Americans to believe, most people did not have a lot of faith in government. Worse yet, those who did think trust could be restored in Washington thought Carter was more likely to do it by nearly 2 to 1 (Gallup Poll, July 1976). And unlike Eisenhower or Reagan, there was nothing Ford could do to demonstrate his trustworthiness. There were no SALT treaties to negotiate or wars to declare ends to. He had already proclaimed the long nightmare's end—and though he had not done anything to make matters worse, he had pardoned Richard Nixon. Ford was an inside man, and nothing he could do would get him out. Ford ran a solid clarifying campaign, but even his focus on the economy could not dislodge voters' memory of him as part of the problem.

Like the Missile Gap, Carter's outsider campaign was broad in scope and thematically centered. All sorts of issues were discussed under this rubric, therefore any time Carter spoke, he reinforced his insurgent message: "trust me, I am not them, I will not disappoint you." Even if people wanted to trust Ford, he *was* "them" and he *did* disappoint people by pardoning the president.

Figures 5.1 through 5.13 illustrate a campaign's content in ads, speeches, and news and contrast the clarifying candidate's campaign content with the insurgent candidate's.

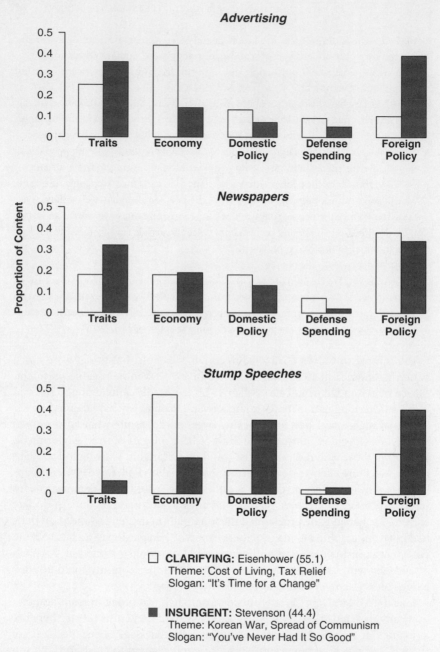

Figure 5.1 Campaign Messages in Ads, Speeches, and News, 1952
Data are from *New York Times* A Section from September 1 until Election Day
and from primary sources of candidate ads and speeches over same period.

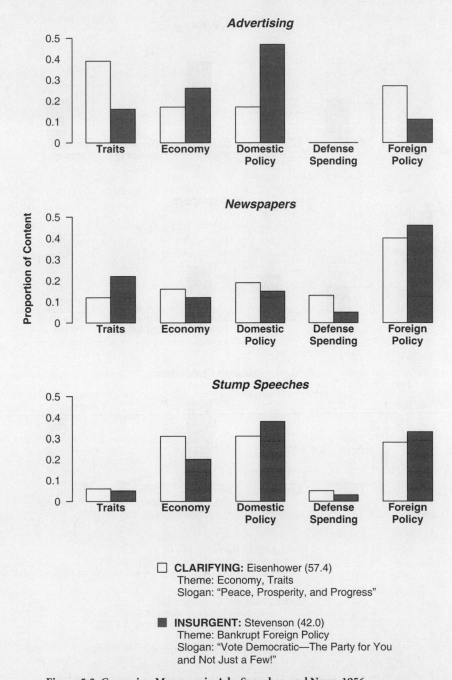

Figure 5.2 Campaign Messages in Ads, Speeches, and News, 1956
Data are from *New York Times* A Section from September 1 until Election Day
and from primary sources of candidate ads and speeches over same period.

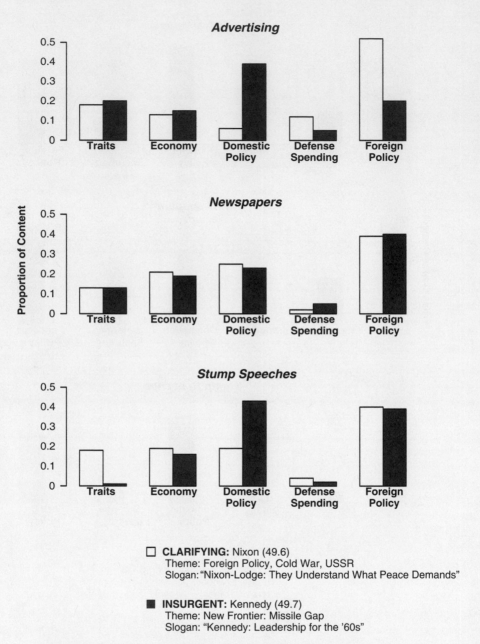

Figure 5.3 Campaign Messages in Ads, Speeches, and News, 1960
Data are from *New York Times* A Section from September 1 until Election Day
and from primary sources of candidate ads and speeches over same period.

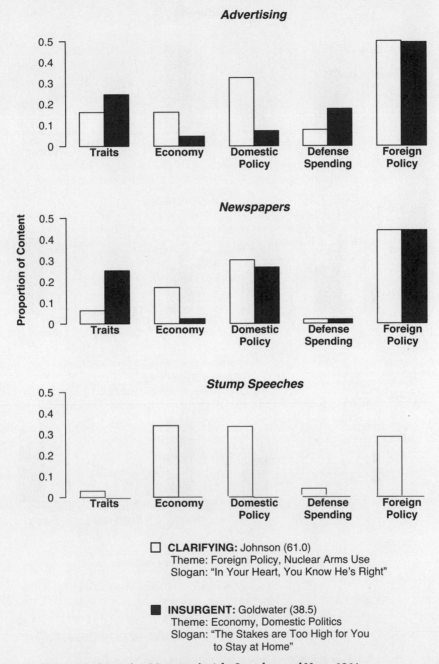

Figure 5.4 Campaign Messages in Ads, Speeches, and News, 1964
Data are from *New York Times* A Section from September 1 until Election Day
and from primary sources of candidate ads and speeches over same period.
Goldwater speeches unavailable.

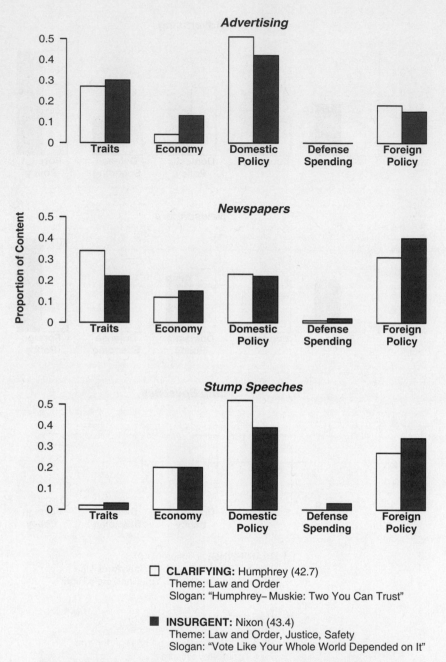

Figure 5.5 Campaign Messages in Ads, Speeches, and News, 1968
Data are from *New York Times* A Section from September 1 until Election Day
and from primary sources of candidate ads and speeches over same period.

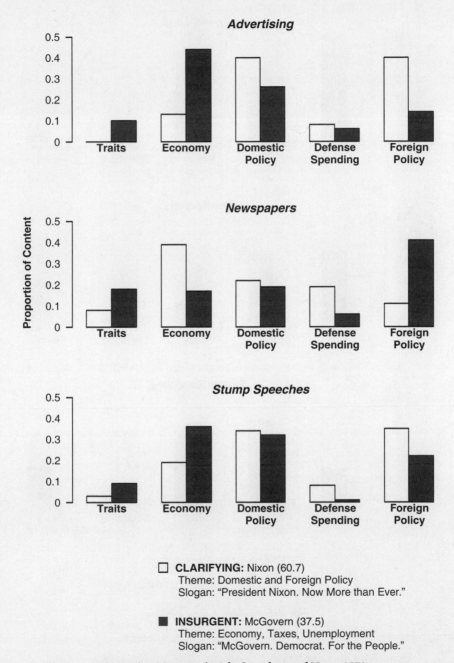

Figure 5.6 Campaign Messages in Ads, Speeches, and News, 1972
Data are from *New York Times* A Section from September 1 until Election Day
and from primary sources of candidate ads and speeches over same period.

97

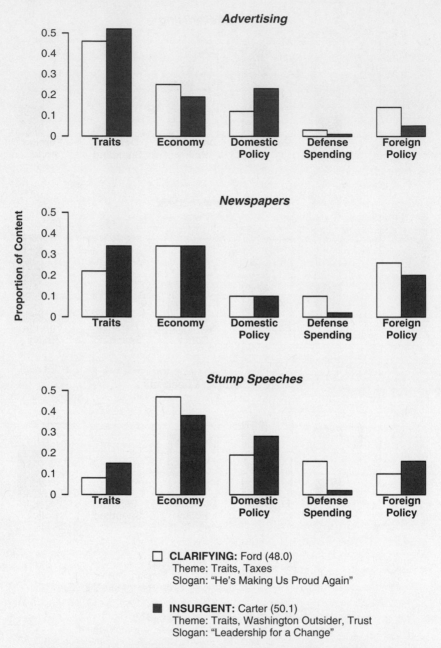

Figure 5.7 Campaign Messages in Ads, Speeches, and News, 1976
Data are from *New York Times* A Section from September 1 until Election Day
and from primary sources of candidate ads and speeches over same period.

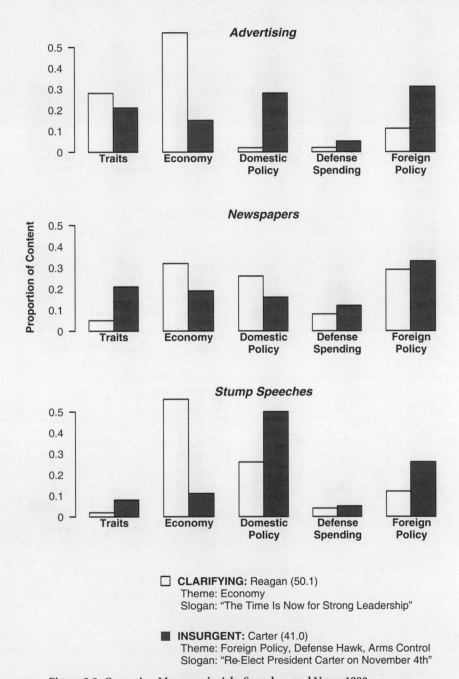

Figure 5.8 Campaign Messages in Ads, Speeches, and News, 1980
Data are from *New York Times* A Section from September 1 until Election Day
and from primary sources of candidate ads and speeches over same period.

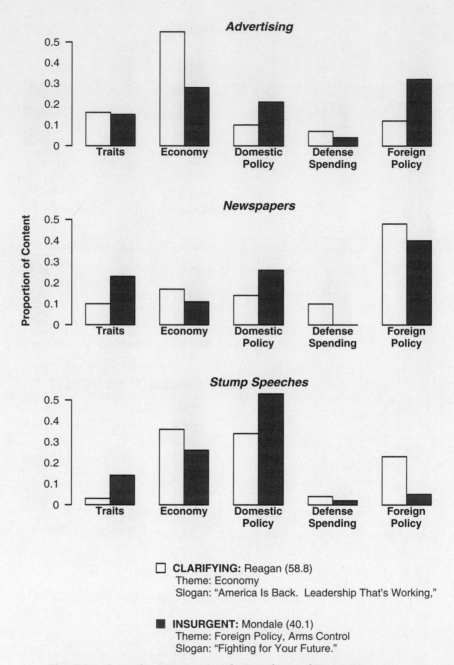

CLARIFYING: Reagan (58.8)
Theme: Economy
Slogan: "America Is Back. Leadership That's Working,"

INSURGENT: Mondale (40.1)
Theme: Foreign Policy, Arms Control
Slogan: "Fighting for Your Future."

Figure 5.9 Campaign Messages in Ads, Speeches, and News, 1984
Data are from *New York Times* A Section from September 1 until Election Day
and from primary sources of candidate ads and speeches over same period.

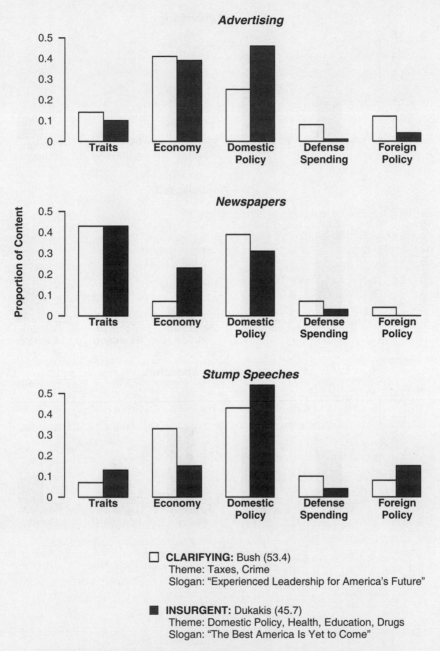

☐ **CLARIFYING:** Bush (53.4)
    Theme: Taxes, Crime
    Slogan: "Experienced Leadership for America's Future"

■ **INSURGENT:** Dukakis (45.7)
    Theme: Domestic Policy, Health, Education, Drugs
    Slogan: "The Best America Is Yet to Come"

Figure 5.10 Campaign Messages in Ads, Speeches, and News, 1988
Data are from *New York Times* A Section from September 1 until Election Day
and from primary sources of candidate ads and speeches over same period.

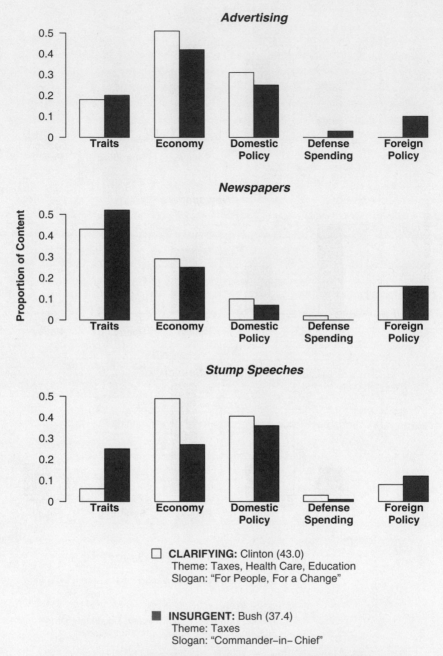

Figure 5.11 Campaign Messages in Ads, Speeches, and News, 1992
Data are from *New York Times* A Section from September 1 until Election Day
and from primary sources of candidate ads and speeches over same period.

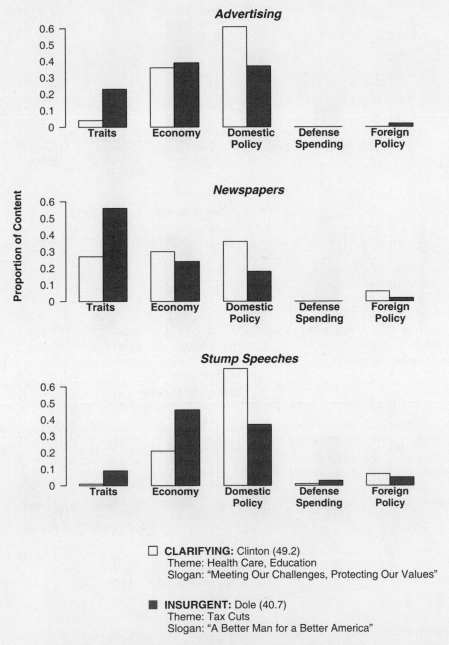

Figure 5.12 Campaign Messages in Ads, Speeches, and News, 1996
Data are from *New York Times* A Section from September 1 until Election Day
and from primary sources of candidate ads and speeches over same period.

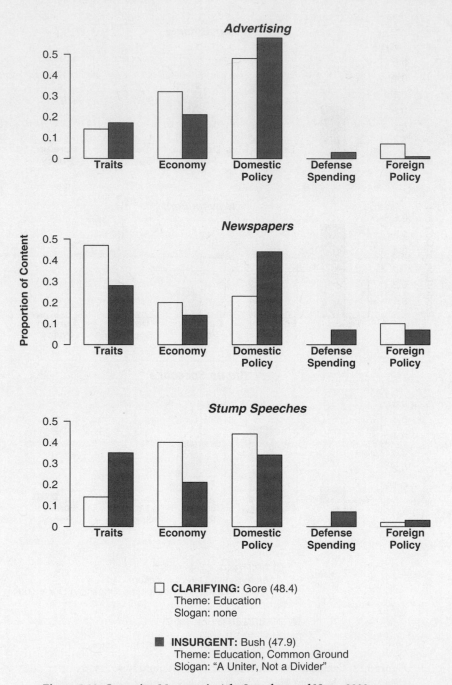

Figure 5.13 Campaign Messages in Ads, Speeches, and News, 2000
Data are from *New York Times* A Section from September 1 until Election Day
and from primary sources of candidate ads and speeches over same period.

These descriptions of insurgent candidates running campaigns that highlight the theory's prescriptions demonstrate the importance of appreciating the context of an election campaign. The nation's conditions and the candidates' characteristics matter a great deal. But they are not deterministic. The context provides candidates with the raw material on which their campaigns can be run, but what candidates do with those raw materials makes a difference to the outcome.

It is not enough to be advantaged by the economy. Nixon (1960), Humphrey, Ford, and Gore had economic conditions on their side, and except for Ford, they talked about something else and lost their elections. Nixon again (in 1972) and Clinton (1996) did the same thing but won. Two important differences are evident: Nixon (1972) and Clinton (1996) were incumbent presidents running for re-election and might have had to work less hard to establish their link to the economic conditions. Moreover, their opponents both ran insurgent campaigns focused on economic issues (taxes). The others—Nixon (1960), Humphrey, Ford, and Gore—all forwent economic discussion although conditions benefited them; but their opponents exploited characteristics and conditions on which they were more popular among voters and on which these clarifying candidates were constrained.

The elections of 1964 and 1988 are good illustrations of clarifying candidates talking about economic conditions and insurgent candidates struggling to find issues on which they have an advantage. Goldwater simply took unpopular positions and, as he admitted, probably should have known better. And Dukakis, also in his own words, reaffirmed his decisions, saying that a presidential candidate's campaign is determined by his long career in politics, not by the nature of the current election. But the candidates who recognize the value of the current context and who leverage their opponent's constraints are more likely to win elections. The context of an election is not deterministic. What candidates do with the context is.

Two More Tests of the Theory at the Candidate Level

A More Rigorous Test of Compliance

Now that I've discussed the details from the content analyses of campaigns, I would like to revisit table 5.2 and change the definition of what it means for a candidate to meet the theory's prescriptions. The test in table 5.2 took into consideration only the main arguments of the theory—did clarifying candidates talk mainly about the economy and did insurgent candidates talk mainly about something else. In table 5.5, I use a more strict test of theoretical compliance by evaluating the candidates' behavior in light of the theory's main arguments *and* its corollaries. In order to be in compliance with the theory for the purposes of this more strict test, a clarifying candidate must talk about the economy more

TABLE 5.5
Theoretical Predictions and Election Outcomes, Strict Test

	Follows Theory	Violates Theory	Total
Loses	8.33	85.71	50.00
	(1)	(12)	(13)
Wins	91.67	14.29	50.00
	(11)	(2)	(13)
	100	**100**	**100**
	(12)	**(14)**	**(26)**

Notes: Candidates are the unit of observation. Period covers 1952–2000.
Chi Square = 15.5, p = 0.00.
Fisher's Exact = .00.

than his opponent, and an insurgent candidate must choose an issue on which he is closer to most voters and one on which the clarifying candidate is constrained to an unpopular position. A violation of any one of these corollaries puts the candidate in the noncompliance category.

When the two corollaries for insurgent candidates are accounted for, an even more striking dependency emerges. With this new classification, only 14 percent of candidates who violate the typology's prescriptions go on to win elections, compared to 92 percent of candidates who behave as the theory suggests they should. Once again, the null hypothesis of independence between these two variables is rejected. Candidates who violate the theory's prescriptions lose elections.

This is the second statistical demonstration of the theory's power. The dependency results are robust to different classifications of violations and are not dependent on party, incumbency, or clarifying candidate status. A clarifying candidate who violates the typology may lose the election (and most often will), but an insurgent candidate who violates the typology always loses. Following the theory's prescriptions seems to be most important for insurgent candidates. This is nicely illustrated by considering the cases in which the candidates violated the most basic prescription for insurgents—they talked about the economy when it helped their opponent to do so (McGovern, Bush 1992, Dole). In these cases, the insurgent candidate always loses. Talking about something other than the economy is a necessary condition for insurgent candidates, although it may not be sufficient (Stevenson, Goldwater, Carter, Dukakis). On the other hand, focusing on the economy is not a necessary condition for winning elections, but it is nearly sufficient for clarifying candidates, as only one clarifying candidate who talked about the economy lost (Ford).[4]

[4] Or perhaps I should say the state of a good economy itself is a sufficient condition for winning elections. At this point, I have not demonstrated that it is anything these clarifying candidates did that garnered them a victory, only that they were benefiting from a good economy, talked about it,

Explaining the Errors in Forecasting Models

For a more exacting test of the theory's power, I now ask whether we learn any-thing more from this classification of campaigns than from basic economic forecasts. This is another attempt to illustrate, at the candidate level, whether candidate messages matter to outcomes separate from the state of the economy in general. In chapter 3, I discussed the power of simple economic forecasts to predict election winners. While economic forecasts can identify the winning party most of the time, the models often mis-estimate the margin of victory by significant amounts. The point estimates are usually on the correct side of the 50 percent mark, but they do not isolate the predicted outcomes with much precision. For example, using data from 1952 to 2000, a very simple model of outcomes using change in GNP from the fourth quarter of the year before the election to the second quarter of the election year results in an R^2 of .38 and a root mean square error (RMSE) value of 4.7. Thirty-eight percent of the vari-ation in election outcomes is explained by the simple model, and on average, the predictions are off by about 4.5 points, which, however, often cover 50 per-cent—making it difficult for candidates to learn much from the forecasts other than an understanding that the election is likely to be quite close.

Election forecasters are sensitive to this critique and make great efforts to sharpen their predictions. Incumbency can be added to the model as an indica-tor for whether one of the party nominees is actually the sitting president. When incumbency is added to the forecast, the model's ability to explain the variation in outcomes improves. Forty-seven percent of the variation is ex-plained by changes in these variables and the RMSE drops to 4.4, still large enough to straddle the 50-percent mark in a few elections over the last sixty years. Substituting other objective measures of economic performance (stock-market performance, leading indicators, real disposable income, or job growth) does little to improve the error.[5]

But what if forecasters add variables to their models that might pick up opin-ion dynamics? One obvious baseline measure of opinions about the upcoming election is the Gallup measure of presidential approval in July of the election

---

and subsequently won. The fact that two candidates won, who benefited from the economy and didn't talk about it, lends some credence to the view that it is the actual economy that matters, not the candidates' talking about it. Finally, the fact that Ford had a good economy, talked about it, and still lost gives further support to the possibility that what the candidates are saying may be irrele-vant. The strongest support for the notion that clarifying-candidate behavior matters is the fact that three of the five clarifying candidates who ignored the good economy lost their elections by very narrow margins.

[5]Using RDI instead of GNP does not significantly change the results or trends reported above. Table 5.7 presents the summaries for GNP as well as RDI. Included in the RDI model are an indi-cator for whether the country is at war (and the incumbent is to blame) and a count of the number of terms the incumbent party has been in office. These variables are coded by Bartels and Zaller (2001) and are based on Hibbs's (1987) "bread and peace" model.

year. When this variable is added to the forecast along with GNP change, the model explains 71 percent of the variation in outcomes—a thirty-three-point improvement from the GNP-only model. The RMSE drops to 3.2, still rather large for someone in the business of telling a candidate whether he or she is likely to win an upcoming election, and hardly an improvement over the model with incumbency and GNP change together.

Turning the forecasting models a bit on their side—what happens if I evaluate them in retrospect and add a variable indicating whether the out-party candidate followed the campaign theory's prescriptions? Can candidate behavior in campaigns explain the errors in forecasting models of presidential elections? The results strongly suggest that what the candidates do in campaigns matters in important ways.[6]

The forecasting model that includes the previous indicators and whether the out-party candidate followed the theory's prescriptions explains 93 percent of the variation in election outcomes and the RMSE drops to 1.67. That is a 65 percent reduction in the model's error when compared to the straightforward forecast using only change in GNP. Additionally, this model correctly predicts the outcomes of all but one presidential election since 1952. These comparisons are presented in table 5.6 along with other popular forecasting models, like the bread and peace model.

Of course, for these years, these are in-sample predictions, since it is only possible to observe whether the candidates followed the theory's mandates once the election is over—or at least substantially under way. In this sense, the forecast with campaign variables is less an actual prediction and more an illustration of two potential election outcomes. In advance of the election, the existing "correct campaign forecasting models" can be used to predict what will happen *if* the nonincumbent-party candidate follows the typology's mandates.[7] Essentially, a prediction can be made from a model that sets the "correct campaign" variable to one—meaning the out-party candidate met the theory's criteria—and another prediction can be made setting the value of the correct campaign variable at zero, indicating that the out-party candidate did not run the predicted campaign type.

The results of the model with the correct campaign variable suggest that running the predicted type of campaign results in roughly a six-point gain in two-

---

[6]The model is a linear regression of two-party vote share for the incumbent party candidate with the following independent variables: GNP change as described above, an indicator for incumbency status, and an indicator for whether the nonincumbent-party candidate followed the theory's prescriptions.

[7]It is worth noting that sometimes this is the insurgent candidate and sometimes the clarifying candidate. Most of the out-party candidates are insurgent candidates. Adding an additional indicator for whether the incumbent party candidate behaved as the theory prescribes does not change the results and actually results in a small increase in RMSE. Seven out-party candidates meet the criteria, three of them are clarifying candidates and four are insurgents.

TABLE 5.6
Forecasting Models, Explained Variation, RMSE, and Accuracy

Model	R^2	RMSE	Correctly Predicted
GNP Q4-Q2	.38	4.7	8/13
GNP and Incumbency	.47	4.4	9/13
GNP and July Approval	.71	3.2	10/13
GNP, July, and Incumbency	.79	2.8	12/13
GNP, July, Incumbency, and Out-Party Campaign	.93	1.7	12/13
RDI Q12-15	.50	4.2	10/13
RDI, War, and Terms	.69	3.34	11/13
RDI, War, Terms, and Out-Party Campaign	.81	2.6	11/13

Notes: Period covers 1952–2000. Full model results in Appendix.

party vote share for the nonincumbent party. This trumps the effects of incumbency, which are slightly less than 2 points.[8] The campaign variable is able to explain 67 percent of the variation in the residuals of a basic economic forecasting model using only GNP change. Put more clearly, knowing whether a candidate leverages the nation's economic conditions or refocuses the election onto some other issue explains two-thirds of the random noise in basic forecasting models. It turns out the noise is not random at all—it captures the behavior of candidates in campaigns and the messages they send, which political scientists rarely measure.

This implies that candidates should heed the nation's economic context and make decisions about what type of campaign to run accordingly. Candidates can leverage the state of the economy by highlighting good times or downplaying bad times. Their behavior in campaigns magnifies the effects of the economic situation. Incumbents in good economies can do better than merely resting on their accomplishment—they can talk about the economy in their campaigns in order to increase their vote shares by nontrivial amounts. But perhaps more importantly, out-party candidates who recognize how the structural conditions determine their campaign content can dramatically increase their vote shares on Election Day. In close elections, this magnitude (six points) improvement in two-party vote share could be critical. Eleven of the last fifteen presidential elections have been decided by smaller margins. Only 1972, 1964, 1984, and 1956 had bigger margins.

[8]Complete models and results are in the Appendix.

PART III

Chapter Six

THE MESSAGE MATTERS: MICROLEVEL
TESTS OF THE THEORY

S O FAR, I HAVE DESCRIBED candidate behavior in presidential campaigns as predictable long before the candidates are known or the first
general election campaign dollar is spent. I have described a campaign environment in which the economy plays a starring role and both candidates react
to it. I have shown that candidates seem to understand this world and generally
behave as the typology predicts they should, or they lose elections. Presidential
candidates, at least some of them, understand that national context matters and
that the decisions about where to center their campaigns have consequences.
Some of them are better at it than others, and some of them are exemplary (Kennedy, Nixon, Carter, and George W. Bush). Candidate behavior in campaigns
and its effects are predictable and systematic, across candidates, across elections,
and across varying national contexts. We no longer need to resort to *New York
Times* editorial board explanations like President Bush turning into "nasty-man"
in 1992 after brilliantly outcampaigning Dukakis in 1988 in order to understand campaign effects. My theory of campaigns brings some structure to a process previously described by analysts as wildly idiosyncratic or even irrelevant.

This argument requires the belief that what candidates say to voters affects
citizens in systematic and important ways. I have shown that the messages
matter to outcomes in general—but now, I attempt to get specific. Do voters
connect the clarifying candidate to economic prosperity if he talks about it more
than his opponent? How, exactly, do economic messages affect people? How
difficult is it for insurgent candidates to increase the importance of noneco-
mic issues in voters' minds? Is it even *possible* for insurgent candidates to prime
issues among the electorate? Even those insurgent candidates who choose issues
unwisely should have some success making those issues more important among
voters, but what does the evidence suggest? In order to understand why the theory explains outcomes and candidate behavior so well, it is necessary to explore
individual-level voting data that can demonstrate how voters are affected by the
different types of campaigns. In this chapter, I investigate the individual-level
mechanisms that drive the aggregate results presented heretofore. These individual-level data help to make sense of the pattern of aggregate results observed
earlier and bolster the theory's credibility.

Before I introduce these data, I want to set some expectations. Any argument is only as good as the evidence on which it is based. Sometimes we lose sight of this. For a long time now, the divide between scholars of politics and practitioners of politics over whether and how much campaigns matter has grown. The people who work on campaigns for a living, the candidates, the news media— they *know* that campaigns are important. Their evidence is anecdotal and personal, but real. And the people who analyze campaigns, study them, and look deeply for patterns of effects over time have decided campaigns matter only in minimal ways, and only at the margins. Their evidence is observational, limited in quantity, but also real. Both sets of evidence suffer from limitations, and I fear it is the limitations, not the evidence itself, that is motivating the arguments. Too often we hear anecdotal stories about a campaign strategist's successes while tending not to hear about the failures. Similarly, we hear about the lack of change in voters' attitudes or survey responses over the course of "the campaign" without hearing that the campaign is being defined as a few weeks before the election.

To make stronger arguments we need better evidence. In order for analysts to argue that campaigns are important to voters, we need evidence showing the initial perceptions and affinities voters have for candidates, and by initial, I mean in the early stages of the nominating process, before the nominees are announced. Further, we need these data for lots and lots of people in order to isolate what might be a small (in size) yet important effect on people's decisions. Then, we ideally need many interviews with these same people over the course of the campaign and over many years of elections in order to track how opinions change leading up to vote choice. And, the interviews would be quite long so that we could ask people about all the possible sources of impact on their political attitudes and behavior. The costs of such a study would be astronomical, and as such, it is not surprising that no study like this has been done.

What has been done, and done quite well, is no less impressive in size, continuity, and scope. For every presidential election year since 1952 (and most midterms, too), the American National Election Study (ANES) completes at least one thousand interviews with American citizens before and after the election.[1] The project is currently funded mainly by the National Science Foundation, but had many grantors over the years.[2] The content of the study changes year to year, but a surprising number of items have been retained over time. These data are analysts' only and best shot at uncovering a pattern of effects for

[1] The ANES has undergone a series of name changes over the years, the most recent from the National Election Study to its current name in 2005. Prior to that, it was called the Michigan Election Study (1948–76)

[2] Funding sources included the University of Michigan Survey Research Center, Office of the Provost, and Department of Political Science; the Social Science Research Council, the Carnegie Corporation, the Rockefeller Foundation, IBM, the National Science Foundation, the Ford Foundation, the National Institute of Mental Health, the Markle Foundation, Russell Sage Foundation, Center for Investigation and Research on Civic Learning and Education, and Stanford University (IRISS program).

presidential campaigns that span the last half-century. It is to these data that I append my data on the content of campaigns and news coverage in an effort to learn whether the things candidates say and do in campaigns affect voters in elections. Of course, these data are not perfectly suited for this task, and the limitations will significantly impact the conclusions I can draw about campaign effects, but they will allow me to clearly identify patterns in most cases and, in others, to carefully suggest relationships at work. Because the nature of the argument I am making is temporal—within but also across elections—the ANES is the best source of political time-series data available. No single coefficient's test of significance will make this argument. But through repeated tests with consistent results, across years and candidates, these data show how messages affect people.

Clarifying Candidate Campaign Effects: Do Campaign Messages Shape Voters' Evaluations of Candidates?

Among other things, the ANES contains measures that reflect the way ordinary Americans talk about presidential candidates. In each election since 1952, the ANES has asked a nationally representative sample of survey respondents the following set of questions about each of the major party candidates:

> Now I'd like to ask you about the good and bad points of the major candidates for President. Is there anything in particular about [insert candidate's name] that might make you want to vote for him? What is that? Anything else?

> Is there anything in particular about [insert candidate's name] that might make you want to vote against him? What is that? Anything else?

Interviewers code up to five reasons for voting for and against each candidate for a total of up to twenty reasons for the two major party candidates.[3] These open-ended questions have the distinct advantage of allowing respondents to convey whatever voting considerations they may hold. Closed-ended questions, in contrast, restrict respondents to a set of predetermined considerations that the survey writers have identified in advance. The flexibility of the open-ended questions is especially important in tracing changes in the bases of presidential voting over time, since survey writers are likely to do a better job some years than others in anticipating the considerations that will be uppermost in Americans' minds.[4]

The candidate likes/dislikes questions are coded by the ANES into hundreds

---

[3]In 1972 the ANES recorded three rather than five items for each question.

[4]While concerns are sometimes expressed that these open-ended questions are overly sensitive to the momentary accessibility of one or anther consideration in respondents' minds, Geer (1991) shows that respondents' comments do not indiscriminately reflect recently encountered informa-

of different substantive categories, which I recoded into the same groups as those that describe the candidate and news content of campaigns: the economy, domestic policy, foreign policy and defense, and traits or character. The combination of data on campaign content in advertisements and speeches, news coverage of campaigns, and voters' evaluations of candidates makes this a unique and powerful dataset for testing whether the things that candidates talk about in their campaigns influence voters in elections. In other words, before I can argue that it matters to voters what clarifying candidates say about the economy, I want to demonstrate that what candidates say during campaigns makes it at all into voters' thoughts.

In order to test the fidelity of this candidate-voter relationship, I reduce these open-ended data to the proportions of comments in each issue area for each candidate in any given year. If voters are affected by the campaign such that the more candidates talk about something, the more voters either believe that thing is important or learn more about the candidate's position on that issue (the two modes of campaign influence derived from the spatial model of voting), then voters' evaluations of the candidates ought to reflect the things candidates are raising in their campaigns. And to some degree, the comments ought to be responsive to changes in the composition of candidates' campaigns—maybe not over the course of a single election, but historically we would expect that voters make fewer comments about foreign policy in years when the candidates do not talk about foreign policy than in years when this issue is discussed with great frequency. Even if voters are merely sampling off the "top of their heads" (Zaller 1992), we would expect there to be more considerations about foreign policy available for random sampling when candidates or the media talk about it a lot compared to a paucity of considerations about foreign policy at the top of one's head when candidates do not mention the issue much at all.

High Fidelity?

To show the relationship between what candidates and media talk about during campaigns and what voters say they like about the candidates, I present the figures below, grouped by the four issue areas under consideration.[5] Each figure plots the percentage of voters' comments about an issue on the vertical axis and the percentage of candidate or news discourse about that same issue on the horizontal axis. Each point is a candidate in a given year. A 45-degree line represents

---

tion. Similarly, the NES recently expressed concern about the quality control of the coding of these responses. From 1990 to 1992, while working as Warren Miller's research assistant at Arizona State University, I coded similar responses to questions on the mass-elite-linkages project (the Convention Delegate Study). My training, by Professor Miller, was thorough and clear. I assume that my counterparts working on the NES questions were equally prepared for their work even if documentation of the training appears haphazard in retrospect.

[5] I do not present results for defense spending since so few candidates talk about this at all.

perfect fidelity—if the points fall on (or near) the 45-degree line, a 1-percent increase in candidate or news discourse on a topic is reflected in a 1-percent increase in voters' comments on that topic. As I mentioned earlier, we might not expect this relationship to be perfectly reflective, but it serves as a benchmark from which we can evaluate the fidelity of this system.[6]

As is evident in figure 6.1, high fidelity relationships rarely exist. In some cases, voters rarely talk about issues (the economy), making it difficult for changes in candidate or news content to register effects. In other cases, voters talk a lot about the topic (traits), which also makes it difficult for changes in candidate or news content to have an effect. Most of the relationships, however, are positive, with the exception of trait coverage in the news, which seems to negatively affect how much voters talk about these things. A few relationships are flat, indicating no fidelity between candidate or news content and voters' thoughts, but most of these relationships are with news content. The conclusion for campaign-voter fidelity seems to be that voters are subtly responsive to changes in campaign content, but their comments do not necessarily reflect the overall composition of the campaign very well.[7]

Each row of the figure represents a different issue, and each column a mode of campaign communication (ads, speeches, news). There are several ways to evaluate the trends in figure 6.1. One way is to examine the tightness of the fit of the data, in other words, how closely are the data points scattered about the regression line? It is clear that the economy is the issue for which the relationship between campaign discourse and voters' thoughts is the tightest—regardless of whether the information comes from ads, speeches, or news. This suggests that the issue itself may drive the relationship, not a specific method of campaign content delivery. Domestic and foreign policy, on the other hand, trend slightly more parallel to the 45-degree line than the economy, but the data have a lot of dispersion around the regression lines. This suggests that the general relationships move in the right direction, but that there is a lot of variation in the relationships between domestic and foreign-policy campaign content and voters' evaluations of candidates on these topics.

In terms of the mode of communication, the relationship between ads, speeches, news, and voters' evaluations of candidates is positive and significantly different from zero for advertising about the economy, foreign policy, and traits. Speech content is only significantly related to voters' comments on domestic and foreign policy, and news content is not significantly related to voters' thoughts on any of these issues. Surprisingly, news coverage seems to have

---

[6]For all of the data presented in the remainder of this chapter, information about numbers of cases for each election year, for each subset (clarifying v. insurgent, partisanship, information level, etc.), can be found in the Appendix. For the years under investigation, the NES data has 25,502 respondents. From 1972 forward, when NES began asking the seven-point issue scales used at the end of this chapter, the total number of respondents is 16,870.

[7]These analyses use the things that voters say they "like" about a candidate.

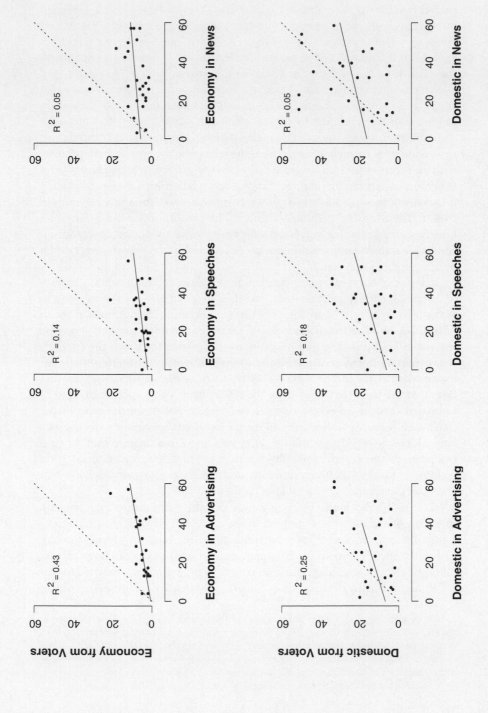

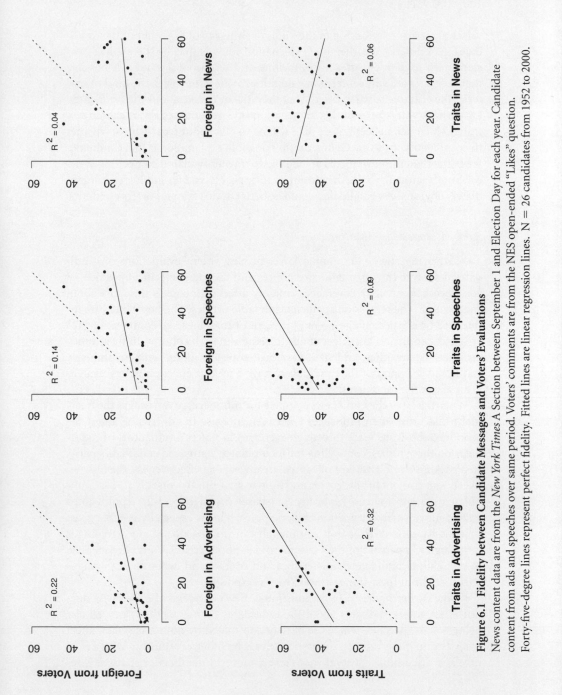

Figure 6.1 Fidelity between Candidate Messages and Voters' Evaluations

News content data are from the New York Times A Section between September 1 and Election Day for each year. Candidate content from ads and speeches over same period. Voters' comments are from the NES open-ended "Likes" question. Forty-five-degree lines represent perfect fidelity. Fitted lines are linear regression lines. N = 26 candidates from 1952 to 2000.

very little if any relationship to the kinds of things people say about the candidates. As I described earlier, one explanation for this may be the media's constant need to define stories in compelling and sensational ways. It is possible that news stories, while interesting, do not provide voters with the kind of material they can recite when asked what they like or dislike about the candidates. Or perhaps voters turn all this information into generalities about candidates' traits, which people seem more than willing to talk about regardless of whether the candidates or the media do. Another possible explanation is that candidates are better than the news media at judging what voters will find compelling, however, both actors have worthy incentives to appeal to voters, and it is not immediately obvious why candidates would be better at this than reporters or editors.

Ads: Messages That Matter

To further investigate the unique forces driving voters' evaluations of candidates, I analyze the open-ended responses and ascertain specifically which, of ads, speeches, or news coverage, is mainly affecting people's thoughts about candidates.[8] The regression coefficients in table 6.1 describe how voters are influenced by a 1-percentage-point (1 percent of total message composition) increase in candidates' messages about the issues in each column. In these models, the ads, speeches, and news coverage compete along with incumbency status and the party of the candidate to have a unique effect on voters' evaluations about the candidates.

When ads, speeches, and news compete for influence, advertising is the treatment that most often influences voters. An increase in advertising about the economy and traits leads directly to increases in voters' evaluations of candidates on these topics, controlling for incumbency status and candidate's party. In a striking demonstration of campaign advertising effectiveness, the link between trait content in advertising and trait evaluations by voters is 1.5 : 1. A candidate need only increase his or her trait-based message in ads by a point and a half to move voters' evaluations by one point. This is especially notable given that the baseline level of trait commentary in the absence of any signaling is quite high (35 percent of their comments are about traits). Voters are inclined to talk about candidate characteristics and traits—and, when the campaigns advertise about these things as well, voters respond.

As the earlier figure (6.1) demonstrated, news coverage of campaigns does not affect voters' thoughts about the candidates on any of the issues, all else being equal. Speeches, which are heavily dominated by domestic policy, affect voters' evaluations only on domestic issues. The other relationship with a positive and discernible effect on voters' evaluations is incumbency status as it re-

[8] I do this using OLS regression and controlling for incumbency status and party. I cluster the standard errors around campaign year.

TABLE 6.1
Do Ads, Speeches, or News Affect Voters' Evaluations of Candidates?

	Economy	Foreign Policy	Domestic Policy	Traits
Advertising	.19 (.08)	.17 (.10)	.07 (.16)	.65 (.17)
Speeches	.01 (.06)	.14 (.13)	.48 (.21)	−.04 (.28)
News Coverage	.01 (.11)	−.06 (.10)	.14 (.30)	−.21 (.21)
Incumbency	.02 (.02)	.04 (.02)	−.04 (.04)	−.01 (.07)
Republican	−.01 (.01)	.05 (.02)	.05 (.04)	.05 (.05)
Constant	−.01 (.01)	.00 (.02)	−.09 (.06)	.35 (.10)
R^2	.52	.45	.41	.42

Note: There are twenty-five cases for each column because Goldwater speeches were not available. Cell entries are OLS regression coefficients with standard errors in parentheses. Standard errors are clustered for campaign year. Campaign content is measured in percent of appeals in ads, speeches, or news coverage about each issue in the columns. The content analysis is done for each candidate in every year from 1952 to 2000. Voters' comments are from the ANES open-ended likes-dislikes questions (likes only). Full model results in Appendix.

lates to foreign policy, although the effect is substantively very small. The small size of this effect, however, is important to the story about how much the candidate messages matter. Controlling for the things candidates say in campaigns, incumbency status matters very little to the kinds of comments voters make about the candidates.

It would not have been surprising to learn that it is easier for people to say things about incumbents since people presumably know a lot about them already, but in fact, the direct effects for incumbency status are basically negligible in this context. Another possibility is that incumbency conditions the effectiveness of campaign communication, but there is little evidence that this is true either. In tests of the four models presented in table 6.1 when the models are fully interacted with incumbency, significant differences exist only for advertising on the economy and traits. For economic advertising, voters respond more to challenger advertising. But, for traits, they respond more to incumbent advertising. There were no differences for other modes of communication or other issues. The messages of campaigns affect people, regardless of candidate party or incumbency status.

To detail this relationship with a bit more nuance and to put the theory to a tough individual-level test, I am going to focus solely on campaign advertising, since that is the method of campaign communication with the strongest relationship to voters' evaluations. My theory of campaigns suggests that clarifying and insurgent candidates send voters different messages during campaigns because real economic circumstances condition the kinds of things they should talk about. In chapter 5 I showed that some candidates figure this out and some do not. The aggregate data demonstrate that the candidates who understand that context matters greatly to the formation of their messages are more likely to win elections. But can this powerful aggregate result be seen at the individual level—and if so, how does it operate?

To establish the relationship between campaign messages, voter evaluations, and economic context at the individual level, I am going to use two sets of voter evaluations—the first is the proportion of economic statements people make when they talk about liking a candidate. The second is the proportion of economic statements people make when they talk about liking a candidate *and disliking his opponent*. The second measure allows me to test whether economic messages shape the positive considerations about one candidate, presumably the candidate sending the message, while also influencing the negative considerations about the other. If messages truly matter, the analyses should show advertising effectiveness for both types of candidates, clarifying and insurgent, but the things voters *say* about the candidates may be different depending on their type. This pattern is demonstrated nicely in table 6.2.

Clarifying candidates prime economic considerations in the minds of voters by increasing their economic messages in ads. Clarifying candidates benefit from the economy and should talk as much as possible about this issue so voters associate the clarifying candidate with the economy. The data in the first column of table 6.2 show that voters respond to clarifying messages. For every three-point increase in economic content, clarifying candidates increase the economic content in voters' evaluations by one point. This same level of responsiveness is not observed for insurgent candidates. Their ability to shape the things voters like about them does not change when they talk about the economy. This is the role of context. The insurgent candidate is sending messages about the economy in an environment that does not reinforce his positive association with this issue. Reality neutralizes the effect of this positive association. This, however, does not mean that insurgent messages on the economy do not matter. In fact, quite the contrary is true.

The insurgent messages may not prime positive economic evaluations of insurgents, but given the content of insurgent messages about the economy, these messages might affect the things voters associate negatively with the clarifying candidates—especially since the clarifying candidate is likely to have identified the economy as the central issue in his or her campaign. The last column of table 6.2 demonstrates this effect. When the things voters like about a candidate and the things they dislike about the opponent are considered jointly, the messages of insurgent candidates become equally as effective as the messages of clarifying candidates. Insurgent candidates cannot shape their own positive images with economic campaign messages, but they can influence the negative things voters say about their opponents.

Table 6.2
Effects of Campaign Messages about Economy on Evaluations of Candidates

	Candidate Likes		Candidate Likes and Opponent Dislikes	
	Clarifying	Insurgent	Clarifying	Insurgent
Advertising	.30 (.08)	.06 (.05)	.23 (.09)	.23 (.08)
Speeches	−.11 (.12)	.15 (.07)	−.06 (.13)	−.19 (.12)
News Coverage	−.03 (.12)	−.03 (.09)	−.01 (.13)	.27 (.15)
Incumbency	.04 (.02)	−.01 (.01)	.01 (.02)	−.02 (.02)
Republican	−.00 (.02)	−.02 (.02)	−.00 (.02)	−.01 (.02)
Constant	.00 (.02)	.02 (.03)	.00 (.04)	−.01 (.03)
R^2	.72	.73	.57	.66
N	13	12	13	12

Note: Cell entries are OLS regression coefficients with standard errors in parentheses. Campaign content is measured in percent of appeals in ads, speeches, or news coverage about the economy. The content analysis is done for each candidate in every year from 1952 to 2000. Voters' comments are from the ANES open-ended likes-dislikes questions.

The difference in where these individual-level effects operate is compelling and reinforces the theory's fundamental claims. Clarifying candidates help themselves by talking about the economy (and they damage their opponent's images too), but insurgent candidates do not help themselves directly by talking about the economy. The best they do is damage their opponent's position relative to this issue. To boost their own evaluations among voters, insurgent candidates have to send messages about something other than the economy. These open-ended comments suggest that insurgents' messages about traits in ads and domestic-policy coverage in the news are most likely to shape their positive images.

Clarifying Candidate Campaign Effects: Do Campaign Messages Help Voters Learn about Candidates' Issue Positions?

Campaign messages about the economy affect the composition and direction of voters' evaluations of the candidates. Specifically, these messages interact with the nation's economic context to influence voters' considerations, both positive and negative, of clarifying candidates. As candidates increase the economic content in their message, voters respond by using the economy more in their assessments of the candidates. Economic messages affect whether voters like or dislike the clarifying candidate over the course of the campaign, but are voters actually learning anything about the candidates' positions on economic (or other) issues during the campaign? On the one hand, it is normatively appealing to believe that campaigns educate voters about important issues, so a campaign effect illustrating learning seems important. On the other hand, candidates do not so much care why voters like them or they vote for them, just that they do. From this perspective, increasingly positive evaluations about candidates may be equally satisfying as evidence that people learn about issue positions over the course of the campaign. As an investigator of the process, I am agnostic about whether learning should occur, but I would like to know if it does. In a further effort to elucidate the individual-level mechanisms that drive the aggregate results from the previous chapter, I turn now to an investigation of campaign learning. The next several pieces of evidence use the ANES data, but not the open-ended questions. Instead, I use closed-ended questions about specific policies.

The ANES introduced a regular battery of issue questions in 1972 to tap into citizens' perceptions of candidates' positions on issues. Respondents are asked to place themselves, and if they can do that, they are asked to place each of the presidential candidates on the same issues.[9] Several issues have been asked repeatedly over the last thirty-four years and some of them coincide with the kinds of things candidates were talking about or getting news coverage of in their campaigns; they are: whether the government ought to be responsible for making sure every American who wants a job can find one; whether we should cooperate with Russia; whether we are spending the right amount of money on national defense; whether the government ought to increase spending and services or cut both; whether health insurance should be universally provided; whether the government has provided too much or too little help to minorities; and whether women should enter the workforce or stay home. The general question text, which changes for each issue and for whether the respondent is placing him- or herself or the candidates, reads:

> Some people feel that the government in Washington should see to it that every person has a job and a good standard of living. Suppose these people are at one end of a scale, at point 1. Others think the government should just let each person get ahead on his/their own. Suppose these people are at the other end, at point 7. And, of course, some other people have opinions somewhere in between, at points 2, 3, 4, 5 or 6. Where would you place yourself on this scale, or haven't you thought much about this?[10]

---

[9]After 1996, the ANES sometimes asked respondents to place the candidates even if they could not place themselves. For consistency's sake, I only use candidate placements for respondents who could place themselves.

[10]This wording was used in some years, and in other years it was not specified, "suppose these people are at one end . . ." For exact question wording, see Appendix.

Additionally, the ANES asks respondents to place themselves and candidates on an ideology scale that ranges from very liberal to very conservative.[11]

Measuring Uncertainty

These issue questions give us great leverage on whether voters know enough to place the candidates on the issues, and if so, whether those issues are important in evaluating candidates. Roughly a quarter to one-third of respondents cannot make a placement about themselves or the candidates on these issues. I assume this means they know so little about the candidates or the issue that they cannot even guess what position on the scale might be reasonable. If the campaigns are reducing uncertainty on candidates' issue positions, especially clarifying candidates' positions on economic issues, then over the course of the campaign more people should be able to offer placements of the candidates on these scales. By dividing the campaign into two-week intervals, I measure the changes in how many people can place candidates on these issues during the campaign. I expect to see greater levels of reduction in nonplacement for clarifying candidates who talk about the economy compared to those clarifying candidates who focus on something other than the economy. The theory is less clear about whether insurgent candidates ought to be able to reduce uncertainty about the insurgent issue, since their main goal is to change the coefficient on this issue from zero to something greater than zero, not to clarify their position—reductions in uncertainty are a luxury good candidates can purchase after the issue on which they are campaigning is salient and they are advantaged.

In figure 6.2, I show changes in the average level of nonplacement on six issues from the first two weeks of September to the last two weeks before Election Day aggregated across all years. The data show that clarifying candidates are in fact able to reduce the average level of uncertainty about their positions on economic issues, like whether the government should guarantee jobs to everyone who wants to work. They also reduce uncertainty on their positions on the general left-right ideological placement scale and on the level of cooperation they desire with Russia. The largest reduction, as expected, is on the jobs issues. Insurgent candidates, on average, are not able to reduce voters' levels of uncertainty on any of the issues over the course of the campaign.

Admittedly, a one-point movement is small. Many people are inclined to treat such small differences as unimpressive or unimportant, but small in size is not synonymous with negligible. The one-point reduction in uncertainty for clarifying candidates on the jobs issue corresponds to roughly a 4-percent decrease in nonplacement on this issue. And, given that nonplacement on this issue is limited to a small range (13–34 percent), the one-point shift taken over the observable range of nonplacements is actually more like the equivalent of

[11]For exact question wording, see Appendix.

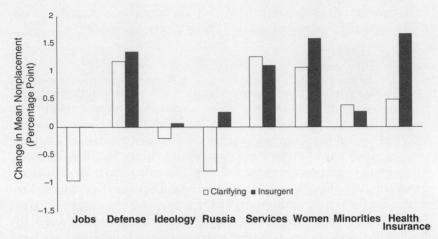

Figure 6.2 Changes from September to Election Day in Mean Levels of Issue Uncertainty by Candidate Type
Each bar in the figure represents the average change across all years (1952–2000) from the first two weeks of September to the two weeks before Election Day in respondents' inability to place the clarifying candidate on an issue compared to their inability to do the same for the insurgent candidate. Decreases in uncertainty indicate learning over the period of the campaign. Data are from ANES seven-point placement scales.

what would be a five-point shift over the entire range of possible outcomes. A simple regression of the change in nonplacement on the jobs question controlling for year and using only candidate type as a regressor shows that the one-point reduction in uncertainty is not due to sampling error (the standard error on the coefficient of 1.0 is .39).

Further, nonplacement is a rather blunt operationalization of uncertainty reduction or learning. In truth, I am using this dichotomous observation to measure something continuous (and unobservable), thus the small reductions in uncertainty for clarifying candidates suggest that everyone is becoming more certain of the clarifying candidate's position on economic issues, but not so for insurgent candidates. Clarifying candidates show an advantage on the economy.

In figure 6.3, I break out the clarifying candidates by year and examine those who talk mainly about the economy separately from those who do not. As the figure demonstrates, and as we saw with the aggregate content data, sometimes talking about the economy yields desired effects, but sometimes it does not. In 1976 Ford talked mainly about the economy in his speeches (and about traits in his ads) but was not able to reduce voter uncertainty about the economy. The same is true in 1980 for Reagan, who talked about the economy in both ads and speeches. In 1984, 1988, and 1992, however, Reagan, Bush, and Clinton were all able to reduce voter uncertainty about the issue of jobs over the course of the

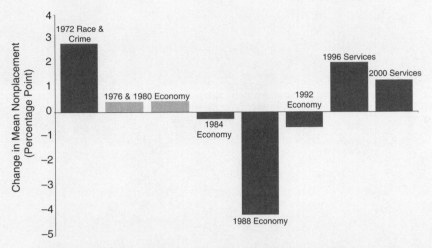

Figure 6.3 Changes in Mean Levels of Uncertainty from September to Election Day for Clarifying Candidates by Dominant Topics of Campaign Messages
Each bar in the figure represents the change from the first two weeks of September to the two weeks before Election Day in respondents' inability to place the clarifying candidate on the issue on which they focused their campaign messages. Decreases in uncertainty indicate learning over the period of the campaign. Dark shades indicate a theoretically anticipated effect.

campaign. In 1972 and 2000, the clarifying candidates talked about something other than the economy and were unsuccessful at reducing uncertainty on those issues. It is not enough just to be the clarifying candidate or just to talk about any issue—clarifying candidates cannot reduce voter uncertainty about any issue and are especially advantaged on the economy. In the three years (1972, 1996, 2000) in which the clarifying candidates talked mainly about something other than the economy, reductions in economic uncertainty are observed for two of them (1972 and 2000). Since I previously showed that insurgent candidates who talk about the economy influence what people think about clarifying candidates, it is worth mentioning what the insurgent candidates were talking about in these years. In 1972 McGovern talked mainly about the economy, and Dole did the same in 1996. In 2000 neither candidate did, although one-third of Gore's campaign content was about the economy and roughly a quarter of Bush's.

Dole's and McGovern's economically centered insurgent campaigns in 1996 and 1972 leave only one election—2000—in which neither candidate talked mainly about the economy. This makes it very difficult to separate the effects of messages about the economy from the effects of simply being advantaged on the economy. As a first step toward sorting this out as much as possible, in figure 6.4 I present the changes in average levels of uncertainty about insurgent issues from Labor Day to Election Day for insurgent candidates.

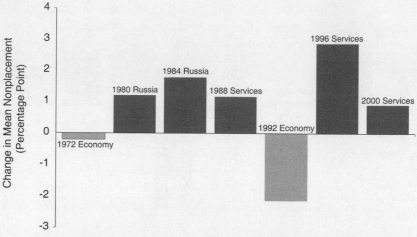

Figure 6.4 Changes in Mean Levels of Uncertainty from September to Election Day for Insurgent Candidates by Dominant Topics of Campaign Messages
Each bar in the figure represents the change from the first two weeks of September to the two weeks before Election Day in respondents' inability to place the insurgent candidate on the issue on which they focused their campaign messages. Decreases in uncertainty indicate learning over the period of the campaign. Dark shades indicate a theoretically anticipated effect.

It is difficult to reduce uncertainty on issues that are not salient to voters—and some of these insurgent issues may be only mildly salient, or not so at all. Interestingly, the two years in which insurgent candidates were able to reduce uncertainty about their insurgent issues—1972 and 1992—are both years in which insurgents talked about the economy even though it did not benefit them. There simply are not enough cases to sort out whether this is an incumbency effect, an effect of the economy as an issue, or both. The fact is, though, that except for 1976 and 1980, every candidate who talked about the economy reduced voters' uncertainty about the issue. Some of these candidates were advantaged by the economy, but two were not. Four candidates who did not talk about the economy still experienced reduced uncertainty about their positions on guaranteed jobs (both candidates in 2000, Nixon in 1972, and Dukakis in 1988). Except for 2000, these other candidates could have been affected by their opponents' dominant discussions of the economy. One fact, however, is clear: candidates who talked about other issues never decreased the average aggregate levels of uncertainty on those issues when all the years are examined together.

Reducing Uncertainty

The patterns in figures 6.3 and 6.4 are mixed, and with so few cases, it is not easy to understand exactly what forces are at work and in what magnitudes. It is time to dig into the data a little deeper. Using all the issue-candidate-year data, I test whether dominant campaign messages reduce voters' uncertainty about the candidates' positions on those issues. This multivariate test will help to clarify the size and pattern of the effects by tying specific candidate messages to actual effects within election years on related issues. I present these results in table 6.3. The results are from a linear regression using ninety-four candidate-issue-year observations on the proportion of respondents who are unable to place the candidate on each issue at different points during the campaign. The first column presents the mean level of uncertainty for those interviewed near Labor Day, and the second column reports the changes occurring for those interviewed during the campaign between Labor Day and Election Day. Reductions in uncertainty are indicative of learning about where candidates stand on issues. The

TABLE 6.3
Reductions in Mean Levels of Issue Uncertainty for Eight Issues

	Labor Day	Labor to Election Day
Clarifying Candidate	−.13 (.07)	.37 (.45)
Message: Economy	−4.3 (1.3)	−1.1 (.58)
Message: Domestic	−9.6 (2.0)	−2.4 (.72)
Message: Foreign	−.9 (2.0)	−.06 (.29)
Economic Issue and Message	−2.9 (1.8)	−1.42 (.29)
Domestic Issue and Message	−4.3 (1.2)	.32 (.90)
Foreign Policy Issue and Message	−1.3 (1.8)	.16 (.86)
Constant	.41 (3.9)	2.85 (.82)
N	94	94
R^2	.71	.44
Difference due to Economic Message	−7.2	−2.5

Note: Data are respondents' abilities to place each candidate on eight different issues: guaranteed jobs, defense spending, cooperation with Russia, services v. spending, the role of women, aid to minorities or blacks, government-supplied health insurance, and the ideological left-right scale in every year from 1972 to 2000. Not all issues are asked in each year. The dependent variable is coded 1 if the respondent cannot place the candidate on the issue, thus negative coefficients indicate reductions in uncertainty levels. Cell entries are regression coefficients generated by regressing whether the candidate in question was the clarifying candidate, whether the candidate talked predominantly about the economy, domestic policy, or foreign policy, and the interaction of these messages with whether the issue placement is on one of those issues. Indicators for each year are also included (coefficients suppressed), except 1972. Changes between Labor Day and Election Day are defined as the difference between the first two weeks of September and the first two weeks of November. Standard errors are clustered on issue.

model includes indicators for each year (except 1972), an indicator for being the clarifying candidate, indicators for whether a candidate talked about a given issue in a specific year, and interactions between the issues candidates talked about and voters' abilities to place those candidates on the particular issue on which their message focuses.[12] For example, I include both the direct effect of talking about the economy and its interaction with whether the issue placement we observe is an economic one in order to pick up the full force of message effectiveness. It is possible that focusing on the economy reduces people's uncertainty about placing the candidates on economic issues, but also reduces uncertainty about the candidates' preferences over domestic spending or federally funded health insurance, or even how sympathetic they are to the role of women in the workforce. I want to illustrate these "spillover" effects where they exist, but also test the stronger hypothesis that messages about the economy help voters learn about economic policy positions in particular.

Candidate's campaign messages, specifically about the economy and domestic policy, successfully reduce voters' levels of uncertainty about the candidates' positions on issues in general. In the campaign period prior to Labor Day, candidates who focus their messages on the economy decrease the average nonplacement rate on issues by 4.3 percentage points. Campaigns that focus on domestic policy are more than twice as effective, decreasing the average rate of nonplacements by 9.6 points (these results are in the first column of the table). After Labor Day, the effects are smaller, but still important: a 1.1-point reduction from economic messages and a 2.4-point reduction from domestic messages (these results are in the second column of the table). These effects establish the "spillover" effects mentioned above. Even though the candidates are talking mainly about the economy or domestic policy, they are successful at reducing uncertainty on average—across all the issues in the dataset—by substantial amounts. It is not hard to imagine how this happens. The eight issues in the dataset cover aid to minorities, the role of women in society, government-sponsored health insurance, and general ideological placements, along with whether the government should guarantee a job for everyone who wants to work and two questions on defense spending and relations with Russia. Learning about a candidate's position on domestic spending for education could help voters figure out where to place the candidate on the ideological spectrum. Similarly, hearing that a candidate wants to lower taxes might suggest to voters that the candidate is not in favor of large government programs like federally administered health care.

That voters make these connections is at the same time intuitive and remarkable. It makes sense that people could learn about ideology from hearing candidates speak about specific policies, but effects like this, directly from campaign messages, have been difficult to document. These kinds of connections

---

[12]Results are robust to different specifications. Standard errors are clustered on issues.

are at the heart of Popkin's (1991) "reasoning voter," yet there have been few demonstrations of this kind of inferential thought process by voters. As Popkin argued and these data show, candidates send messages or signals about one thing during a campaign, and voters actually learn about other political dimensions as well. Popkin argues that this is a result of voters making inferences about a candidate's position on various issues because of the things the candidate says and does in the campaign. Voters, according to Popkin, are constructing narratives in their heads about the candidates. The "scripts" are generated from the kind of generalizations I call spillover effects from messages.

An equally compelling finding is the effect of specific messages on only those issues related to the campaign message. When the effect of the messages is conditioned by whether the issue is in the same policy area as the message, additional reductions in uncertainty occur. In the period prior to Labor Day, the average nonplacement rate on economic issues alone goes down another three points when campaigns are about the economy—making the total reduction in uncertainty on economic issues slightly more than seven points. The average nonplacement rate for domestic issues is reduced an additional four points, for a total reduction from domestic messages of about fourteen points. These are dramatic effects from campaign messages especially when considering the observable range on nonplacement on most issues ranges from roughly 10 to 40 percent. Fourteen points on a thirty-point range is nearly a 50-percent reduction in the rate of nonplacement directly attributable to the things candidates talk about in their campaigns.

In the traditional campaign period, between September and November, however, one set of issues stands out as responding directly to campaign messages, and that is the economy. Over the course of the campaign, as candidates focus on the economy, average rates of nonplacement decrease by roughly 2.5 points (a 1.1-point effect from the message directly and another 1.42 points on economic issues specifically). The other issues show no decreases in uncertainty over the course of the campaign on the issues on which candidates focus. The economy is slightly privileged in this regard—messages about it matter to voters over the campaign period in a way that they do not for other issues. This finding demonstrates a microfoundation for an effect that has long been accepted as an aggregate regularity: the economy is a good predictor of election outcomes. The trends in table 6.3 suggest one microlevel reason why this is true—because people learn about the candidates' positions on economic issues over the course of the campaign *if the candidates talk about the economy* in a way that they do not learn about other issues.

Campaign Learning about the Economy

I know there will be skeptics who question this result, so I want to come at this from one more, somewhat different, angle. Average rates of nonplacement are indicative of people's levels of uncertainty about candidates over the course of the campaign, but one of the advantages of individual-level data is the ability to allow different people to have different reactions to conditions or messages. It is time to investigate whether these learning results are robust to individual-level controls, and to push the test of the clarifying message to the most difficult level I can with these data. In order to do this, I model issue nonplacements *separately* for the eight issues mentioned above and include controls for age, race, gender, education, and fixed effects for election year. As above, the dependent variable is an indicator for whether the respondent can place a specific candidate on a specific issue. Since I am interested in documenting reductions in uncertainty, a one on the dependent variable indicates an inability to place the candidate on that issue. I expect coefficients on campaign variables to be negative. To this simple probit model I add a final test of the theory. The NES asks respondents how much attention they pay to the campaign in various forms of media. I use these measures to scale a person's likelihood of receiving campaign messages. I expect the campaign messages to reduce uncertainty in greater magnitudes for people who have high likelihoods of experiencing the campaign messages when compared to those who have low likelihoods of getting the messages. The scale is a simple additive measure using attention to the campaign on television, in newspapers, on the radio, and in magazines.[13] I add this variable to the model and interact it with the time of the person's interview. This interaction is the test of campaign message effectiveness and follows the spirit of Bartels (1986). Reductions in uncertainty should be greatest for those people who pay attention to the campaign in the media between Labor Day and Election Day. More specifically, uncertainty about economic issues should be reduced over the course of the campaign for clarifying candidates. I show these effects in figure 6.5 as predicted probabilities of nonplacement on each issue for an average respondent in an average year.

The predicted levels of nonplacement, broken out by particular issues, confirm the story told by the mean levels of nonplacement. There does not appear to be anything special about just being the clarifying candidate—there are issues on which uncertainty about clarifying candidates is decreased, but there are also issues on which uncertainty about clarifying candidates is increased, all else being equal. The left side of the figure shows the predicted probabilities of nonplacement on each issue for people with no exposure to the campaign through the media. In comparison to the right side of the figure, it is easy to see that people with no media exposure to the campaign are not as affected by the campaign during the six weeks before the election—several issues actually show increases in nonplacement over the course of the campaign for both candidates.

[13]In some years, one or two of these questions are not asked. In those years, straightforward media-use questions were substituted with the outcome categories made similar to the campaign-attention questions by treating each two-day set as a category of attention. For example, zero to one day of watching TV news is equivalent to "none" in the attention-to-campaign news question.

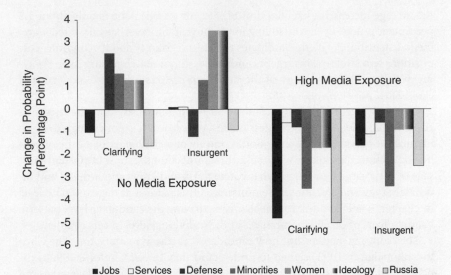

■Jobs □Services ■Defense ■Minorities ▥Women ▪Ideology □Russia

Figure 6.5 Changes in Predicted Probability of Issue Nonplacement over Course of Campaign by Levels of Attention to Campaign in Media
Each bar in the figure represents the change in an average respondent's predicted probability of nonplacement for the candidate on the related issue from the first two weeks of September to the two weeks before Election Day. Decreases in uncertainty indicate learning over the period of the campaign. Predicted probabilities of nonplacement are generated from fourteen probit analyses with inability to place each candidate on each issue as the dependent variable. Explanatory variables include level of attention to the campaign in the media, date of interview, demographic controls, and indicators for campaign year. Standard errors are robust and clustered on campaign year. Full model results appear in the Appendix.

The right side of the figure, for people paying high levels of attention to the campaign in the media, shows reductions in uncertainty, on average, for all issues and all candidates. This is evidence of campaign learning. From September to November, people who pay attention to the campaign in the news are better able to place candidates on all issues at the end of the campaign, controlling for basic demographic indicators. This is not true for people who do not encounter the campaign in the news.

The largest reduction in uncertainty over the course of the campaign is for the placement of clarifying candidates on the economy and on cooperation with Russia. The reduction in uncertainty for clarifying candidates is more than twice as large as the reduction for insurgent candidates. People are, on average, approximately five percentage points more likely to place the clarifying candidate on the issue of guaranteed jobs at the end of the campaign than they are at the beginning of the campaign, all else being equal. For insurgent candidates, the average increase in likelihood of placement on this issue is only about 1.5 percentage points. Even controlling for demographics, year-specific effects, and media attention, clarifying candidates reduce uncertainty about economic issue positions to a level that insurgent candidates cannot match on any issue.[14] Paying attention to the messages of the campaign matters to voters' knowledge of candidates' positions on issues.

Table 6.3 together with figures 6.1 and 6.5 demonstrate that the messages clarifying candidates send to voters make a difference. It is not enough to be an incumbent party nominee in a good economy or a challenger in a time of economic decline. Candidates who make this connection the most important message of their campaigns affect what voters think and know about them, and ultimately, they win elections. I demonstrated this pattern at the candidate level in chapter 5; and, as a test for mechanisms driving the candidate-level pattern, I show effects of candidate messages at the individual level in this chapter.

The economy matters, but how candidates react to it matters, too. The Clinton campaign in 1992 seemed to understand this. In Bill Clinton's 1992 campaign headquarters, a sign read, "It's the economy, Stupid." This adage turns out to be more right than maybe even Clinton and his strategist James Carville imagined. The economy matters because it determines which candidates can talk about which issues in campaigns; it is always an important consideration to voters; and, it is critical that candidates advantaged by the economic situation talk about it during the campaign more than they talk about anything else and more than their opponents talk about it, even if they are incumbents. Clinton and Carville probably knew this, as the sign was inward facing, to remind people who were talking to the press, writing ad copy, or drafting speeches, and to remind the candidate himself that the campaign's message was simple: remind voters that times were not as good as they seemed at the hands of George H. W. Bush.

Insurgent-Candidate Campaign Effects: Changing the Debate by Increasing the Importance of Issues

The previous section detailed the connections between what candidates talk about on the campaign trail and what voters say about candidates during the same time period—particularly for clarifying candidates and economic messages. Citizens make more comments about the economy when asked to de-

---

[14]Results from the issue models show that the interaction between media attention and time of interview (the test for learning) is significantly different from zero for clarifying candidates on the economy, but not for any other issues. The results are discernible from zero for insurgent candidates on no issues. This indicates that the changes between the no attention and high attention predicted probabilities on the same issue calculated for the same period of the campaign are statistically different from one another, but it does not indicate that predicted probabilities across issues are statistically different from one another.

scribe the candidates, and they are better able to place clarifying candidates on economic-issue scales if the clarifying candidate talks mainly about the economy in ads or speeches. But sometimes, clarifying candidates lose elections. These losses are not merely caused by errors on the part of clarifying candidates (a few win even though they do not talk mainly about the economy). The other important element of electioneering is, of course, what the insurgent candidate is doing alongside the clarifying candidate.

Because the economic context does not benefit him or her, the insurgent candidate needs to focus the election off the economy and onto some other issue. Specifically, an issue on which he or she is closer to the average American than his or her opponent, and an issue on which his or her opponent is committed to an unpopular position. It also helps if public opinion on the issue is lopsided, that is, that opinion on the issue is not split between the two candidates' positions. It does little good to increase the importance of an issue on which half the people will favor the opponent's position. The kinds of things insurgent candidates choose to talk about vary across year and party, but typically they fall into two broad categories: foreign and domestic policy.

In the fifties Stevenson tried to refocus the elections onto Eisenhower's mishandling of the Korean War. In 1960, Kennedy painted a picture of both foreign and domestic decline as he compared the United States to the Soviet Union. Mondale wanted to portray Reagan in 1984 as reckless and aggressive in his possible reactions to the Soviets. And in 2000 George Bush offered leadership for solving domestic problems that was bipartisan, kinder, compassionate—yet conservative and market driven. A few insurgent candidates centered their campaigns on economic issues (McGovern, George H. W. Bush, Dole) and thereby, according to the theory and the results presented earlier, helped their opponents win the election.

How successful are the insurgent candidates at increasing the importance of their chosen insurgent issues? Using the ANES data, I create a measure for "insurgent issue" that varies by election year. The insurgent issue questions I use in the remainder of the book are constructed such that each year relates to that specific candidate's insurgent issue. So, the observations on the insurgent issue for 1980, for example, always refer to foreign policy—specifically, our relations with the Soviet Union and the willingness of the United States to go to war. For 2000 they always deal with domestic policy—education, social security, and health care.[15]

To organize the analyses that follow in a tractable manner, I define two different classes of insurgent candidates, which escalate in accordance with how well

[15]These issues are: 1972 economy—guaranteed jobs; 1976 outsider status/morality; 1980 and 1984 foreign policy—relations with Russia; 1988 domestic policies—services/spending; 1992 economy—guaranteed jobs; 1996 economy—guaranteed jobs; 2000 education/healthcare—services/spending. All NES variables are seven-point issue scales with the exception of 1976 for which I use the seven-point trait-evaluation scales on morality.

the insurgent candidate followed the theory's prescriptions. I will present results for each group and its complement. This results in four different groups
for which I analyze the data.

At the high end of the adherence scale are those insurgent candidates who
meet all the insurgent candidate criteria laid out by the theory. That is, they talk
about something other than the economy; they are closer to most voters than
their opponent on this issue; and their opponent is committed to his unpopular position on this issue. I defined these candidates as Kennedy (1960), Nixon
(1968), Carter (1976), and George W. Bush (2000). For the remainder of the
book, I classify these candidates as fully meeting the theory's criteria. The label
"Meets Criteria" in the remaining figures represents them. The candidates who
are not in this category are those who failed to meet both of the theory's criteria in one way or another. These include McGovern, Bush in 1992, Dole (who
failed to meet both), and the others who failed to meet just one criterion,
Stevenson twice, Goldwater, Carter in 1980, Mondale, and Dukakis. In the
figures that follow, this group of candidates is labeled the "Violates Criteria"
group. The Meets Criteria and Violates Criteria groups are complements of
each other, and together they exhaust the list of candidates under investigation.

Because decisions about whether the candidates satisfy the theory's corollaries may seem subjective to some (it is a matter of some judgment to determine
whether Eisenhower actually was "soft on communism" or whether Reagan
truly was "a hawk" who preferred military solutions to diplomatic ones), I create a second class of candidates by relaxing the theory's requirements and
counting those candidates who satisfy the first criteria—they talk about something other than the economy—as meeting the requirements. These insurgent
candidates include the four above and Stevenson twice, Goldwater, Carter in
1980, Mondale, and Dukakis. I will refer to this class of candidates as the "Meets
Topic" group in subsequent tests because they meet the theory's criteria for
choosing a campaign message. The three remaining insurgents who talked
about the economy (McGovern, Bush in 1992, and Dole) make up the complement or opposite group to this one—those who violate the theory and its corollaries in total. I label this group "Violates Topic" in the pages ahead. As above,
the Meets Topic and Violates Topic groups taken together exhaust the list of
candidates under investigation. This latter group allows any insurgent candidate whose message is on a topic other than the economy to be counted as a success. It provides a more relaxed test of the theory.

If the theory is a good explanation of how insurgent candidates win elections, and if messages matter, the candidates who meet the theory's criteria will
show the greatest effects of priming their insurgent issues during the campaign.
Further, the candidates who talk about something other than the economy
should do better in terms of the insurgent issue helping them gain votes than
those candidates who use the economy as their insurgent issue (since this issue
favors the clarifying candidate).

The Most Important Problem in the Nation

Each year, the NES asks respondents to name the nation's most important problem. I use this measure as a first test for whether the various classes of insurgent candidates are successful at increasing the importance of their insurgent issues over the course of the campaign.[16] For what group of insurgents do voters think the insurgent issues are the nation's most important problem? The answer is as expected—insurgents who meet the theory's criteria convince more voters (27 percent) that the insurgent issues they stress are important. Their complement group, those who violate at least one of the theory's mandates, convince only 21 percent of the people this is the case. Relaxing the criteria, insurgents who choose a topic other than the economy convince 25 percent of the public the insurgent issue is important, and the complement to this group, those insurgents who talk mainly about the economy even though it benefits the other candidate, convince only 17 percent of voters that this issue is the most important.[17] Each of these differences is significantly different from zero at a 99 percent level of confidence.

More compelling than just the marginal distributions of these issues is the way they change over the course of the campaign. Can insurgent candidates who choose wisely increase the importance of their issues as the campaign wears on? In figure 6.6, I plot the mean percent of respondents who named the candidates' insurgent issues as the nation's most important problem by date of interview (broken into roughly two-week segments) for each of the classes of insurgent candidates over all the years. Care should be taken not to make too much of the time trend in these figures, since prior to the 1990s the ANES did not employ a

---

[16]The NES began asking the Most Important Problem question in its current form 1960. These analyses are done on data from 1960 to 2000. Because the insurgent issue in ads in 1976 is a characteristic or trait (honesty, trust, morality), and these kinds of qualities are not expressed as answers to the most important problem question, I drop 1976 from the analysis on this question. Results are robust to its inclusion (if I operationalize the concept using a question about "trusting the government to do the right thing," findings do not substantively change), but for clarity's sake I do not include it when looking at data on this question.

[17]It may seem odd that the economy is not very important since I argued earlier that it is always one of the most important issues in elections. Interestingly, it is among the top three issues mentioned in these years, but in 1972 and 1996 there are unusually high rates of missing data on the most important problem question. For this question, missing represents a respondent saying they "don't know" or do not have an answer to the question. In 1972 the level of missingness is 63 percent. In 1996 it is 55 percent. In most years it is between 10 and 25 percent. Except for 2000—the only year in which neither candidate talked about the economy. The incidence of missing on this question in 2000 is 51 percent. These data suggest that when the clarifying candidate does not talk about the economy, people have a hard time identifying what the nation's most important problems are. Of people who offer an answer, the economy is always important, but fewer people offer answers when the clarifying candidate is not talking about the economy. This makes its overall percentage lower in some years than in others.

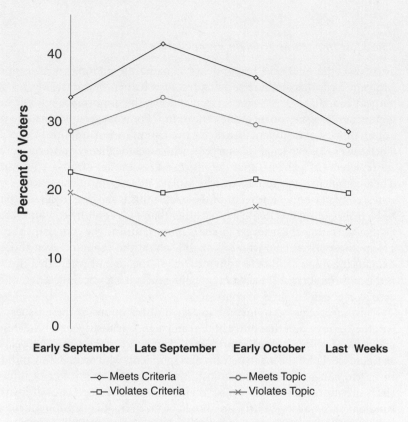

Figure 6.6 Mean Percent of Respondents Who Offer Insurgent Issue as Nation's Most Important Problem over Time for Different Classes of Insurgent Candidates
Data are from the NES (1960–2000, 1976 omitted), N = 24,840. Insurgent campaigns are grouped according to their level of adherence to the theory's prescriptions. Within each class of candidate for each time period, the figure demonstrates the mean percent of respondents who volunteered the insurgent candidate's insurgent issue as the nation's most important problem when asked. Results with confidence intervals appear in the Appendix.

sampling design that generated representativeness at the daily, weekly, or monthly level. After 1990, they released the sample in representative quarter-samples. There is, however, little reason to believe that the people who partici-pate in the face-to-face interviews in the first weeks of the period are systemat-ically different from those who participate in the last few weeks on the things we care about that would introduce bias. Any interesting trends based on time of interview, however, should be taken as suggestive of a larger pattern, with this caveat in mind.

Generally speaking, none of the insurgent candidates do a very good job of increasing their issue's importance over the course of the campaign when the beginning is compared directly to the end. Nevertheless, the differences between the groups are telling, especially as they move over time. As the campaign is getting into full swing, late September into October, those candidates who meet both criteria (Meets Criteria) and those who talk about something other than the economy (Meet Topic) are able to increase the importance of their insurgent issues by eight and five points, respectively. In early October they are still doing marginally better than when they started, but the gains are lost in the last weeks before the election. Both groups finish below where they started.[18] Still, when compared to the dynamics of the candidates who violate one or both of the theory's criteria, the candidates who meet the mandates fare well. The violators never rise above their starting point, and at the height of the campaign their incidence rate is declining instead of increasing. Compare the candidates who meet both criteria (Meets Criteria) to those who violate both criteria (Violate Topic): the difference in the number of people who think the insurgent issue is the most important problem is tripled for those candidates who meet the theory's criteria.

Further support for the robustness of these trends comes from looking at the data for insurgent candidates who talk about something other than the economy (Meets Topic). The percentage of respondents who think the noneconomic insurgent issue is the most important in the country reaches a high of 34 in the first half of October. This number is between the numbers for insurgent candidates who get it wrong in one way or another (between 14 and 20 percent) and those who get it right (42 percent). In other words, getting it "half-right"— talking about something other than the economy, but not something on which you are uniquely advantaged vis-à-vis your opponent—lands a candidate halfway between the individual level effects of those who violate in some way and those who fully meet the theory's criteria.

Like the volatility and reversion Gelman and King (1993) illustrate with public opinion polls over the course of the campaign, these individual-level data show movement during the campaign period with reversion to starting points. This is a pattern that will emerge again and again throughout the remainder of this chapter. It is a set of trends worth pondering. For now, I introduce the idea that this reversion is the result of campaigning from the other candidate(s) in the race. In the beginning of the campaign, the insurgent candidate gains traction on his issue, but as the clarifying candidate works to neutralize insurgent gains, much of the insurgent candidates' early successes are lost.

---

[18]These differences are robust to varying definitions of time periods. The middle and end part of the campaign are systematically different than the beginning.

Most Important Problem and Vote Choice

The evidence from figure 6.6 suggests that insurgent candidates who behave as the theory suggests they should are successful at priming their issue in the minds of voters, increasing the percentage of people who think the issue is the most important by a high of twenty-eight points relative to those who violate the theory—in late September. But, the question remains: does the importance of this issue matter to a vote choice on Election Day? In order to learn whether increasing the importance of the insurgent issue helps these insurgent candidates at the polls, I present the results in figure 6.7. The vertical bars represent the changes in reported vote share for the insurgent candidate as a function of whether respondents name the insurgent issue as the nation's most important problem.[19] I present these comparisons for each of the four classes of insurgent candidates and across different levels of respondents' political information.

The set of bars on the left side of the figure present the changes in vote for the insurgent candidate when the entire set of respondents is taken as a whole. The differences between the insurgent candidates' vote shares, depending on whether people think the insurgent issue is the most important problem in the country, are not large for any class of insurgent candidate. Only the three- and five-point increases in vote for those insurgents who violate the theory are different from zero using conventional tests. This may seem counterintuitive, especially for those candidates who talked about the economy because the economy ought to be helping the clarifying candidate. But, recall from above that only 17 percent of respondents think the economy is the most important problem in these years, the lowest of any of the classes of insurgent candidates. One interpretation of this result is that challengers running against incumbents in good economies (McGovern and Dole) cannot prime the economy the way clarifying candidates can. In these years, neither Nixon nor Clinton talked predominantly about the economy, leaving only their insurgent challengers to send an economic message. Although it appears that the message is persuasive to those who are primed, very few people (comparable to other insurgent issues) end up believing the economy is the single most important issue in these years. In 1972, 8 percent of the people named it most important and, in 1996, 9 percent did so. The other year in this category of insurgent candidate is 1992—and in that year, both candidates talked about the economy more than anything else.

---

[19]These results are generated from twelve cross-tabulations using postelection vote report and an indicator for whether the respondent named the insurgent issue as the nation's most important problem. These results can be thought of as the change in the probability of vote for the insurgent candidate depending on whether respondents think the insurgent issue is the most important one. Significant differences (at the 95-percent level of confidence) in the proportion of insurgent vote exist for all classes of insurgent candidates in the low-information group. In the full sample, the change is significant for those in the Violates Criteria group only. None of the differences in the high-information group are significantly different from zero.

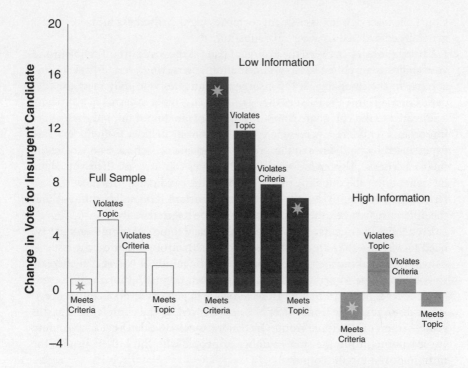

Figure 6.7 Change in Insurgent Candidate Vote Share Depending on Whether Respondent Named Insurgent Issue as Most Important Problem in Nation for Each Class of Insurgent Candidate by Levels of Political Information
Data are from NES (1960–2000). Bars represent mean change in insurgent candidate vote share within each class of candidate for people who name the candidate's insurgent issue as the nation's most important problem compared to those who do not. Classes of insurgent candidates are defined previously. Levels of respondent political information determined by NES interviewer. Results are from twelve cross-tabulations. Full tables appear in the Appendix.

Not surprisingly, 32 percent of the electorate thought it was the most important problem in the country.

The connection between the insurgent issue's importance and vote share for the insurgent candidate gets much more interesting when the sample is broken down by respondents' levels of political information. There are a lot of different ways to measure this concept. I use an assessment made by the NES interviewers about how knowledgeable the respondent appears as they complete the survey. The assessment is the interviewer's judgment. Although it is possible to scale people based on how many correct answers they give to questions about who the vice president is or how many members there are on the Supreme

Court, the interviewer's assessment correlates highly with these measures and is generally considered an acceptable substitute.[20]

The relationship between the insurgent issue as most important problem and vote choice is amplified for low-information voters, who seem especially susceptible to the campaign. If the insurgent candidates who fully meet the theory's criteria prime their issues they gain sixteen-points in terms of vote share (compared to the vote share from those people who do not think the issues are important). This large increase in vote is statistically distinct from the increase experienced by candidates in this group's complement—those who violate the theory's criteria. Although even these candidates can increase their vote share by eight points, the doubling of this effect for the candidates who meet the criteria is both substantively and statistically important. The null hypothesis that the difference between the groups is zero can be rejected easily.

Even those insurgents who meet only the broad topic criterion—and pay no heed to whether they are advantaged vis-à-vis their opponent on the issue—benefit from making their issue important in the minds of voters. The increase in vote share due to priming their issue is seven points. Although this seven-point effect is notably different from zero at a 95 percent level of confidence, it is not distinguishable from the effects experienced by the complement to this group—the Violates Topic group. Once more, these candidates get a large bump (twelve points) from the small number of people who think their issue is the most important in the country.

The high-information voters show very small and nondistinguishable effects. When considered in light of the effects among high-information voters, the presence of campaign effects among low-information voters is striking. The high-information voters seem impervious to campaign appeals. High-information respondents may have such a large store of previously acquired political knowledge that the new information and messages provided by the campaigns do not persuade them. In the words of Zaller (1992), the high-information people have a host of considerations with which to filter out information that is inconsistent with their previously held beliefs. Low-information people do not have these filters, and thus any new information they receive affects them.

As interesting as the changes in vote share due to changes in importance of the insurgent issue are the levels at which voters are casting ballots for the insurgent candidate. Taken together, the changes *and* the levels paint a sensible and responsive campaign environment. The first thing that any candidate is

[20]There are five categories of information level as recorded by the NES interviewers. I use the two highest and two lowest to define the categories of information I use in subsequent analyses. This leaves the middle group, which the NES calls "average." Results are robust to including this group with one or the other of the divisions I use, but doing so only dampens the differences between the high- and low-information people. The average people, in the middle, seem truly to be between the high- and low-information people in terms of the things I am interested in presenting. For simplicity of presentation, and because the middle is not so interesting, I leave them out.

concerned about is getting more votes than his or her opponent. I have reduced all the vote shares under analysis to two-party votes—so candidates in this framework aim to get 50 percent plus one single vote. The insurgent candidates are only successful at crossing the 50-percent threshold in four cases—all of them for groups of candidates who meet the theory's mandates in some way. These effects are marked with stars in figure 6.7. In the whole sample and for both levels of information, insurgents who meet both criteria of the theory rise above the 50-percent mark. Additionally, insurgent candidates who talk about something other than the economy (Meets Topic) also cross this line for low-information voters only. Interestingly, and consistent with expectations about political knowledge, high-information people are already voting for the insurgent candidates who meet both criteria of the theory even if they do not think the candidate's insurgent issue is very important. Highly informed voters do not need to be primed by the candidates' campaigns—they already understand the issues and how the candidates relate to them.

When the results in figures 6.6 and 6.7 are taken together, a compelling impression emerges: Candidates can affect how important their insurgent issue becomes to voters—and for any type of insurgent—the more important the better. But, the gains they make early in the campaign are lost as Election Day draws near, perhaps a result of campaigning to neutralize the insurgent issue by the clarifying candidate. If insurgent candidates can keep some of those gains they achieve early in the campaign period, they can persuade voters in important ways—gaining election-winning critical votes if they meet the theory's criteria and keep voters from waning on the importance of their insurgent issues. The dynamics of the story are most impressive for low-information voters, who show substantial changes in outcomes (sixteen points) due to the success and longevity of insurgent campaign messages.

The use of respondents' self-reports of the nation's most important problems to explain changes in vote shares, however, is not ideal for a number of reasons. Primarily, it is possible that the campaign influences both of these things in real time. It may not be possible to isolate the causal direction in this relationship. Maybe ideas about the nation's most important problem drive vote, but maybe vote preference drives ideas about the nation's most important problem. The worst-case interpretation is that insurgent candidates who meet the theory's criteria are the most qualified candidates (after all, they could figure out how to beat the economically advantaged candidate) and that the campaign just reveals this information to voters over time. In this scenario, increases in vote share and issue priming are simultaneously driven by the revelation of information—not by the particular messages these candidates send. The best reassurance I can offer about the spuriousness or endogeneity of these effects comes from the strong, historical relationship between economic performance and election outcomes. Incumbents in good economies usually win (similarly challengers in bad economies), but in a few years this does not happen—and it is in those years that we see the insurgent candidates convincing people about the importance of their issue. The movements on this over the campaign period are dramatic even though the real election outcomes are narrow to say the least; and in one year, 2000, the outcome is in the wrong direction! I settle on this point: even if the relationship works in the opposite direction from what I claim, the fact that voters change their minds and decide to vote for the insurgent candidate in these situations—and then begin to mimic his or her campaign message—is evidence that the things candidates say in campaigns reach voters and that people use this information when they talk about the candidates or the election. Even if it is just to justify the change in their vote choice, it is a campaign effect nonetheless.

INSURGENT-CANDIDATE CAMPAIGN EFFECTS: BEING CLOSER TO MOST VOTERS ON THE INSURGENT ISSUE

These results hint at intricate and compelling campaign effects at the individual level, yet thus far, I have reduced even the individual-level data to aggregate indicators. As in the previous section on clarifying candidate effectiveness, it is time to dig a little deeper into these data. In addition to making the insurgent issue more important to voters over the course of the campaign, insurgent candidates can also gain advantages by persuading people that the relative distance between the voter's position on the insurgent issue and the candidate's position is closer for insurgent candidates than it is for clarifying candidates. In other words, they can attempt to demonstrate or even change their advantage on the issue. This is a test of the insurgent candidate's ability to persuade voters. To elucidate whether insurgent candidates can do this over an eight-week campaign period, and assess again whether they are increasing the importance of their issues, I return to the seven-point issue-position scales I used in the section on uncertainty.

The Difference in Distances

As the spatial theory of voting illustrates, I take the difference between the candidate's position and the voter's position for each issue and square the value such that all distance measures are expressed in positive numbers.[21] Greater values indicate there is a larger distance between the voter and the candidate. I do this for both the clarifying and insurgent candidates on each issue. To answer the question, "To which candidate is the voter closest?" I simply subtract the clarifying candidate's squared distance from the insurgent candidate's squared

---

[21]A fair number of people are unable to place the candidates or themselves on these issue scales. In the analyses that follow, missing values on issue scales are imputed. Results are robust to this process.

distance. This gives me a relative measure of proximity for this issue. I call this measure the "Difference in Distances." Negative values of this difference in distances indicate the voter is closer to the insurgent candidate. Positive numbers indicate the opposite. For example, if the voter places both of the candidates and him- or herself at exactly the same point on the issue scale (regardless of where that was on the scale), the squared differences for each candidate are 0 and the difference in distances is 0. If a voter places both candidates at positive 6 and him- or herself at 1, each squared distance is 25 and again, the difference in distances is 0. On the other hand, if a voter places the clarifying candidate at 6, the insurgent at 1, and him- or herself at 4, the squared distance to the clarifying candidate is 4 ($6 - 4 = 2$ and $2^2 = 4$), and the squared distance to the insurgent candidate is 9 ($1 - 4 = -3$ and $-3^2 = 9$). Thus the difference in distance would be $9 - 4 = 5$. Since this is a positive number, we know that the voter is closer to the clarifying candidate. Because the issue scales have 7 points where people can place candidates and themselves, the difference in distance measure can range from -36 to $+36$. In truth, most values fall near the 0 mark, but are not actually 0.

If insurgent candidates are successful, they not only prime the importance of their insurgent issue, but they choose an issue on which they are closer to voters than the clarifying candidate—or they try to convince voters of this over the course of the campaign. Figure 6.8 presents the changes in average values of the difference in distance measure for the insurgent issues over the course of the campaign. Again, I present these data for the four different classes of insurgent candidates (with the complementary groups matched by the shading of the lines). I also break out the results by levels of respondent political information in the bottom two panels. Of primary importance is the fact that the classes of insurgent candidates "stack" in the correct order—with the average distance between the voters and candidates being closest to the insurgent candidate for those candidates who meet both the theory's prescriptions. The next closest distance is for those candidates who talk about something other than the economy, and so on. The largest distance from the insurgent candidate appears for those insurgents who talk about the clarifying issue—the economy. The stacking of the lines is important because it demonstrates why issue selection is critical to insurgent-candidate success. The candidates who meet both criteria (talk about something other than the economy and something on which they are advantaged) are *closer* to voters than the candidates who pick issues on which they are not advantaged—but even these candidates are closer to voters than the insurgents who run on an issue that benefits their opponent (the economy). The ordering of the lines shows why and how the theory's corollaries are powerful.

Not only do the lines stack in the expected order, the values of the distances for the candidates who meet the theory's criteria (whether defined loosely or strictly) are negative—in other words, voters think they are closer to the insurgent candidate than the clarifying candidate on these insurgent issues. The

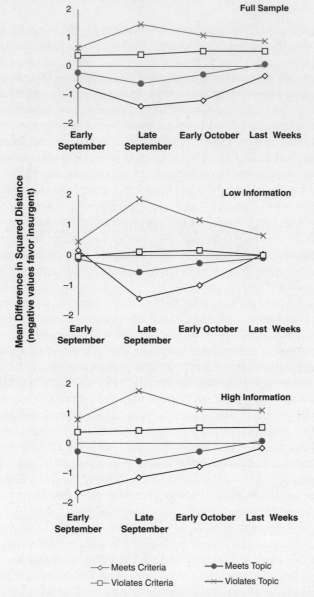

Figure 6.8 Mean Differences in Squared Distances on Insurgent Issues over Campaign Period for Each Class of Insurgent Candidate by Levels of Political Information

Data are from the NES (1972–2000), N = 16,870. Difference in distances are calculated for each insurgent candidate on the insurgent issue of their choice by differencing their proximity to voters relative to the clarifying candidate's proximity to voters on the same issue. Negative values favor the insurgent candidate. Levels of political information are interviewers' assessments. Results with confidence intervals appear in the Appendix.

other two sets of insurgents, those who violate the typology in any way, consistently show small advantages for the clarifying candidate (positive values on the Y-axis).

The dynamics over the course of the campaign are interesting as well. Looking at the sample as a whole (the top panel) the familiar pattern of movement during the early part of the campaign with reversion to starting values appears again. The last time we saw this pattern it was for changes in the percentage of people who think the insurgent issue is the most important issue in the country (figure 6.6). The data in this figure (6.8) are from the same dataset, but do not use the same question and are not asking about the importance of the issue at all. These data are showing how close respondents think they are to the candidates on the insurgent issue. For candidates who meet the theory's criteria, taken together these results suggest that the early period of the campaign does two important things: it increases the importance of the insurgent issue as the insurgent candidates talk about it *and* it persuades voters that their own positions on this issue are closer to the insurgent candidate's than to the clarifying candidate's. Critically important, however, is the fact that these gains are lost by Election Day.

This illustrates again the possibility that the clarifying candidate is telling voters that he or she holds exactly the same position as the insurgent candidate. He or she neutralizes the issue because it costs nothing to do so—this is why the theory's second corollary is so important: the clarifying candidate should be committed to the unpopular position. Examples of candidates doing this include Eisenhower pointing out that he in fact was not soft on communism by referencing the Berlin Air Lift and declaring, "I shall go to Korea, I shall end the War!" to neutralize Stevenson's insurgent issue. Similarly, Reagan argued against the claim that he was reckless and prone to start a nuclear war by holding up as evidence START-nuclear arms reduction talks he initiated with the Soviets during his first term.

As with the previous analysis, the results among low-information voters (middle panel) are slightly amplified compared to the sample as a whole. These unsophisticated voters show slightly greater movement over the campaign period for those candidates who fully meet and fully violate the theory's criteria. But while the movement over the period is active, at the end of the campaign, low-information voters end up closer to the zero point than the full sample. They are equally influenced by both campaign messages such that at the end, they find fewer differences between themselves and each candidate than they found as the campaign began. Voters with low levels of political knowledge again appear to be the most susceptible to campaign messages.

The results for high-information voters demonstrate the sophistication that these voters bring with them at the beginning of the campaign. They are immediately able to place themselves close to those insurgent candidates who meet the theory's criteria. It is almost as if they do not need to hear the message over and over again to understand that the insurgent candidate has an advantage on this dimension—they get it at once. We might think of them as opinion leaders, one "period" ahead of the other voters in terms of the effects of campaign messages. In figure 6.8 one can see this by looking at the bottom line of the bottom panel. Even though these high-information voters begin by giving the insurgent candidates who meet the theory's expectations benefits on the insurgent issue, over the course of the campaign, even the high-information voters are persuaded by the messages from the clarifying candidates that attempt to neutralize this issue. By Election Day, even sophisticated voters have attenuated the advantage given to the most successful insurgent candidates on the insurgent issue to the point of indifference between the two candidates on this issue.

One more interesting comparison can be drawn from figure 6.8. Looking at the candidates who meet the theory's criteria in one way or another (the diamond and circle lines) it is easy to see that for every period of the campaign, for each type of voter, the strict definition of adherence to the theory (the diamonds) results in greater advantages for the insurgent candidate. What this shows is that insurgent candidates who talk about something other than the economy *and* pay attention to whether their opponent is committed to an unpopular position on this issue (and whether they are advantaged) do better than those candidates who only choose an issue other than the economy and pay no heed to their relative position vis-à-vis their opponents. This is the difference between being Barry Goldwater in 1964 and Richard Nixon in 1968. Goldwater did not run on the economy, but neither did he choose an issue on which he had an advantage among voters relative to Johnson. Nixon, on the other hand, did not run on the economy, but chose an issue on which he knew he would be more popular with most voters and an issue on which he knew Humphrey could not take the identical position. Finding the latter type of insurgent issue has benefits—as the difference in distances between respondents and the candidates is always closer to the insurgent candidate for candidates who find issues as Nixon did.

The evidence to this point shows that there are some groups of voters who react to the campaign in volatile ways and some who remain more steady throughout the campaign. Low-information voters show more instability over the course of the campaign than high-information voters, but low-information voters may not be the only vulnerable ones in the population. Campaigns may also exhibit greater effects among self-described independents, or those with no political party affiliation. Figure 6.9 presents the results for differences in distances broken out by party type.

For the ease of presentation, I eliminate one class of insurgent candidates from this picture—those who talk about the economy (Violates Topic). These lines look similar to the trends for the Violates Criteria group and including them makes the overall pattern of the figure more difficult to discern. Of primary importance again is the fact that the lines, within each category of party

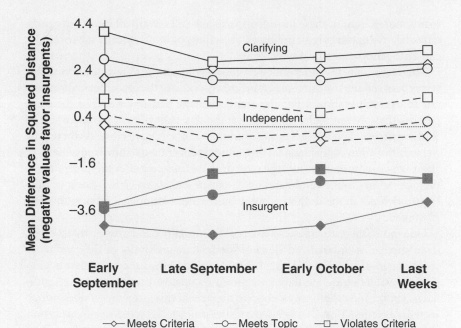

—◇— Meets Criteria   —○— Meets Topic   —□— Violates Criteria

Figure 6.9 Mean Differences in Squared Distances on Insurgent Issues over Campaign Period for Each Class of Insurgent Candidate by Respondent's Party Identification
Data are from the NES (1972–2000), N = 16,870. Difference in distances is calculated for each insurgent candidate on the insurgent issue by differencing their proximity to voters relative to the clarifying candidate's proximity to voters on the same issue. Negative values favor the insurgent candidate. Clarifying and insurgent partisanship is measured using the traditional NES seven-point party identification scale. In some years, clarifying partisans are Republicans (1972, 1976, 1980, 1984, 1988), but in some years they are Democrats (1992, 1996, 2000). Results with confidence intervals appear in the Appendix.

identification, stack in the correct order. Even among respondents who identify with the clarifying candidate's party (this can change in a given election year, sometimes it is the Democrats and sometimes the Republicans), insurgent candidates who behave as expected (whether defined strictly or loosely) fare better in voters' minds than those who violate the theory's prescriptions in one way or another. Of course, even with these effects for insurgent candidates who choose their messages well, the clarifying partisans always believe they are closer to the clarifying candidate than they are to the insurgent candidate on the insurgent issue. Similarly for the insurgent partisans. Although they understand that those candidates who violate the theory's prescriptions are farther away from their ideal positions on the insurgent issue than the insurgents who choose their issues more carefully, these insurgent partisans still reward all insurgent candidates relative to clarifying candidates, regardless of how carefully the insurgent candidate chooses the insurgent issue.

This leaves only the independent voters—who appropriately position themselves between the two partisan groups of voters. Like the low-information voters, independents show a familiar trend over the first few weeks of the campaign—they are most affected by the candidates' behaviors in the latter part of September, but then slowly revert to ending points that are close to where they started. Both low-information voters and independents show movement of about a two-point range over the course of the campaign on the difference in their proximity to the candidates on the insurgent issue. This is not a terribly large difference in the distances, but it is the largest among all groups of voters examined.

One more interesting pattern emerges from figure 6.9. Partisan voters begin the campaign with polarized views of the relative proximity of the candidates to voters' ideal positions on the insurgent issue. But as the campaign begins, partisan voters moderate their perception of relative proximity to the candidates. Unlike the other movements we have seen, this attenuation does not go away by Election Day. Clarifying partisans move toward the insurgent candidate on the insurgent issue over the course of the campaign and insurgent partisans move toward the clarifying candidate on the insurgent issue as the campaign progresses. This is an unexpected overall pattern of movement, but one that paints a charitable picture of partisan voters in America over the last fifty years. It seems that even partisan voters consider the messages sent by both candidates during the campaign and allow themselves to be influenced slightly by candidates of the opposing party. Granted, this persuasion is not changing the partisan voters' overall assessments of which candidates they prefer on the insurgent issues, nonetheless, this move toward the middle shows a level of campaign responsiveness that is surprising in light of the power of party identification to shape attitudes. Partisans are still, well, partisan, but they are responsive to campaign messages in an unexpected way.

These data show that low-information voters and independents are the most easily influenced by the campaign in its initial period, and that the advantages they give to candidates during this time dissipate as the campaign wears on. As I have mentioned repeatedly in this chapter, it is difficult to isolate the cause of this reversion with these data. Campaigning from the opposition seems like the most obvious explanation, especially since the probability of voting for the insurgent candidate remains positive (despite the reversion) for insurgents who choose theoretically correct issues, but becomes negative for those insurgents who choose poorly. Other more complicated explanations are imaginable, including the possibility that even low-information and independent voters are predisposed to support one or the other of the candidates, and despite being swayed by short-term information during the campaign, these movable voters return to their original preferences on Election Day. Fortunately, each of these explanations is interesting from a campaign perspective. Unfortunately, one of them implies that campaigns matter a great deal to voters (the first explanation), and the other implies that they do not matter at all. More and better data are needed to sort out exactly what is going on with this pattern.

Differences in Distances and Vote Choice

I have shown that the candidates can move voters' assessments of these distances during the campaign, but the main question remains. How important are these relative distances in predicting the vote? To assess this, I model vote for the clarifying candidate as a function of the difference in distances on two issues—the insurgent issue and the clarifying issue (the latter of which is an economic question about guaranteed jobs for those who want to work). I will finally let the insurgent and clarifying issues compete for influence over people's vote choice. Controls in these models include gender, age, race, and party identification.[22] I am not trying to model the vote in an explanatory way in these tests; I aim only to show the effects of each candidate's message, controlling for basic considerations like gender, race, and age.

Results show that both issues have substantively and statistically significant effects on the vote in the expected directions. Coefficients are expected to be positive for both issues such that if there is no perceived difference in the comparable distances by voters (a difference in distance observation of zero), the issue is neutralized and the issue has no effect on the vote choice. But, for increasing values of the difference in distances (increasing values favor the clarifying candidates), the issue increasingly benefits the clarifying candidate. Negative values of the difference in distances benefit the insurgent candidate such that increasing distances are a drain on the probability of a clarifying vote choice.

When voters see no difference between the candidates on the insurgent issue and only a slight advantage on the economy for the clarifying candidates (two points), voters are more likely to cast ballots for the clarifying candidate, all else being equal. In this situation, the probability of an average voter in an average year voting for the clarifying candidate is .63. This strong likelihood of voting for the clarifying candidate holds whether the insurgent candidate meets or violates the theory's criteria, because the leverage of the insurgent issue is essentially neutralized in the calculation of these probabilities. Relative issue proximity matters to voters in predictable ways.

An interesting pattern emerges when I change the perceived differences between the voter's proximity to the candidates on the insurgent issue. I allow the difference in distances to take on three values for each class of insurgent candidate: zero, negative four, and negative fifteen. I hold the difference in distances

---

[22]Standard errors are robust and clustered on campaign year.

for the clarifying issue at two (a modest net gain for the clarifying candidate). For each level of difference, I calculate the probability of voting for the clarifying candidate holding other variables at their means. Again I will leave out the insurgent candidates who campaign on the economy since I cannot make this distance simultaneously close to the insurgent and the clarifying candidate.

Figure 6.10 illustrates the importance of issue-position proximity to election outcomes separately for those with low and high levels of information. If there is no difference between the candidates on the insurgent issue, the clarifying candidate will win the election handily regardless of voters' levels of information. All the data points in figure 6.10 are above the dotted 50-percent line (clarifying candidate territory) when voters see no differences between the candidates on the insurgent issue and a slight benefit for the clarifying candidate on the economy. Moving away from indifference between the two candidates, if voters perceive they are closer to the insurgent candidate on the insurgent issue than they are to the clarifying candidate on this issue (while still slightly closer to the clarifying candidate on the economy), the insurgent candidate gains votes. The gently downward sloping lines tell the story of why it is important to leverage the difference in voters' proximity to the candidates on issues. This is why insurgent issues with lopsided public opinion and opponents committed to the wrong side of the distribution are so attractive.

When voters perceive slight advantages for the insurgent candidate, the probability of voting for the clarifying candidate drops below the 50-percent point for insurgent candidates who meet all the theory's criteria. And, among low-information voters even those who meet only the topic requirements are more likely to win. The importance of relative-issue proximity is easily appreciated when the differences are large. When voters perceive a fifteen-point advantage for the insurgent candidate, nearly every voter is likely to vote for the insurgent candidate, regardless of voters' levels of information. Insurgent candidates who meet the theory's prescriptions have a higher likelihood of winning voters than those who violate the theory's mandates, but at very large levels of distinction between the candidates, all types of insurgent candidates benefit.

High political-information voters show slightly greater rates of change in the probability of voting for the clarifying candidate as the relative proximity between the candidates changes. Unlike the previous evidence on changes in mean placements on issues or average salience of the insurgent issue, this evidence seems to suggest that the high-information people are more affected by the campaign—not the low-information people. In truth, what these data show is that the high-information people know how to use the proximity measures in their political calculations, while the low political-information people are less affected by these changes in relative distance to the candidates. Low-information voters may be more susceptible to campaign efforts at persuasion, as demonstrated by their marked shifts on differences in distances over the course of the campaign, but once the relative differences have changed, they affect the

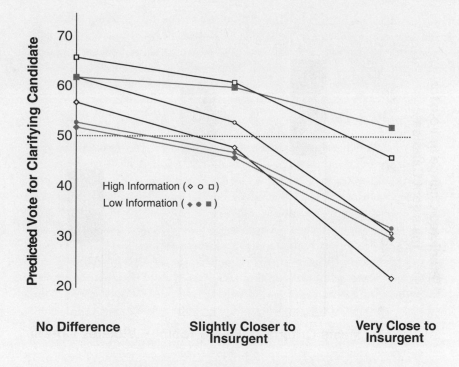

-◇- Meets Criteria   -○- Meets Topic   -□- Violates Criteria

Figure 6.10 Predicted Vote for Clarifying Candidate at Varying Differences in Distances on Insurgent Issues by Levels of Political Information
Data are from the NES (1972–2000), N = 16,870. Difference in distances is calculated for each insurgent candidate on the insurgent issue by differencing their proximity to voters relative to the clarifying candidate's proximity to voters on the same issue. Negative values favor the insurgent candidate. Levels of political information are interviewers' assessments. Results are predicted probabilities based on twelve probit analyses. "Slightly closer" category sets difference to –4. "Very close" category sets distance to –15. Full model results appear in the Appendix.

low-information voters less than they would those who are more politically aware. This is an interesting conundrum for candidates—*precisely those people they are able to persuade are the ones for whom issue proximity matters the least.*

I present the differences in the way high- and low-information voters respond to the changes in relative issue distances in figure 6.11. For each type of insurgent candidate, the bar represents the increase in predicted vote for the insurgent candidate (using the model described above) when no differences are perceived on the insurgent issue compared to the vote when the insurgent candidate is thought to have a fifteen-point advantage in relative proximity. The

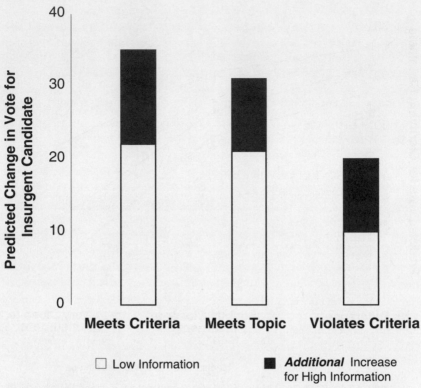

Figure 6.11 Change in Predicted Probability of Voting for Insurgent Candidate by Levels of Information for Varying Degrees of Differences in Distances
Data are from the NES (1972–2000), N = 16,870. Difference in distances is calculated for each insurgent candidate on the insurgent issue by differencing their proximity to voters relative to the clarifying candidate's proximity to voters on the same issue. Negative values favor the insurgent candidate. Levels of political information are interviewers' assessments. Each bar represents the change in predicted probability of voting for insurgent candidate moving from no difference between the candidates on the insurgent issue to –15 points of difference. White bars are the increase in probability for low-information voters. Shaded bars demonstrate the *additional change* experienced by high-information voters. Results are changes in predicted probabilities from eight probit analyses. Full model results appear in the Appendix.

white portion of the bar is the increase in predicted vote for the insurgent candidate for low-information voters, all else being equal.

The shaded portion of the bar adds the additional increase in probability of voting for the insurgent candidate for high-information voters, given the same change in relative insurgent-issue proximity. For every class of insurgent candidate, high-information voters increase their probability of voting for the insurgent candidate by greater amounts than low-information voters as the insurgent candidate becomes closer to the voters on the insurgent issue. Just to make the campaign environment even more challenging for candidates (and political scientists), high-information voters are the hardest to persuade with campaign messages, but are more likely to use campaign information when making a vote choice.

The Message and Its Effects

With the previous series of analyses I attempted to show that campaign messages affect voters in elections. The nature of the survey data available to test for message effectiveness, and the competitive essence of campaigning, make it difficult to execute a single, definitive test for campaign effects at this level, but the ten sets of findings in this chapter suggest that the messages of campaigns matter to voters.

Tables 6.4 and 6.5 summarize the series of findings about each type of campaign in an effort to illustrate the repeated patterns in these data that demonstrate how candidates' messages influence people. These theoretically derived patterns allege that clarifying candidates will associate themselves with the economy and reduce voters' uncertainty about that association over the course of the campaign, and that insurgent candidates will refocus the election off of the economy and onto an issue on which they are closer to most voters and on which the clarifying candidate is committed to an unpopular position. In chapter 5, the candidate-level data showed that candidates behave as the theory predicts and that those candidates who do not do so lose elections. The analyses in this chapter demonstrate why those candidate-level patterns exist by using individual-level data to identify microlevel mechanisms that explain the aggregate patterns. This collection of evidence substantiates the theory's value.

Economic messages from clarifying candidates help voters positively associate the economy with clarifying candidates and negatively associate it with insurgents. Clarifying candidates who talk about the economy more than anything else and more than their opponents reduce voters' levels of uncertainty about economic issues like jobs and unemployment by substantial amounts. These effects are amplified for people who report paying a lot of attention to campaign news in general.

Table 6.5 further illustrates the importance of candidates' messages. Insurgent candidates can prime issues over the course of the campaign if they choose issues on which they have a solid advantage (they are closer to most voters, and their opponent is constrained to an unpopular position). Voters increasingly think these issues are important problems in the country and these assessments affect vote choice in important ways. All of this is particularly true for voters with low levels of political information or sophistication, and for self-identified independents.

TABLE 6.4
Summary of Individual-Level Campaign Effects for Clarifying Candidates
and Messages

What Is Changing?	What Is the Effect?
Fraction of campaign ads, speeches, and candidate's news about the economy, domestic policy, foreign policy, and traits.	Voters' comments are reflective of changes in campaign messages but the fidelity is low. Comments are responsive to changes but do not reflect overall composition of campaign message very well. Strongest relationships come from advertisements.
Content of campaign ads, speeches, and news compete with incumbency and party to affect voters' comments about the candidates on particular issues.	Clarifying ads on the economy shape positive images of clarifying candidates and negative images of insurgents. Insurgent ads on economy only shape negative images of clarifying candidates (not positive images of insurgents).
From Labor Day to Election Day, change in average number of people who can place clarifying candidate on issues compared to insurgent candidate.	Biggest reductions in uncertainty are for clarifying candidates on economic issues. Insurgents do not reduce uncertainty on any issues.
Same as above but separately for people with varying levels of attention to the campaign in the media.	Biggest reductions in uncertainty are for clarifying candidates on economy among those who pay high levels of attention to the campaign.
Same as above, but allowing each issue/year pair to be affected by campaign messages for all candidates and all issues.	Messages make a difference. Talking about an issue reduces uncertainty on that issue. Biggest effects for economic and domestic issues. Only economic messages work as election draws near.

Note: Data about voters' comments and candidate placements on issues are from ANES. Data on content of campaigns is from the content analysis discussed in chapter 4.

Those with low levels of information are the most susceptible to campaign influences, especially in the early weeks of the campaign. As time wears on, however, the advantages gained are lost. Moreover, these voters actually use the new information they receive from campaigns less than their more informed counterparts when making a vote decision.

The individual-level data presented here is in some cases only suggestive of trends in the right direction. Nonetheless, the data illustrate nicely the mechanisms that drive the spatial model of campaign competition. Aggregate election

TABLE 6.5
Summary of Individual-Level Campaign Effects for Insurgent Candidates and Messages

What Is Changing?	What Is the Effect?
From Labor Day to Election Day, percentage of people who think insurgent issue (II) is nation's most important problem (MIP).	Increases in the middle of the campaign for insurgents who follow theory's prescriptions. Not so for insurgents who fail to meet criteria. Despite dynamics during campaign, percent finishes where it started—it reverts to starting level for all types of insurgent candidates.
From Labor Day to Election Day, change in vote for insurgent candidate depending on whether II is thought of as nation's MIP.	Sixteen-point increase for candidates who meet criteria among low-information voters. Eight-point increase for those who talk about something other than the economy.
From Labor Day to Election Day, change in average difference in distances (DID) between two candidates on II.	Movement in middle of campaign toward insurgent for candidates who follow theory's prescriptions. Movement for others less pronounced. Despite movement, finishes near indifference between candidates. Amplified for low-information voters and self-described independents.
From Labor Day to Election Day, changes in predicted vote for insurgent as DID on II vary (all else at mean).	At indifference on II between two candidates, probability of voting for insurgent is very low for all insurgent candidates. At modest levels of advantage, probability becomes greater than .5 for insurgents who meet theory's criteria. At large differences, probability is very high for all insurgents. Amplified for high information voters.

Note: Data about voters' distance from candidates on issues are from ANES.

forecasts and candidate-level tests establish the theory's explanatory and predictive capabilities, but these individual-level data corroborate the foundations on which the theory is built.

The dynamics of presidential campaigns, given these data, are found in the late-September to early-October period. As the election approaches in the last week of October and into November, however, on measure after measure, average positions and effects return to their early September values. A charitable explanation for this pattern is that candidates are reasonably good at what they do—they know when they are getting beaten or when their opponent is gaining the advantage, and they adjust their messages and strategies accordingly. Voters seem to respond. This back-and-forth results in nearly neutral advantages for either candidate come Election Day. Another possibility is that the predispositions held by voters are so strong that despite being persuaded by candidates during presidential campaigns, voters return to their previously held beliefs.

Why is the economy a strong predictor of election outcomes? Finally, there is a campaign-based, individual-level explanation for this regularity beyond sociotropic voting. The economy matters because the candidate who benefits from it talks about it a lot during the campaign and this makes voters more aware of the condition and this candidate's relationship to it. Why is it so difficult for a challenger to defeat an economically advantaged candidate? Because finding the right issue onto which the electoral agenda can be reset is difficult, and candidates are challenged by it. Those who find such an issue, however, can make it more important to voters over the course of the campaign and narrowly edge out the economically advantaged candidate if voters are made to clearly see the differences between the candidates on this issue. Candidates and campaigns matter to outcomes despite—or alongside—the importance of the nation's economy.

Chapter Seven

CANDIDATES CREATING CONTEXT

A N IMPRESSIVE BODY OF systematic evidence that voters reward incumbent politicians for good economic times and punish them for bad times precedes my work here, and in fact, motivates the puzzle I set out to resolve. The causal path between economic conditions and electoral outcomes is demonstrated with great regularity, and the mechanism that drives this link is often identified as pocketbook or sociotropic voting, a more specific case of retrospective voting—yet no one had linked the importance of economic voting to campaigns and candidate behavior. Now that link is clearer. The economy matters, but candidates' discourse about the economy matters, too. Further, candidates' rhetoric about other issues can drive out the importance of the economy if they choose the right issue. The structural conditions matter, but they can be overcome.

Key famously described retrospective voting on the economy as a demonstration that "voters are not fools" (1966, 7). People may not be able to name their member of Congress, but they are able to respond to long-term, important economic conditions when choosing the nation's chief executive. Kramer (1971) and Fiorina (1981) were equally pleased in their descriptions of how retrospective voting on the economy delivered "rough justice" to incumbents who failed to manage the economy. Key, Kramer, and Fiorina carved out and illustrated a role for citizens in elections after voting-behavior scholars of the mid-twentieth century implicitly discredited them as irrational, impressionable, and habitual oafs (Berelson et al. 1954; Campbell et al. 1960; Converse 1964).

Almost by proxy, candidates were deemed oafs as well. If voters could not "cognize the issues" then everything candidates did toward that end in campaigns was irrelevant. Early scholars of voting behavior could not demonstrate that campaigns mattered in consequential ways, so they concluded that campaigns took a backseat to long-standing social and psychological attachments. But as Tufte (1978, 5) said, "the absence of evidence is not convincing evidence of absence." "Small" or "minimal" effects are not synonymous with unimportant effects.

My intention here has been to chip away at the absence of evidence linking candidate behavior in campaigns to voters in elections, and to do so in a theoretically motivated and very specific way. The impressive relationship between citizens and national economic context can be intensified if candidates choose to talk about the economy in their campaigns. And the link between voters and the nation's economy can be diluted if candidates prime other dimensions on which they have advantages. Being from the incumbent party in a good economy certainly sets candidates up with electoral advantages, but Ford, Humphrey, Gore, and even Nixon (in 1960) show us that this advantage alone is not enough. Claiming credit for good times is an important element in the retrospective voting model—this rhetoric is part of the mechanism that makes retrospective voting work. It is, surprisingly, a part of the mechanism that has been missing from descriptions and tests of the theory for over thirty years. My theory of campaigns helps us understand the behavior of candidates in campaigns and how it affects voters. It also provides a clear message to candidates about leveraging their strengths in campaigns.

CAN CANDIDATES CREATE THE CONTEXT?

This is not to say that voting-behavior scholars have ignored the relationship between candidates, particularly incumbents, and the economic context of elections. If the electoral fortunes of incumbents and their parties are so tightly tied to the state of the economy, is it possible for incumbents to create good economic times at exactly the right moment—the moment when voters are looking—and to deal with the consequences (if any) of their actions after the election is over? In other words, can incumbent candidates create the economic context?

Indeed, an entire literature on the political business cycle argues that sitting presidents can and often do use the institutional powers of their office to manipulate macroeconomic conditions for electoral gain (Nordhaus 1975; McRae 1977; Frey 1978; Frey and Schneider 1975,1978,1979; Tufte 1978). An incumbent president, for example, seeking re-election or the re-election of his party, might exploit a lag in the tradeoff between unemployment and inflation by enjoying the short-term benefits of lower unemployment in an election year and not have to address increases in inflation until well after the votes are counted. This possibility creates an opportunity for strategic behavior by sitting presidents. Nordhaus (1975) and McRae (1977) each find evidence of this pattern for up to five postwar presidents, and Tufte (1978) demonstrates that these cycles are driven by increases in transfer payments in the years preceding a presidential election. Tufte shows that of the six years between 1946 and 1976 in which unemployment and inflation were reduced simultaneously, four of them were in presidential election years. Early efforts at uncovering strategic, election-seeking behavior by incumbent presidents offered sound support for the idea that incumbents try to create an economic context from which they will benefit.

Subsequent work, however, was not as clear. Presidents, it turns out, have limited ability to directly manipulate the macroeconomy (Golden and Poterba 1980), and the evidence that they try to do so is limited (Keech 1980; Alt and

Chrystal 1983). More precisely, many of these scholars agree that elections *seem* to magnify the performance of the nation's economy, but the link to presidential manipulation of monetary policy is not easy to make (Lowery 1985; Beck 1987; Grier 1989; Williams 1990).

A recent series of papers by Chris Achen and Larry Bartels examine the link between economic performance and voting behavior from various vantage points. Achen and Bartels's goal is to answer questions about how economic policy, the ensuing income distribution, and voter decision-making demonstrate democratic ideals such as representation and accountability. In one of these papers (2004), Achen and Bartels (and Bartels separately in *Unequal Democracy*, 2008) demonstrate empirically that voters only care about the short-term economic performance around presidential elections—they are not, as Ferejohn (1986) describes, punishing current incumbents to ensure good performance by future incumbents. If voters were doing this, Achen and Bartels argue, they would consider economic growth over the incumbent's entire term in office, not just the most recent couple of weeks before the election. Achen and Bartels's demonstration of the power of short-term economic conditions on vote choice works in concert with the economic forecasting literature that includes in its models recent performance (most often the change in GDP from the fourth quarter of the year before the election to the second quarter of the election year). In more sophisticated approaches to forecasting elections, scholars have allowed economic changes over the president's entire term to play a role, but they weight recent performance more heavily than earlier performance (Hibbs 1987, 2000; Erikson 1989; Bartels and Zaller 2001). Achen and Bartels conclude that, "the clear consensus in the literature is that recent economic performance is much more relevant at election time than what happened earlier."

Achen and Bartels take the evidence of short-term economic effects and pose the question, "how would we expect re-election seeking incumbents to respond to electoral incentives of the sort we have described?" Their answer, of course, is that rational candidates will seek to increase growth right before the election. Whatever result their economic policies produced in the prior quarters of their tenure becomes irrelevant as the election draws near. Achen and Bartels find evidence that presidents do in fact behave this way. The average difference in real disposable income between election years and nonelection years is 1.5 percentage points. The income growth rates during election years are 80 percent higher than in nonelection years. Further, they show that the patterns of economic growth by presidents of both parties look identical in election years, but differ markedly in nonelection years.

The assumption in this work is that the myopia of voters leads incumbents to strategically manipulate the economy in the quarters just before the election. Indeed, this might explain why so many of the clarifying candidates are from the incumbent party. The argument and evidence provided in the preceding chapters, however, lead me to believe that Achen and Bartels may have the arrow pointing in the wrong direction. The myopia of voters is not evidence of their inability or unwillingness to "think" (another article by Achen and Bartels is titled, "It Feels Like We're Thinking") rigorously about politics, but is driven by the things candidates say in their campaigns. This, contrary to Achen and Bartels's conclusions, is exactly how democracy should work.

Voters' obsession with recent economic performance does not drive incumbent behavior; it is the *result* of candidate behavior that primes the nation's economic conditions in the minds of voters in a specific way. Why is the recent growth rate more important than the entire growth rate during the incumbent's tenure? Because candidate messages in campaigns focus on what is happening to voters *now*—not what happened to them three years earlier. Consider this excerpt from a speech that John F. Kennedy gave in1960 at the National Stockyards in East St. Louis, Illinois:

> I am glad to be here in this stockyard because this proves an important point. I come from Massachusetts, which is not a great agricultural center, but I can tell you that Massachusetts will not be prosperous unless the farmers of the United States are prosperous. We heard today that International Harvester, which makes farm machinery, has closed down today, and John Deere plants have closed down; and the reason is that agricultural income has dropped in the past few years almost 20 to 25 percent, and because when farmers go down the rest of the economy sooner or later goes down. The farmers are the No.1 market for the auto industry of the United States and the auto industry is the No.1 market for the steel industry, and the steel is 50 percent of capacity. That is what we are producing this week. The Soviet Union last week produced more steel than we did, because we are only using half of our capacity and only slightly more than half of our people. The economy of the United States is tied together. If the farmer prospers, the city prospers, and if the city prospers the farmer prospers, and I think the Democratic Party has understood that from the beginning. I think Franklin Roosevelt and Truman and Woodrow Wilson fought for the people of this country, fought to advance their progress, and we must fight in 1960 and 1961 and 1962. (October 3, 1960)

In keeping with his theme of comparing America to the Soviet Union (and always finding America to be lagging behind), Kennedy compares American steel production to Soviet production. But notice the immediacy of the language, "We heard *today*," Kennedy says when referring to the closing of International Harvester. Sure, Kennedy references the drop in agricultural productivity over the last few years, but his concrete examples are from "this week" and he compares the United States to the Soviet Union's levels of productivity "last week." Similarly, Ronald Reagan in 1984 said to supporters in North Carolina:

> Well, we cut inflation, and I'll tell you what it means: that 8.8 percent weekly—or decline in weekly earnings—within the last 2 years, weekly earnings have increased by 3.2 percent. . . . And as we freed up the economy to grow, we created over 6 million

new jobs in the last 21 months. More people are working this year than ever before in our history, and a job is the surest escape from poverty. (October 8, 1984)

Like Kennedy, Reagan references changes in policy over the previous two years, the previous twenty-one months. "More people are working this year than ever before," he says. While these anecdotes are not representative of campaign speeches more generally, they do raise at least the possibility that voters weight recent economic performance more heavily than earlier performance because candidates are telling them to do so.

Although the evidence is mixed over the last thirty years, there is a substantial and convincing set of findings that support the idea that candidates, particularly incumbent presidents, can create economic context before elections—and try to do so. Once the context is created, incumbents talk about it in their campaigns, encouraging voters to make the connection between their presidency or party and the good times. Meanwhile, the insurgent candidate is likely struggling to find an issue on which he or she is closer to most voters and on which the clarifying candidate is committed to an unpopular position.

Creating Salience: Finding the Right Insurgent Issue

Relative to claiming credit for a good economy or placing blame for a bad economy, the insurgent candidates have their work cut out for them. Not all candidates are in the position of Kennedy in 1960 or Carter in 1976, when natural, nonspecific policy dimensions were obviously salient to voters leading up to the election. In 1968 Nixon capitalized on Americans' existing racial prejudices and general sense of fear (and frustration with the chaos coming out of the protest movements of the period) in order to leverage the valence issue of law and order—and Bush, in 2000, cleverly seized voters' disappointment with the dalliance of sitting president Bill Clinton to promote himself and his domestic policies as "uniters" not dividers, the implicit argument being similar to Carter's "A Leader, for a Change" appeal in 1976.

But what happens if the insurgent candidate is Walter Mondale in 1984, running against an incumbent who presided over a period of sustained growth and economic repair? Or John McCain in 2008 running as the incumbent party in a period of global financial crisis? Was there an insurgent issue for Mondale in 1984 or McCain in 2008? Mondale surely thought a Kennedyesque appeal to American's fear of "Star Wars" (the Strategic Defense Initiative) and Reagan's likelihood of taking us to the point of having to deploy nuclear missile-defense systems would work to his advantage, but Reagan was not in Nixon's position (in 1960). And this dissimilarity was critical to Reagan's ability to counter Mondale's argument by raising the Strategic Arms Reduction Talks in which he was instrumentally involved. Nixon in 1960 believed Kennedy was (or could be) right about the Missile Gap; Reagan knew Mondale was wrong (or could at least be made to look wrong).

As American politics moves toward more elite partisan polarization, it might seem that insurgent issues are harder for candidates to find. Candidates have to find the plurality of voters and align close to them, which may be hard to do if most people are camping out at the extremes (although see Fiorina 2005). But at the same time, many Americans refuse to align themselves with either of the parties, suggesting that there may be issues on which public opinion does not merely mimic the partisan divide in the country. As we move beyond the 2008 election, what issues might insurgent candidates consider priming?

Recent polls suggest a host of issues on which Americans hold one-sided opinions. The issue that stands out most prominently is energy. A Quinnipiac College poll conducted in June of 2007 asked people if they thought the rising price of gasoline was a serious concern. Seventy-three percent of Americans said they thought this was a serious problem. Interestingly, however, the seriousness of the problem does not seem to stem from an economic foundation, because only 51 percent of the same respondents report cutting back on household spending for other items due to the increase in gas prices. Further, only a third of these people have changed their summer vacation plans because of the change in the price of gasoline.

Health care is another area with unequal distributions of opinion. An ABC News/*Washington Post* poll released in September of 2007 reports that 56 percent of Americans believe Democrats are better able to handle health care as a public-policy issue; only 26 percent give Republicans the nod here. The other 19 percent mostly believe neither party is better. Further, 72 percent of respondents to this poll favor increasing federal funding to insure currently uninsured children, and paying for it with cigarette taxes. And poll results show that 61 percent of Americans support embryonic stem-cell research. The same ABC/*Washington Post* poll shows that most Americans (67 percent) believe that not enough is being done to keep illegal immigrants from entering the country. Finally, a CBS/*New York Times* poll from 2005 reports that 92 percent of Americans think their Social Security system is in trouble.

These are some of the issues on which American opinion is not equally divided. Of course, each of the issues varies in terms of whether one of the candidates will have committed to unpopular positions in the past; and some are so tied to partisan positions that it would be impossible for a candidate of one party to campaign on the side of public opinion. But without knowing who the candidates will be and without knowing which party will have to run the next insurgent presidential campaign, is there anything that can be said about the insurgent candidate's ability to find the right issue or idea?

I think history and the patterns of evidence presented here suggest that the right insurgent strategy is often one that amalgamates a number of issues into one coherent theme: Kennedy's "New Frontier," Bush's "Compassionate Conservatism," or even Nixon's holistic leveraging of fear, best expressed in the tagline to his advertisements, "This November, vote like your whole world depended on it." The topics of energy policy, insuring children, immigration, medical research, and Social Security are all squarely domestic issues and can be woven tightly into an overarching message like these. A clever insurgent candidate might be able to mix these issues together into one broad message. In the face of years of Homeland Security initiatives and spending on war, it might be possible for an insurgent candidate to focus his or her campaign on Homeland *Prosperity*—not in terms of the economy, of course, but in terms of domestic conditions on important matters like energy, immigration, making advancements in cures for cancer, helping those with spinal-cord injuries walk again, or quite simply, just bringing basic health care to millions of children. An insurgent candidate running against a clarifying candidate with a record on the wrong side of a number of these domestic initiatives might have success advocating a true focus on the "homeland"—to ensure that we have something worth securing.

In *The Reasoning Voter* (1991), Popkin summarizes work from psychology and economics arguing that people use narratives to help them make sense of choices. Stories help us organize and understand the world around us. For the clarifying candidate, the story is easy for voters to appreciate—you are doing better today than you were before. But for the insurgent candidate, the story most likely has to be created. The Soviets launched a satellite and they are talking about orbiting the moon! It was easy to construct a story around our fear of communism that put Kennedy in charge of the New Frontier. America would send a man to the moon, and Kennedy told voters he was going to get it done. The story was so easy to play over and over again—if Kennedy could get it done it must be true that Nixon could not; he certainly had not done so in his eight years in the administration. The narratives candidates create, whether through their campaign rhetoric or through manipulation of economic policy or through a clever weaving and packing of issues, affect voters. Evidence from the last fifty years of presidential campaigns in America demonstrates that the best stories for candidates are the ones that are easy for them to tell, the ones on which they are naturally advantaged. Only two of the twenty-six candidates who have run since 1952 won elections by telling stories about things other than their natural advantage—and both of them were incumbents in good economies (1972 and 1996). Candidates, particularly incumbents, may be able to create the context of elections, but what is more important is that they recognize where their advantages are, where their opponents' weaknesses are, and that they leverage these opportunities at every opportunity.

What makes all of this even more challenging for candidates is that they cannot rely on the media to spread their story. The fidelity between the composition of candidates' campaigns and media coverage of them is low, although the media do respond somewhat to changes in the composition of campaign rhetoric over the course of a campaign. Candidates have to work hard to tell their own stories, which may explain the increase in paid advertising in presidential campaigns over the last twenty years. And now, with a crowded advertising arena, candidates struggle to tell their own stories before independent groups make advertisements that tell it for them. Being a major party presidential nominee is hard work.

To make it more complicated, the stories candidates tell play differently on different types of voters. Most notably, independents and voters with low levels of political sophistication and information are more likely to remember the candidates' narratives and mimic their rhetoric when asked about the candidates, but these voters use this information less at the polls. Candidates are in the uncomfortable position of needing to influence a very specific group of voters who are willing to believe their stories, but whose decision-making machine does not use this information as effectively as it could.

The single most impressive feature of presidential elections in the last fifty years must be the importance of national economic circumstances. The state of the economy conditions what kind of campaigns candidates are likely to run, it affects the stories candidates will weave about themselves and their policy agendas, and it predicts the winner of a good many elections well in advance of the vote. Despite this strong role for the structural conditions, there is still a role for candidates, their histories, their ideas, and their campaigns. The economy is the backdrop in front of which the great play of modern presidential campaigns is performed. The scenery is important. But as Shakespeare said, "the play's the thing."

APPENDIX

CHAPTER 2: SPATIAL MODEL OF VOTING

Assume that there are two candidates under evaluation by voters, candidate J and candidate G. For simplicity's sake, assume that voters are examining these two candidates over two issue dimensions, 1 and 2, that are relevant to the choice facing voters in this election. The two dimensions are not equal in importance, thus each issue has a weight attached to it, β and γ, respectively. Because voter i has uncertain information about the position of each candidate along these issue dimensions, the voter's perception of each candidate's true position on each issue under consideration is represented as a random variable, P_{ij1} (similarly for issue 2). This random variable is assumed to be normally distributed with mean, p_{ij1} and variance σ^2_{ij1}/n_{j1} where n is the number of messages candidate J sends about issue 1, (similarly for candidate G and issue 2). A voter's belief about each candidate's location on each issue is a combination of a central point and a distribution of points around the central point. The smaller the distribution of points around the central point, the less uncertainty the voter has about the candidate's position on that particular issue.

Assume that voters have quadratic utility functions, are utility maximizers, and that preferences can be expressed with a Euclidean distance measure. Let voter i's evaluation of candidate J on this particular issue be composed of a set of non-policy-oriented variables such as party identification, age, sex, and race. We will call these influences, c_{ij} for characteristics. Also, assume a voter's issue preferences can be measured by the squared distance between the voter's placement of him- or herself on the issue (x_{i1}) and the voter's placement of the candidate on the issue (P_{ij1}). Thus, voter i's utility for candidate J is

$$U_{ij} = \tau c_{ij} - \beta(P_{ij1} - x_{i1})^2 - \gamma(P_{ij2} - x_{i2})^2. \tag{1}$$

Note that P_{ij1} is a random variable, over which voters take expectations, such that

$$E[U_{ij}] = E[\tau c_{ij} - \beta(P_{ij1} - x_{i1})^2 - \gamma(P_{ij2} - x_{i2})^2]. \tag{2}$$

Expanding the squares in equation 2 reveals

$$E[U_{ij}] = E[\tau c_{ij} - \beta(P^2_{ij1} - 2P_{ij1}x_{i1} + x^2_{i1}) - \gamma(P^2_{ij2} - 2P_{ij2}x_{i2} + x^2_{i2})]. \tag{3}$$

Now, move the expectations operation through the right-hand side of the equation, noting that as defined above $E[P_{ij1}] = p_{ij1}$ and $E[P^2_{ij1}] = p^2_{ij1} + v_{ij1}$. When the expectation operation moves through these terms, other terms will be generated, so note that $v_{ij1} = \sigma^2_{ij1}/n_{j1}$. This gives

$$E[U_{ij}] = \tau c_{ij} - \beta(p_{ij1}^2 + (\sigma_{ij1}^2/n_{j1}) - 2p_{ij1}x_{i1} + x_{i1}^2)$$
$$- \gamma(p_{ij2}^2 + (\sigma_{ij1}^2/n_{j1}) - 2p_{ij2}x_{i2} + x_{i2}^2). \tag{4}$$

Finally, collect the terms on the right-hand side:

$$E[U_{ij}] = \tau c_{ij} - \beta[(p_{ij1}^2 - 2p_{ij1}x_{i1} + x_{i1}^2) + (\sigma_{ij1}^2/n_{j1})]$$
$$- \gamma[(p_{ij2}^2 - 2p_{ij2}x_{i2} + x_{i2}^2) + (\sigma_{ij2}^2/n_{j2})]. \tag{5}$$

And then,

$$E[U_{ij}] = \tau c_{ij} - \beta[(p_{ij1} - x_{i1})^2 + (\sigma_{ij1}^2/n_{j1})]$$
$$- \gamma[(p_{ij2} - x_{i2})^2 + (\sigma_{ij2}^2/n_{j2})]. \tag{6}$$

And the expected utility for candidate G can be written similarly:

$$E[U_{ig}] = \tau c_{ig} - \beta[(p_{ig1} - x_{i1})^2 + (\sigma_{ig1}^2/n_{g1})]$$
$$- \gamma[(p_{ig2} - x_{i2})^2 + (\sigma_{ig2}^2/n_{g2})]. \tag{7}$$

In an election between J and G, the decision rule for the voter is simple. A voter would vote for candidate J if $E[U_{ij}] > E[U_{ig}]$.

Because of the assumption that utility functions are quadratic, uncertainty depresses the voter's utility for a candidate. This theoretical prediction implies that the more uncertain voters are about a candidate's policy position, the lower their utility for that candidate, ceteris paribus.[1] This is a direct result of the risk-aversion assumption. In other words, the more a voter knows about candidate J, the more the voter's utility for J increases, regardless of other factors such as proximity to the candidate's issue placement and the weight of the issue.[2]

1. Shepsle (1972) notes that this prediction will not generally hold if voters have utility functions with convex regions.

2. This may seem counterintuitive at first. The increase in utility due to a reduction in uncertainty is an example of a mean preserving spread. This means that as the "spread" of dispersion around the mean becomes smaller, the mean remains unchanged. Thus the increase in utility is due to the decrease in dispersion or uncertainty, not to a change in other factors. Even if the voter places the candidate far from his own position on the dimension, the voter's utility for this candidate will increase as the uncertainty around that placement is reduced. For example, if a candidate were placed far to the right by a voter whose position was central, the voter would still experience an increase in his utility for this candidate if he learned that the candidate was not as far right as some threshold, d. Whereas prior to the new information, the voter thought the candidate could be as far right as d, he now knows that the candidate is not that far to the right and therefore his utility for this candidate increases.

Chapter 5 and Chapter 6: Results

Table A1
Forecasting Models 1952–2000 (Table 5.6)

	Coefficient	SE	R^2	Correctly Predicted
GNP (4th to 2nd)	2.52	.87	.38	8/13
Constant	47.77	2.11		
GNP	2.43	.81	.47	9/13
Incumbent	4.26	2.50		
Constant	45.32	2.42		
GNP	1.21	.69	.71	10/13
July Approval	.27	.07		
Constant	37.13	3.21		
GNP	1.23	.60	.79	12/13
Incumbent	3.38	1.61		
July Approval	.25	.06		
Constant	35.92	2.83		
GNP	1.10	.36	.92	12/13
Incumbent	1.45	1.07		
July Approval	.12	.05		
Meets Criteria	−5.95	1.44		
RDI (12th to 15th)	2.45	.67	.50	10/13
Constant	46.40	2.10		
RDI	1.98	.56	.69	11/13
War Dummy	−2.89	2.80		
No. of Terms	−4.60	2.11		
Constant				
RDI	1.20	.53	.81	11/13
War Dummy	−1.54	2.24		
No. of Terms	−1.30	2.10		
Meets Criteria	−6.52	2.51		
Constant	54.03	2.20		

Notes: GNP and RDI data from Bureau Economic Advisors.
July Approval from the Gallup Organization.
Incumbent indicates incumbent candidate.
No. of Terms counts number of terms party is in office.
War Dummy indicates whether country is at war.

TABLE A2
Media Attention and Uncertainty (Figure 6.5)

| | Guaranteed Jobs | | | | Defense Spending | | | |
| | Clarifying | | Insurgent | | Clarifying | | Insurgent | |
	Coef.	SE	Coef.	SE	Coef.	SE	Coef.	SE
Media	−.13	.02	−.14	.02	−.17	.03	−.15	.02
Media*Time	−.01	.01	−.01	.01	−.01	.01	−.02	.01
Time	−.01	.02	.001	.02	.02	.03	.03	.03
Female	.34	.05	.34	.04	.56	.014	.56	.02
Black	−.11	.05	−.17	.07	.25	.10	.23	.07
Education	−.17	.01	−.18	.01	−.20	.03	−.19	.02
Young	−.32	.08	−.27	.06	−.25	.07	−.21	.09
Midlife	−.34	.05	−.28	.04	−.26	.05	−.21	.07
Senior	−.25	.03	−.22	.03	−.21	.06	−.20	.07
1976	.11	.01	.06	.01	*	*	*	*
1980	.30	.01	.02	.01	.32	.03	.06	.004
1984	−.12	.01	−.04	.01	−.09	.03	.06	.02
1988	.12	.01	.05	.01	.02	.02	−.18	.003
1992	.09	.01	−.20	.01	.32	.03	.05	.01
1996	−.36	.01	−.32	.01	−.05	.02	−.18	.02
2000	−.20	.02	−.29	.02	*	*	*	*
Constant	.35	.1	.46	.09	.08	.16	.11	.12
R^2	.11		.11		.15		.15	
N	14153		14151		10776		10777	

Table A3
Media Attention and Uncertainty (Figure 6.5)

	Aid to Minorities				Services/Spending			
	Clarifying		Insurgent		Clarifying		Insurgent	
	Coef.	SE	Coef.	SE	Coef.	SE	Coef.	SE
Media	−.09	.03	−.10	.03	−.17	.03	−.16	.02
Media*Time	−.02	.01	−.01	.004	−.00	.01	−.00	.003
Time	.02	.02	.01	.02	−.01	.02	.00	.02
Female	.36	.03	.35	.03	.31	.03	.3	.04
Black	−.31	.08	−.40	.07	.16	.06	.11	.07
Education	−.18	.02	−.18	.02	−.22	.02	−.20	.02
Young	−.33	.04	−.32	.04	−.31	.11	−.32	.10
Midlife	−.35	.04	−.32	.03	−.31	.06	−.29	.07
Senior	−.32	.05	−.29	.04	−.26	.11	−.24	.10
1976	.49	.03	.42	.03	*	*	*	*
1980	.54	.04	.16	.04	*	*	*	*
1984	.16	.03	.18	.03	.46	.03	.76	.01
1988	.43	.01	.35	.01	.63	.01	.81	.02
1992	*	*	*	*	.71	.03	.69	.01
1996	−.27	.02	−.17	.03	−.59	.02	.19	.02
2000	.22	.02	.09	.01	*	*	*	*
Constant	.01	.10	.20	.08	.01	.11	−.17	.08
R^2	.12		.12		.19		.16	
N	12808		12807		9164		9160	

TABLE A4
Media Attention and Uncertainty (Figure 6.5)

| | Role of Women | | | | Liberal/Conservative | | | |
| | Clarifying | | Insurgent | | Clarifying | | Insurgent | |
	Coef.	SE	Coef.	SE	Coef.	SE	Coef.	SE
Media	−.10	.04	−.10	.04	−.12	.03	−.12	.03
Media*Time	−.01	.01	−.01	.01	−.01	.01	−.13	.01
Time	.01	.02	.03	.01	−.01	.03	.01	.03
Female	.11	.06	.15	.09	.31	.03	.32	.03
Black	−.003	.08	−.14	.08	.27	.05	.20	.05
Education	−.17	.01	−.15	.02	−.29	.01	−.28	.01
Young	−.35	.03	−.46	.03	−.13	.05	−.16	.05
Midlife	−.31	.03	−.32	.04	−.17	.05	−.17	.05
Senior	−.23	.05	−.23	.03	−.15	.05	−.16	.06
1976	.44	.09	.27	.09	.39	.04	.34	.04
1980	.23	.08	−.25	.07	.59	.03	.49	.03
1984	*	*	*	*	−.26	.03	−.27	.03
1988	.27	.03	.09	.02	.31	.01	.27	.01
1992	*	*	*	*	.32	.03	.15	.03
1996	−.49	.05	−.62	.04	.10	.02	.05	.02
2000	−.01	.03	−.21	.03	−.53	.01	−.64	.01
Constant	.26	.07	.45	.07	.59	.07	.67	.06
R^2	.11		.11		.18		.18	
N	10651		10652		15165		15164	

Table A5
Media Attention and Uncertainty (Figure 6.5)

	Relationship Russia			
	Clarifying		Insurgent	
	Coef.	SE	Coef.	SE
Media	−.15	.03	−.15	.02
Media*Time	−.01	.01	−.01	.01
Time	−.01	.04	−.01	.03
Female	.56	.04	.53	.05
Black	.43	.10	.30	.18
Education	−.19	.01	−.16	.02
Young	−.34	.06	−.34	.10
Midlife	−.29	.05	−.31	.03
Senior	−.28	.06	−.27	.05
1976	*	*	*	*
1980	.17	.03	−.42	.03
1984	−.15	.01	−.16	.02
1988	*	*	*	*
1992	*	*	*	*
1996	*	*	*	*
2000	*	*	*	*
Constant	.35	.05	.54	.04
R^2	.16		.15	
N	5630		5627	

Note: Inability to place each candidate on each issue is the dependent variable in the above fourteen analyses. Explanatory variables include level of attention to the campaign in the media, date of interview, demographic controls, and indicators for campaign year. Standard errors are robust and clustered on campaign year. These coefficients generate predicted probabilities that are presented in figure 6.5. Each bar in the figure is the change in predicted probability from early September to the last weeks of the campaign for varying levels of attention to the campaign in the media (for each candidate).

Table A6
Mean Percent of Respondents Who Think Insurgent Issue Is Nation's Most Important
Problem by Time of Interview (Figure 6.6)

	N	Mean	Standard Error	Binomial Exact 95% Confidence Interval	
Meets Criteria					
Early September	1557	29.3%	1.2%	27.4%	31.2%
Late September	1705	36.7%	1.2%	34.7%	38.6%
Early October	2050	42.0%	1.1%	40.2%	43.8%
Last Weeks	1230	34.0%	1.4%	31.8%	36.3%
Violates Criteria					
Early September	3715	20.1%	0.7%	19.0%	21.2%
Late September	4151	21.8%	0.6%	20.7%	22.9%
Early October	2986	19.7%	0.7%	18.5%	21.0%
Last Weeks	3534	22.6%	0.7%	21.5%	23.8%
Meets Topic					
Early September	3592	26.6%	0.7%	25.4%	27.8%
Late September	3858	30.3%	0.7%	29.1%	31.5%
Early October	3724	34.0%	0.8%	32.7%	35.3%
Last Weeks	2850	29.0%	0.9%	27.6%	30.4%
Violates Topic					
Early September	1680	14.6%	0.9%	13.2%	16.1%
Late September	1998	18.1%	0.9%	16.7%	19.5%
Early October	1312	14.1%	1.0%	12.5%	15.8%
Last Weeks	1914	20.4%	0.9%	18.9%	21.9%

Note: Data are from American National Election Study, 1960–2000.

TABLE A7
Non-Independence of Vote and Whether Respondent Thinks Insurgent Issue
Is Nation's Most Important Problem (Figure 6.7)

	Not Most Important	Most Important	TOTAL
Meets Criteria[a]			
Insurgent	1,283	806	2,089
	49.88	50.47	50.11
Clarifying	1,289	791	2,080
	50.12	49.53	49.89
TOTAL	2,572	1,597	4,169
	100	100	100
Meets Criteria—Low Information[b]			
Insurgent	171	106	277
	43.96	59.55	48.85
Clarifying	218	72	290
	56.04	40.45	51.15
TOTAL	389	178	567
	100	100	100
Meets Criteria—High Information[c]			
Insurgent	579	251	830
	52.54	50.91	52.04
Clarifying	523	242	765
	47.46	49.09	47.96
TOTAL	1,102	493	1,595
	100	100	100

[a]Pearson chi2(1) = 0.1355   Pr=0.713
[b]Pearson chi2(1) = 11.8812   Pr=0.001
[c]Pearson chi2(1) = 0.3617   Pr = 0.548
Note: Cell entries are raw accounts with column percentages underneath.

TABLE A8

Non-Independence of Vote and Whether Respondent Thinks Insurgent Issue
Is Nation's Most Important Problem (Figure 6.7)

	Not Most Important	Most Important	TOTAL
Violates Criteria[a]			
Insurgent	2,530	879	3,409
	39.1	41.54	39.7
Clarifying	3,940	1,237	5,177
	60.9	58.46	60.3
TOTAL	6,470	2,116	8,586
	100	100	100
Violates Criteria—Low Information[b]			
Insurgent	401	112	513
	41.73	49.12	43.15
Clarifying	560	116	676
	58.27	50.88	56.85
TOTAL	961	228	1,189
	100	100	100
Violates Criteria—High Information[c]			
Insurgent	1,058	367	1,425
	40.54	41.61	40.81
Clarifying	1,552	515	2,067
	59.46	58.39	59.19
TOTAL	2,610	882	3,492
	100	100	100

[a]Pearson chi2(1) = 3.9559   Pr = 0.047
[b]Pearson chi2(1) = 4.1087   Pr = 0.043
[c]Pearson chi2(1) = .3146   Pr = 0.575

Note: Cell entries are raw accounts with column percentages underneath.

Table A9

Non-Independence of Vote and Whether Respondent Thinks Insurgent Issue
Is Nation's Most Important Problem (Figure 6.7)

	Not Most Important	Most Important	TOTAL
Violates Topic[a]			
Insurgent	1,217	347	1,564
	38.32	43.27	39.32
Clarifying	1,959	455	2,414
	61.68	56.73	60.68
TOTAL	3,176	802	3,978
	100	100	100
Violates Topic—Low Information[b]			
Insurgent	174	30	204
	33.4	45.45	34.75
Clarifying	347	36	383
	66.6	54.55	65.25
TOTAL	521	66	587
	100	100	100
Violates Topic—High Information[c]			
Insurgent	581	211	792
	40.63	43.51	41.36
Clarifying	849	274	1,123
	59.37	56.49	58.64
TOTAL	1,430	485	1,915
	100	100	100

[a]Pearson chi2(1) = 6.5711   Pr = 0.01
[b]Pearson chi2(1) = 3.7557   Pr = 0.053
[c]Pearson chi2(1) = 1.235   Pr = 0.266
Note: Cell entries are raw accounts with column percentages underneath.

TABLE A10
Non-Independence of Vote and Whether Respondent Thinks Insurgent Issue
Is Nation's Most Important Problem (Figure 6.7)

	Not Most Important	Most Important	TOTAL
Meets Topic[a]			
Insurgent	2,596	1,338	3,934
	44.26	45.96	44.82
Clarifying	3,270	1,573	4,843
	55.74	54.04	55.18
TOTAL	5,866	2,911	8,777
	100	100	100
Meets Topic—Low Information[b]			
Insurgent	398	188	586
	48.01	55.29	50.13
Clarifying	431	152	583
	51.99	44.71	49.87
TOTAL	829	340	1,169
	100	100	100
Meets Topic—High Information[c]			
Insurgent	1,056	407	1,463
	46.28	45.73	46.12
Clarifying	1,226	483	1,709
	53.72	54.27	53.88
TOTAL	2,282	890	3,172
	100	100	100

[a]Pearson chi2(1) = 2.2964   Pr = 0.13
[b]Pearson chi2(1) = 5.1177   Pr = 0.024
[c]Pearson chi2(1) = .0765   Pr = 0.782
Note: Cell entries are raw accounts with column percentages underneath.

TABLE A11
Mean Differences in Distances on Insurgent Issue over Campaign by Type of Insurgent
Candidate, All Respondents (Figures 6.8 and 6.9)

	N	Mean	SE	90% Confidence Interval	
Meets Criteria					
Early September	1581	−0.34	0.22	−0.70	0.02
Late September	1773	−1.22	0.23	−1.60	−0.84
Early October	2110	−1.39	0.23	−1.77	−1.01
Last Weeks	1246	−0.70	0.24	−1.09	−0.31
Meets Topic					
Early September	4288	0.07	0.12	−0.12	0.27
Late September	5139	−0.29	0.11	−0.47	−0.10
Early October	5100	−0.61	0.12	−0.81	−0.41
Last Weeks	3036	−0.23	0.17	−0.51	0.04
Violates Criteria					
Early September	4343	0.53	0.14	0.30	0.75
Late September	5313	0.53	0.12	0.33	0.72
Early October	4264	0.40	0.13	0.19	0.61
Last Weeks	3664	0.37	0.17	0.09	0.65
Violates Topic					
Early September	1636	0.88	0.28	0.42	1.34
Late September	1947	1.08	0.26	0.66	1.51
Early October	1274	1.47	0.32	0.93	2.00
Last Weeks	1874	0.63	0.26	0.21	1.06

Table A12

Mean Differences in Distances on Insurgent Issue over Campaign by Type of Insurgent Candidate, High-Information Respondents (Figures 6.8 and 6.9)

	N	Mean	SE	90% Confidence Interval	
Meets Criteria—High Information					
Early September	562	−0.16	0.38	−0.79	0.46
Late September	572	−0.79	0.44	−1.51	−0.07
Early October	621	−1.15	0.47	−1.91	−0.38
Last Weeks	372	−1.65	0.55	−2.55	−0.74
Violates Criteria—High Information					
Early September	4018	0.54	0.14	0.32	0.77
Late September	4968	0.52	0.12	0.33	0.72
Early October	3994	0.43	0.13	0.23	0.64
Last Weeks	3238	0.37	0.18	0.08	0.66
Violates Topic—High Information					
Early September	1442	1.11	0.29	0.62	1.59
Late September	1743	1.15	0.26	0.71	1.58
Early October	1126	1.76	0.32	1.23	2.30
Last Weeks	1604	0.80	0.26	0.36	1.23
Meets Topic—High Information					
Early September	3954	0.09	0.12	−0.11	0.28
Late September	4810	−0.28	0.11	−0.46	−0.10
Early October	4772	−0.60	0.12	−0.80	−0.40
Last Weeks	2740	−0.29	0.17	−0.56	−0.01

TABLE A13

Mean Differences in Distances on Insurgent Issue over Campaign by Type of Insurgent Candidate, Low-Information Respondents (Figures 6.8 and 6.9)

	N	Mean	SE	90% Confidence Interval	
Meets Criteria—Low Information					
Early September	538	0.04	0.34	−0.51	0.60
Late September	708	−0.99	0.31	−1.50	−0.47
Early October	931	−1.44	0.28	−1.91	−0.98
Last Weeks	577	0.16	0.26	−0.26	0.59
Violates Criteria—Low Information					
Early September	1989	0.00	0.11	−0.19	0.18
Late September	2767	0.16	0.09	0.01	0.30
Early October	2370	0.11	0.09	−0.05	0.26
Last Weeks	1174	−0.04	0.22	−0.40	0.32
Violates Topic—Low Information					
Early September	347	0.65	0.50	−0.18	1.47
Late September	452	1.16	0.43	0.45	1.87
Early October	317	1.85	0.53	0.98	2.71
Last Weeks	479	0.45	0.43	−0.26	1.16
Meets Topic—Low Information					
Early September	2180	−0.09	0.11	−0.27	0.08
Late September	3023	−0.26	0.09	−0.40	−0.12
Early October	2984	−0.56	0.10	−0.73	−0.40
Last Weeks	1272	−0.13	0.17	−0.41	0.14

TABLE A14
Mean Differences in Distances on Insurgent Issue over Campaign by Type of Insurgent
Candidate, Independents (Figures 6.8 and 6.9)

	N	Mean	SE	90% Confidence Interval	
Meets Criteria—Independents					
Early September	183	−0.39	0.42	−1.07	0.30
Late September	229	−0.62	0.55	−1.54	0.29
Early October	253	−1.33	0.62	−2.36	−0.30
Last Weeks	117	0.06	0.75	−1.18	1.30
Violates Criteria—Independents					
Early September	449	1.26	0.32	0.74	1.79
Late September	562	0.59	0.34	0.04	1.15
Early October	397	1.12	0.37	0.51	1.73
Last Weeks	397	1.20	0.41	0.53	1.88
Violates Topic—Independents					
Early September	196	2.01	0.56	1.07	2.94
Late September	230	1.48	0.61	0.48	2.48
Early October	148	2.33	0.81	0.99	3.66
Last Weeks	198	1.60	0.57	0.66	2.53
Meets Topic—Independents					
Early September	436	0.23	0.27	−0.21	0.68
Late September	561	−0.27	0.32	−0.80	0.25
Early October	502	−0.47	0.36	−1.06	0.12
Last Weeks	316	0.53	0.46	−0.23	1.29

TABLE A15

Mean Differences in Distances on Insurgent Issue over Campaign by Type of Insurgent Candidate, Clarifying Partisans (Figures 6.8 and 6.9)

	N	Mean	SE	90% Confidence Interval	
Meets Criteria—Clarifying Partisans					
Early September	666	2.68	0.30	2.19	3.17
Late September	667	2.49	0.32	1.96	3.02
Early October	839	2.49	0.30	2.00	2.99
Last Weeks	611	2.09	0.25	1.68	2.49
Violates Criteria—Clarifying Partisans					
Early September	1847	3.31	0.19	3.00	3.63
Late September	2298	3.03	0.17	2.75	3.30
Early October	1860	2.79	0.18	2.49	3.08
Last Weeks	1586	4.07	0.23	3.69	4.45
Violates Topic—Clarifying Partisans					
Early September	711	4.78	0.38	4.16	5.41
Late September	861	5.02	0.33	4.47	5.57
Early October	571	5.44	0.43	4.74	6.15
Last Weeks	862	4.45	0.32	3.93	4.98
Meets Topic—Clarifying Partisans					
Early September	1802	2.50	0.16	2.23	2.77
Late September	2104	2.04	0.16	1.78	2.30
Early October	2128	1.96	0.16	1.70	2.21
Last Weeks	1335	2.91	0.22	2.56	3.27

TABLE A16

Mean Differences in Distances on Insurgent Issue over Campaign by Type of Insurgent Candidate, Insurgent Partisans (Figures 6.8 and 6.9)

	N	Mean	SE	90% Confidence Interval	
Meets Criteria—Insurgent Partisans					
Early September	723	−3.16	0.35	−3.73	−2.60
Late September	867	−4.22	0.35	−4.80	−3.65
Early October	1008	−4.58	0.35	−5.15	−4.00
Last Weeks	509	−4.24	0.41	−4.92	−3.56
Violates Criteria—Insurgent Partisans					
Early September	2016	−2.21	0.21	−2.55	−1.87
Late September	2436	−1.84	0.18	−2.14	−1.54
Early October	1979	−2.00	0.20	−2.32	−1.67
Last Weeks	1664	−3.40	0.26	−3.83	−2.97
Violates Topic—Insurgent Partisans					
Early September	724	−3.31	0.44	−4.03	−2.58
Late September	853	−2.99	0.41	−3.66	−2.32
Early October	550	−2.95	0.50	−3.77	−2.12
Last Weeks	810	−3.75	0.41	−4.43	−3.07
Meets Topic—Insurgent Partisans					
Early September	2015	−2.16	0.18	−2.46	−1.86
Late September	2450	−2.28	0.17	−2.56	−2.01
Early October	2437	−2.85	0.19	−3.16	−2.54
Last Weeks	1363	−3.51	0.26	−3.93	−3.08

Table A17
Importance of Differences in Distances to Vote for Clarifying Candidate by Insurgent
Candidate Type, All Respondents (Figures 6.10 and 6.11)

	Meets Criteria		Violates Criteria		Meets Topic		Violates Topic	
	Coef.	SE	Coef.	SE	Coef.	SE	Coef.	SE
Jobs Distance Difference	.04	.005	.03	.006	.04	.005	.06	.01
Insurgent Issue Distance Difference	.04	.007	.03	.005	.04	.005	−.02	.06
Female	.11	.03	−.03	.03	.03	.04	.22	.55
Black	.14	.56	−.23	.29	−.37	.28	−.11	.19
Young	.10	.0002	.04	.13	.19	.07	−.02	.06
Midlife	−.02	.12	.05	.05	.07	.05	.04	.03
Senior	.01	.07	.04	.04	.02	.05	1.8	.29
Clarifying Partisan	1.80	.21	1.87	.16	1.8	.09	−.51	.26
Constant	−.84	.08	−.61	.15	−.70	.09	−.60	.19
R^2	.52		.49		.52		.48	
N	2190		6771		5314		3647	

Table A18
Importance of Differences in Distances to Vote for Clarifying Candidate by Insurgent
Candidate Type, High-Information Respondents (Figures 6.10 and 6.11)

	Meets Criteria		Violates Criteria		Meets Topic		Violates Topic	
	Coef.	SE	Coef.	SE	Coef.	SE	Coef.	SE
Jobs Distance Difference	.06	.00	.04	.01	.06	.01	.07	.01
Insurgent Issue Distance Difference	.07	.01	.04	.01	.05	.01	*	*
Female	.08	.06	−.06	.03	.00	.04	−.04	.05
Black	−.13	.16	−.03	.23	−.24	.14	.21	.38
Young	.17	.20	.01	.08	.07	.14	.06	.11
Midlife	.11	.27	.04	.03	.08	.11	.04	.02
Senior	.14	.15	.10	.09	.07	.10	.19	.01
Clarifying Partisan	1.8	.11	1.95	.19	1.8	.08	1.98	.34
Constant	−.90	.18	−.69	.10	−.79	.09	−.70	.19
R^2	.60		.57		.60		.56	
N	1108		3253		2570		1791	

Table A19

Importance of Differences in Distances to Vote for Clarifying Candidate by Insurgent Candidate Type, Low-Information Respondents (Figures 6.10 and 6.11)

	Meets Criteria		Violates Criteria		Meets Topic		Violates Topic	
	Coef.	SE	Coef.	SE	Coef.	SE	Coef.	SE
Jobs Distance Difference	.03	.004	.03	.01	.03	.01	.04	.01
Insurgent Issue Distance Difference	.04	.004	.02	.01	.03	.01	*	*
Female	.30	.11	.01	.06	.13	.09	−.04	.12
Black	.46	.83	−.52	.40	−.46	.45	.03	.76
Young	.43	.17	.13	.22	.34	.09	−.53	.11
Midlife	.10	.17	−.03	.18	.29	.16	−.40	.16
Senior	.14	.15	−.01	.10	.11	.16	−.17	.14
Clarifying Partisan	1.7	.08	1.64	.22	1.75	.09	1.4	.27
Constant	−1.23	.30	−.37	.30	−.92	.24	.04	.29
R^2	.43		.35		.40		.29	
N	329		1062		850		541	

CHAPTER 5 AND CHAPTER 6: NATIONAL ELECTION
STUDY QUESTION WORDING

Most Important Problem

1960: What would you personally feel are the most important problems the government should try to take care of when the new president and Congress take office in January?

1964: As you well know, there are many serious problems in this country and in other parts of the world. The question is, what should be done about them and who should do it. We want to ask you about problems you think the government in Washington should do something about and any problems it should stay out of. First, what would you personally feel are the most important problems the government should try to take care of when the new president and Congress take office in January?

1966: What do you personally feel are the most important problems which the government in Washington should try to take care of?

1968, 1980, 1982: As you well know, the government faces many serious problems in this country and in other parts of the world. What do you personally feel are the most important problems which the government in Washington should try to take care of?

1970: As you well know, there are many serious problems in this country and in other parts of the world. We'd like to start out by talking with you about some of them. What do you personally feel are the most important problems which the government in Washington should try to take care of?

1972–78, 1984, and later: What do you think are the most important problems facing this country? (If more than one problem:) Of all you've told me (1996–later: Of those you've mentioned), what would you say is the single most important problem the country faces?

Seven Point Scales

GUARANTEED JOBS

Some people feel that the government in Washington should see to it that every person has a job and a good standard of living. (1972–78): Suppose these people are at one end of a scale, at point 1). Others think the government should just let each person get ahead on his/her own. (1972–78: Suppose these people are at the other end, at point 7. And, of course, some other people have opinions somewhere in between, at points 2, 3, 4, 5, or 6.)

Where would you place the Democratic party (yourself, the Republican party) (on this scale)? (7-point scale shown to r)

IDEOLOGY

We hear a lot of talk these days about liberals and conservatives. I'm going to show you (1996 and later: Here is) a 7-point scale on which the political views that people might hold are arranged from extremely liberal to extremely conservative.

Where would you place the Democratic party (yourself, the Republican party) (on this scale)? (7-point scale shown to r)

HEALTH INSURANCE

There is much concern about the rapid rise in medical and hospital costs. Some (1988, 1994–later: people) feel there should be a government insurance plan which would cover all medical and hospital expenses (1984 and later: for everyone). (1996: Suppose these people are at one end of a scale, at point 1.) Others feel that (1988, 1994, 1996: all) medical expenses should be paid by individuals, and through private insurance (1984 and later: plans) like Blue Cross (1984–94: or (1996: some) other company paid plans). (1996: Suppose these people are at the other end, at point 7. And of course, some people have opinions somewhere in between at points 2, 3, 4, 5, or 6.) Where would you place yourself on this scale, or haven't you thought much about this? (7-point scale shown to r).

AID TO MINORITIES/BLACKS

Some people feel that the government in Washington should make every possible effort to improve the social and economic position of blacks (1970: Negroes) and other minority groups (1980: even if it means giving them preferential treatment). Others feel that the government should not make any special effort to help minorities because they should help themselves (1970: but they should be expected to help themselves).

1986 Form A, 1988 Form A, 1990 and later: Some people feel that the government in Washington should make every (prior to 1996 only: possible) effort to improve the social and economic position of blacks. (1996–later: Suppose these people are at one end of a scale, at point 1.) Others feel that the government should not make any special effort to help blacks because they should help themselves.

(1996–later: Suppose these people are at the other end, at point 7. And of course, some other people have opinions somewhere in between, at points 2, 3, 4, 5, or 6).

All years: Where would you place yourself on this scale, or haven't you thought much about it? (7-point scale shown to r)

ROLE OF WOMEN

Recently there has been a lot of talk about women's rights. Some people feel that women should have an equal role with men in running business, industry, and government. Others feel that a woman's place is in the home.

All years exc. 2000 version 2:

Where would you place yourself on this scale or haven't you thought much about this? (7-point scale shown to r)

2000 version 2:

Where would you place yourself on this scale? (7-point scale shown to r)

SERVICES/SPENDING

Some people think the government should provide fewer services, even in areas such as health and education, in order to reduce spending. Other people feel that it is important for the government to provide many more services even if it means an increase in spending. Where would you place yourself on this scale, or haven't you thought much about this? (7-point scale shown to r)

COOPERATION WITH RUSSIA

1980: Some people feel it is important for us to try very hard to get along with Russia. Others feel it is a big mistake to try too hard to get along with Russia.

1984–88: Some people feel it is important for us to try to cooperate more with Russia, while others believe we should be much tougher in our dealings with Russia.

All years: Where would you place yourself on this scale, or haven't you thought much about this? (7-point scale shown to r)

DEFENSE SPENDING

Some people believe that we should spend much less money for defense. (1996: Suppose these people are at one end of a scale, at point 1.) Others feel that defense spending should be greatly increased. (1996: Suppose these people are at the other end, at point 7.) Where would you place yourself on this scale or haven't you thought much about this? (7-point scale shown to r)

REFERENCES

Abramowitz, Alan. 1988. "An Improved Model for Predicting Presidential Election Outcomes." *PS: Political Science and Politics* 21: 843–47.

Achen, Christopher H., and Larry M. Bartels. 2002. "Blind Retrospection: Electoral Responses to Drought, Flu, and Shark Attacks." Paper presented at the Annual Meeting of the American Political Science Association, Boston, August 28–September 1, 2002.

———. 2004. "Musical Chairs: Pocketbook Voting and the Limits of Democratic Accountability." Unpublished manuscript.

Adasiewicz, Christopher, Douglas Rivlin, and Jeffrey Stranger. 1997. "Free Television for Presidential Candidates: The 1996 Experiment," Report No. 11 for the Annenberg Public Policy Center. Philadelphia: University of Pennsylvania Press.

Alt, James E., and Alec K. Chrystal. 1983. *Political Economics.* Berkeley: University of California Press.

Alvarez, Michael. 1997. *Issues and Information in Presidential Elections.* Ann Arbor: University of Michigan Press.

Alvarez, R. Michael, and Charles Franklin. 1994. "Uncertainty and Political Perceptions." *Journal of Politics* 56: 671–88.

Anderson, David C. 1995. *Crime and the Politics of Hysteria: How the Willie Horton Story Changed American Justice.* New York: Random House.

Ansolabehere, Stephen, and Shanto Iyengar. 1995. *Going Negative: How Attack Ads Shrink and Polarize the Electorate.* New York: Free Press.

Arceneaux, Kevin. 2005. "Do Campaigns Help Voters Learn?" *British Journal of Political Science* 36: 159–73.

Bartels, Larry M. 1988. *Presidential Primaries and the Dynamics of Public Choice.* Princeton, NJ: Princeton University Press.

———. 1986. "Issue Voting under Uncertainty: An Empirical Test." *American Journal of Political Science* 30: 709–28.

———. 1996. "Uninformed Votes: Information Effects in Presidential Elections." *American Journal of Political Science.* 40: 194–230.

———. 2000a. "Campaign Quality: Standards for Evaluation, Benchmarks for Reform," in *Campaign Reform: Insights and Evidence.* Ann Arbor: University of Michigan Press.

———. 2000b. "Partisanship and Voting Behavior, 1952–1996." *American Journal of Political Science* 44: 35–50.

Bartels, Larry M., and John R. Zaller. 2001. "Presidential Vote Models: A Recount." *PS: Political Science and Politics* 34: 9–20.

Beck, Nathaniel. 1987. "Elections and the Fed: Is There a Political Monetary Cycle?" *American Journal of Political Science* 31: 194–214.

Berelson, Bernard R., Paul F. Lazarsfeld, and William N. McPhee. 1954. *Voting: A Study of Opinion Formation in a Presidential Campaign.* Chicago: University of Chicago Press.

Berke, Richard L. 2001. "Gore and Bush Strategists Analyze Their Campaigns," *New York Times,* February 12, A19.

Boller, Paul F. Jr. 1996. *Presidential Campaigns.* Oxford: Oxford University Press.

Brasher, Holly. 2003. Capitalizing on Contention: Issue Agendas in U.S. Senate Campaigns. *Political Communication* 20: 453–71.

Campbell, Angus, Philip E. Converse, Warren E. Miller, and Donald Stokes. 1960. *The American Voter*. Chicago: University of Chicago Press.

Campbell, James E. 1990. "Trial-Heat Forecasts of the Presidential Vote." American Politics Quarterly 18: 251–69.

———. 1992. "Forecasting the Presidential Elections in the States." *American Journal of Political Science* 36: 386–407.

Campbell, James E., Lynne Cerry, and Kenneth Wink. 1992. "The Convention Bump." *American Politics Quarterly* 20: 287–307.

Campbell, James E., and Kenneth A. Wink. 1990. "Trial-Heat Forecasts of the Presidential Vote." *American Politics Quarterly* 18 (July): 251–69.

Carsey, Thomas M. 2000. *Campaign Dynamics: The Race for Governor*. Ann Arbor: University of Michigan Press.

Converse, Phillip E. 1964. "The Nature of Belief Systems in Mass Publics." in David E. Apter, (ed.), *Ideology and Discontent*. New York: Free Press.

Cook, Timothy E. 1999. *Governing with the News: The News Media as a Political Institution*. Chicago: University of Chicago Press.

Downs, Anthony. 1957. *An Economic Theory of Democracy*. New York: Harper-Row.

Duch, Raymond M., and Randolph T. Stevenson. 2008. *The Economic Vote: How Political and Economic Institutions Condition Election Results*. Cambridge: Cambridge University Press.

Enelow, James M., and Melvin J. Hinich. 1984. *The Spatial Theory of Voting*. New York: Cambridge University Press.

———. 1981. "A New Approach to Voter Uncertainty in the Downsian Spatial Model," *American Journal of Political Science* 25: 483–93.

Erikson, Robert S. 1989. "Economic Conditions and the Presidential Vote." *American Political Science Review* 83: 567–73.

Fair, Ray C. 1978. "The Effect of Economic Events on Votes for President." *Review of Economics and Statistics* 60: 322–25.

Fallows, James. 1996. *Breaking the News: How the Media Undermine American Democracy*. New York: Pantheon.

Farah, Barbara G., and Ethel Klein. 1989. "Public Opinion Trends." In G. M. Pomper (ed.), *The Election of 1988: Reports and Interpretations*. Chatham, NJ: Chatham House Publishers.

Ferejohn, John. 1986. "Incumbent Performance and Electoral Control." *Public Choice* 50(1): 5–25.

Finkel, Steven E., and John G. Geer. 1998. "Spot Check: Casting Doubt on the Demobilizing Effect of Attack Advertising." *American Journal of Political Science* 42(2): 573–95.

Fiorina, Morris P. 1981. *Retrospective Voting in American National Elections*. New Haven: Yale University Press.

———. 2004. Culture War: The Myth of a Polarized America. NY: Longman.

Franklin, Charles H. 1991. "Eschewing Obfuscation? Campaigns and the Perceptions of U.S. Senate Incumbents." *American Political Science Review* 85: 1193–214.

———. 1992. "Measurement and the Dynamics of Party Identification." *Political Behavior* 14(2): 297–309.

Freedman, Paul, and Ken M. Goldstein. 1999. "Measuring Media Exposure and the Effects of Negative Campaign Ads," *American Journal of Political Science* 43: 1189–208.

Frey, Bruno S. 1978. "Politico-Economic Models and Cycles." *Journal of Public Economics* 9: 203–20.

Frey, Bruno S., and Friedrich Schneider. 1975. "On the Modeling of Politico-Economic Interdependence. *European Journal of Political Research* 3: 339–60.

———. 1978. "An Empirical Study of Politico-Economic Interaction in the United States." *Review of Economics and Statistics* 60: 174–83.

———. 1979. "An Econometric Model with an Endogenous Government Sector." *Public Choice* 34: 29–43.

Gans, Herbert J. 1979. *Deciding What's News.* New York: Pantheon Books.

Geer, John G. 1988. "The Effects of Presidential Debates on the Electorate's Preference for Candidates." *American Politics Quarterly* 16: 486–501.

———. 1998. "Campaigns, Competition, and Political Advertising," in John G. Geer (ed.), *New Perspectives on Party Politics.* Baltimore: Johns Hopkins Press.

———. 2000. "Assessing Attack Advertising: A Silver Lining," in Larry M. Bartels and Lynn Vavreck (eds.), *Campaign Reform: Insights and Evidence.* Ann Arbor: University of Michigan Press.

———. 2006. *In Defense of Negativity: Attack Ads in Presidential Campaigns.* Chicago: University of Chicago Press.

Gelman, Andrew, and Gary King. 1993. "Why Are American Presidential Polls So Variable When Election Outcomes Are So Predictable?" *British Journal of Political Science* 23: 409–51.

Gerber, Alan S., and Donald P. Green. 2000. "The Effects of Personal Canvassing, Telephone Calls and Direct Mail on Voter Turnout: A Field Experiment." *American Political Science Review* 94: 653–64.

Gilens, Martin, Lynn Vavreck, and Martin Cohen. 2007. "The Mass Media and the Public's Assessments of Presidential Candidates, 1952–2000." *Journal of Politics* 69(4): 1160–75.

Glazer, Amihai, and Susanne Lohmann 1999. "Setting the Agenda: Electoral Competition, Commitment of Policy, and Issue Salience." *Public Choice* 99 (3–4): 377–94.

Golden, David G., and James H. Poterba. 1980. "The Price of Popularity: The PBC Reexamined." *American Journal of Political Science* 24: 696–714.

Grier, Kevin. 1989. "On the Existence of a Political Monetary Cycle." *American Journal of Political Science* 33(2): 376–89.

Hagen, Michael G. (1995). "References to Racial Issues." *Political Behavior* 17: 49–88.

Hammond, Thomas, and Brian Humes. 1993. "'What This Campaign Is All About Is . . . : A Rational Choice Alternative to the Downsian Model of Elections," in Bernard Grofman (ed.), *Information, Participation, and Choice.* Ann Arbor: University of Michigan Press.

Hart, Roderick P. 2000. *Campaign Talk: Why Elections Are Good for Us.* Princeton, NJ. Princeton University Press.

———. 1984. *Verbal Styles and the President: A Computer-Based Analysis.* Orlando: Academic Press.

Heckman, James J. 1978. "Dummy Endogenous Variables in a Simultaneous Equation System." *Econometrica* 46: 931–60.

Hershey, Margorie Randon. 1989. "The Campaign and the Media," in Gerald Pomper (ed.), *The Election of 1980: Reports and Interpretations*. Chatham, NJ: Chatham House.

Hess, Stephen. 1981. *The Washington Reporters*. Washington, DC: Brookings Institution.

Hetherington, Marc J. 1996. "The Media's Role in Forming Voters' National Economic Evaluations in 1992." *American Journal of Political Science* 40: 372–95.

Hibbs, Douglas A. Jr. 1982. "President Reagan's Mandate from the 1980 Elections: A Shift to the Right?" *American Politics Quarterly* 10: 387–420.

Hibbs, Douglas A. Jr. 1987. *The American Political Economy: Macroeconomics and Electoral Politics*. Cambridge, MA: Harvard University Press.

Hibbs, Douglas A. Jr. 2000. "Bread and Peace Voting in U.S. Presidential Elections." *Public Choice* 104: 149–80.

Hillygus, D. Sunshine, and Simon Jackman. 2003. "Voter Decision Making in Election 2000: Campaign Effects, Partisan Activation, and the Clinton Legacy." *American Journal of Political Science* 47: 583–96.

Holbrook, Thomas M. 1994. "Campaigns, National Conditions, and U.S. Presidential Elections." *American Journal of Political Science* 38(4): 25–46.

———. 1996. *Do Campaigns Matter?* Thousand Oaks: Sage.

———. 2001. Forecasting with Mixed Economic Signals: A Cautionary Tale. *PS: Political Science and Politics* 34: 39–44.

Huber, Gregory A., and Kevin Arceneaux. 2007. "Identifying the Persuasive Effects of Presidential Advertising." *American Journal of Political Science* 51: 957–77.

Iyengar, Shanto. 1991. *Is Anyone Responsible?* Chicago: Chicago University Press.

Iyengar, Shanto, and Donald Kinder. 1987. *News that Matters: Television and American Opinion*. Chicago: University of Chicago Press.

Jamieson, Kathleen H. 2005. Personal Communication between Kathleen H. Jamieson and Lynn Vavreck on November 30, 2005.

Jamieson, Kathleen H., Paul Waldman, and Susan Sherr. 2000. "Eliminating the Negative? Defining and Refining Categories of Analysis for Political Advertisements," in *Crowded Airwaves*, J. Thurber, C. J. Nelson, and D. Dulio (eds.). Washington: Brookings Institution Press, 44–64.

Johnston, Richard, Andre Blais, Henry E. Brady, and Jean Crete. 1992. *Letting the People Decide: Dynamics of a Canadian Election*. Stanford: Stanford University Press.

Johnston, Richard, Kathleen Hall Jamieson, and Michael G. Hagen. 2004. *The Presidential Campaign of 2000 and the Foundation of Party Politics*. New York: Cambridge University Press.

Just, Marion R., Ann N. Crigler, Dean E. Alger, Timothy Cook, and Montague Kern. 1996. *Crosstalk: Citizens, Candidates, and the Media in a Presidential Campaign*. Chicago: University of Chicago Press.

Kahn, Kim F., and Patrick Kenney. 1999. *The Spectacle of U.S. Senate Campaigns*. Princeton: Princeton University Press.

Keech, William R. 1980. "Elections and Macroeconomic Policy Optimization." *American Journal of Political Science* 24: 345–67.

Kern, Montague. 1989. *30-Second Politics: Political Advertising*. New York: Praeger.

Key, V. O. Jr. 1966. *The Responsible Electorate*. New York: Vintage Books.

Kovach, Bill, and Tom Rosenstiel. 1999. *Warp Speed: America in the Age of Mixed Media*. New York: Century Foundation Press.

Kramer, Gerald. 1971. "Short-Term Fluctuations in U.S. Voting Behavior, 1896–1964." *American Political Science Review* 65(1): 131–43.

Krasno, Jonathan S., and Donald P. Green. 2008. "Do Televised Presidential Ads Increase Voter Turnout? Evidence from a Natural Experiment." *Journal of Politics* 70(1): 245–61.

Lau, Richard R., Lee Sigelman, Caroline Heldman, and Paul Babbit. 1999. "The Effects of Negative Political Advertisemets: A Meta-Analytic Assessment." *American Political Science Review* 93: 851–76.

Lazarsfeld, Paul N., Bernard R. Berelson, and Helen Gaudet. 1948. *The People's Choice: How the Voter Makes Up His Mind in a Presidential Campaign.* New York: Columbia University Press.

Lee, Lung Fei. 1982. "Simultaneous Equations Models with Discrete and Censored Variables," in *Structural Analysis of Discrete Data: With Econometric Applications.* C. Manski and D. McFadden (eds.). Cambridge, MA: MIT Press.

Lewis-Beck, Michael, and Tom Rice. 1992. *Forecasting Elections.* Washington DC: CQ Press.

Lewis-Beck, Michael, and Charles Tien. 2001. Modeling the Future: Lessons from the Gore Forecast. *PS: Political Science and Politics* 34: 21–31.

———. 1996. "The Future in Forecasting: Prospective Presidential Models." *American Politics Quarterly* 24: 468–91.

Lowery, David. 1985. "The Keynesian and Political Determinants of Unbalanced Budgets: U.S. Fiscal Policy from Eisenhower to Reagan." *American Journal of Political Science* 29: 428–60.

Marcus, George E., W. Russell Neuman, and Michael MacKuen. 2000. *Affective Intelligence and Political Judgment.* Chicago: University of Chicago Press.

McCombs, Maxwell, and Donald Shaw. 1972. "The Agenda-Setting Function of Mass Media." *Public Opinion Quarterly* 36: 176–87.

McGuire, William J. 1968. "Personality and Susceptibility to Social Influence." In E. F. Borgatta and W.W. Lambert (eds.), *Handbook of Personality Theory and Research.* New York: Rand-McNally.

McRae, Duncan C. 1977. "A Political Model of the Business Cycle." *Journal of Political Economy* 85: 239–63.

Mendelberg, Tali. 2001. *The Race Card: Campaign Strategy, Implicit Messages, and the Norm of Equality.* Princeton, NJ: Princeton University Press.

Miller, Warren E. 1991. "Party Identification Realignment and Party Voting: Back to Basics." *American Political Science Review* 85: 557–68.

New York Times Editorial Board. 1988 "Why Michael Dukakis Lost," *New York Times,* November 9, A34.

———. 1992. "Ten Reasons to Feel Good," *New York Times,* November 5, A34.

Nie, Norman H., Sidney Verba, and John R. Petrocik. 1976. *The Changing American Voter.* Cambridge, MA: Harvard University Press.

Nordhaus, William D. 1975. "The Political Business Cycle." *Review of Economic Studies* 42(2): 169–90.

Norpoth, Helmut. 1995. "Is Clinton Doomed? An Early Forecast for 1996." *PS: Political Science and Politics* 28: 201–207.

———. 2001. "Primary Colors: A Mixed Blessing for Al Gore." *PS: Political Science and Politics* 34: 45–48.

Page, Benjamin I. 1976. "The Theory of Political Ambiguity." *American Political Science Review* 70: 742.

———. 1996. *Who Deliberates? Mass Media in Modern Democracy*. Chicago: University of Chicago Press.

Paletz, David L. 1999. *The Media in American Politics: Contents and Consequences*. New York: Longman.

Patterson, Thomas E. 1992. *Out of Order*. New York: Vintage Books.

Petrocik, John. 1980. "Contextual Sources of Voting Behavior: The Changeable American Voter," in J. Pierce and J. Sullivan (eds.), *The Electorate Reconsidered*. Beverly Hills, CA: Sage.

Pomper, Gerald M. 1975. *Voter's Choice*. New York: Harper and Row.

Popkin, Samuel L. 1991. *The Reasoning Voter: Communication and Persuasion in Presidential Campaigns*. Chicago, IL: University of Chicago Press.

Powell, G. Bingham Jr., and Guy D. Whitten, "A Cross-National Analysis of Economic Voting: Taking Account of the Political Context," *American Journal of Political Science* 37:2, 391–414.

RePass, David E. 1971. "Issue Salience and Party Choice." *American Political Science Review* 65 (June): 389–400.

Riker, Bill. 1996. *The Strategy of Rhetoric: Campaigning for the American Constitution*. London: Yale University Press.

Robinson, Michael J., and Margaret Sheehan. 1983. *Over the Wire and on TV*. New York: Russell Sage.

Rosenstone, Steven. 1983. *Forecasting Presidential Elections*. New Haven: Yale University Press.

———. 1985. "Why Reagan Won." *Brookings Review* 3: 25–32.

Runkel, David R. (ed.). 1989. *Campaign for the President: The Managers Look at '88*. Dover, MA: Auburn House.

Sanders, David. 1991. "Government Popularity and the Next General Election." *Political Studies*: 235–61.

Schattschneider, E. E. 1960. *The Semisovereign People: A Realist's View of Democracy in America*. New York: Holt.

Shaw, Daron R. 1999a. "The Effect of TV Ads and Candidate Appearances on Statewide Presidential Votes, 1988–1996." *American Political Science Review* 93: 2, 345.

———. 1999b. "A Study of Presidential Campaign Event Effects from 1952 to 1992." *Journal of Politics* 61:2 387–422.

Shepsle, Kenneth A. 1972. "The Strategy of Ambiguity: Uncertainty and Electoral Competition," *American Political Science Review* 66: 555–68.

Sides, John. 2006. "The Origins of Campaign Agendas." *British Journal of Political Science* 36(3): 407–36.

Simon, Adam F. 2002. *The Winning Message: Candidate Behavior, Campaign Discourse, and Democracy*. New York: Cambridge University Press.

Smith, Tom W. 1985. "America's Most Important Problem, Part I: National and International." *Public Opinion Quarterly* 49: 264–74.

Sparrow, Bartholomew H. 1999. *Uncertain Guardians: The News Media as a Political Institution*. Baltimore: Johns Hopkins University Press.

Spiliotes, Constantine J., and Lynn Vavreck. 2002. "Campaign Advertising: Partisan Convergence or Divergence?" *Journal of Politics*. 64(1): 249–61.

Stevenson, Randolph, and Lynn Vavreck. 2000. "Does Campaign Length Matter: Testing for Cross-national Implications." *British Journal of Political Science* 30: 217–35.

Stokes, Donald E. 1966. "Spatial Models of Party Competition," in *Elections and the Political Order.* Angus Campbell et al (eds.). New York: Wiley.

Tufte, Edward R. 1978. *Political Control of the Economy.* Princeton, NJ: Princeton University Press.

Vavreck, Lynn. 2001. "The Reasoning Voter Meets the Strategic Candidate: Signals and Specificity in Campaign Advertising, 1998." *American Politics Research* 29 (September): 507–29.

Vavreck, Lynn, Constantine Spiliotes, and Linda Fowler. 2002. "The Effects of Retail Politics in the 1996 New Hampshire Primary." *American Journal of Political Science* 46 (July): 595–610.

Wattenberg, Martin P., and Craig L. Brians. 1999. "Negative Campaign Advertising: Demobilizer or Mobilizer?" *American Political Science Review* 93(4): 891–99.

West, Darrell. 1997. *Air Wars: Television Advertising in Election Campaigns, 1952–1992.* Washington DC: Congressional Quarterly.

Williams, John T. 1990. "The Political Manipulation of Macroeconomic Policy." *American Political Science Review* 84(3): 767–95.

Wlezien, Christopher, and Robert S Erikson. "Temporal Horizons and Presidential Election Forecasts." *American Politics Quarterly* 24: 492–50.

Zaller, John R. 1992. *The Nature and Origins of Mass Opinion.* New York, Cambridge: Cambridge University Press.

———. 2002. "Assessing the Statistical Power of Election Studies to Detect Communication Effects in Political Campaigns." *Electoral Studies* 21: 297–329.

INDEX

Abramowitz, Alan, 13, 36–37
Achen, Christopher H., 21, 161, 162
Adasiewicz, Christopher, 58
advertisement, 4, 43, 44, 45; coding of, 46–50, 53–54, 56–57; content of, 57–58, 60–62; Daisy Spot, 79; Morning In America, 81; effects of, 116, 165–166
agenda setting, 14, 16, 19–20, 23, 28, 33, 49, 108
Alt, James E., 160–161
Alvarez, Michael, 14, 18
American dream, 82
American Independent Party, 90
American National Election Study, 4, 79, 114, 116–117, 126, 132, 135, 137–138, 142, 146, 168, 149, 153–154
Anderson, David C., 83
ANES, see American National Election Study
Annenberg School of Communication, 46–48, 50
Ansolabehere, Stephen, 15
appeals, 47, 54–57, 60–61, 88, 121, 123, 142
Arceneaux, Kevin, 13, 24, 44
Arizona State University, 47, 116
assassination, of Robert F. Kennedy, 87; of Martin Luther King Jr., 87
assumption, 12, 18, 26, 35, 43, 161
attack campaign, 2, 58, 60, 82
attitudes, 12; change of, 10, 18, 25, 66, 150; as filter, 24; on foreign policy, 30; and party identification, 24; as measured by surveys, 114
Atwater, Lee, 9

"bad news" coverage, 53, 59
Bartels, Larry M., 3, 10, 14, 15, 18, 21, 23, 36, 49, 53, 132, 161–162
Battle of Saigon, 87
BBC, 65
Beck, Nathaniel, 161
Berelson, Bernard R., 10–11, 159
Boller, Paul F. Jr., 79, 85
Boston Harbor, 82
Brasher, Holly, 17
bread and peace model, 108
Brians, Craig L., 15

Bush, George H.W., 1, 2, 9, 23, 46, 82–83, 113, 134; campaign ads of, 51, 61–62, 68, 101–102; and campaign effects, 126; as clarifying candidate (1988), 38, 39, 69, 70, 71, 105, 106, 160; as insurgent candidate (1992), 38, 39, 73, 74–75, 106, 135, 136; newspaper coverage of, 51, 59, 61, 101–102; speeches of, 51, 61–62, 68, 101–102
Bush, George W., campaign ads of, 51, 60–62, 68, 82–83,104; and campaign effects 127; as clarifying candidate (2004), 38, 39, 71; as insurgent candidate (2000), 38, 39, 73, 83, 113, 135, 136, 163, 164–165; newspaper coverage of, 51, 61, 104; speeches of, 47, 51, 60–62, 68, 75, 104

campaign content, 43, 46–47; content analysis of, 47–49, 54–56; by campaign year, 92–104; by candidate, see candidate behavior; effects of 109, 116, 117, 121, 123–129, 131–133, 134, 138, 141, 144, 149, 153–154
campaign effects, 10, 12, 14, 23–24, 26, 43, 46, 115, 118–119, 123, 134, 155; for clarifying candidates, 123–129, 131–133, 156; for insurgent candidates, 134, 138, 141, 144, 149, 153–154, 157; and low information voters, 138, 141–142, 149, 153–154; theory of, 15–16, 18–20, 22, 25–26, 28, 33, 113
campaign effort, 44, 152
campaign events, 15, 44, 49–50, 64, 127–128, 131
Campaign Management Institute, 26
campaign messages, how to measure, 46–49, 52–58; effects of, see campaign effects; by year, 92–104
campaign reform, 2–3, 65
campaigns, advertisements in, see advertisements; by candidate, see candidate behavior clarifying, 31, 69–71, 115, 123–129, 131–133, 156; coverage of, 64–65; effects of, see campaign effects; and individual-level characteristics, 23, 133, 141, 149, 153–154; insurgent, 32, 71–74, 134–137, 138, 144, 146, 149, 153–154, 157; and effects on issue salience, 134, 138, 141; in the literature, 16; messages in, 43, 50–52, 58, 60–61, 68, 106, 109,

campaigns (*continued*)
118–119, 121, 123, 155; and effects on proximity, 144, 149, 153–154; reactions to, 1, 9;
and retrospective voting, 22; and the spatial
model, 19; spending in, 9; theory of, 15,
18–20, 22, 25–26, 28, 33, 113; typology of,
26, 35; and reductions in uncertainty,
123–129, 131–133
Campbell, Angus, 11, 17, 21, 24, 159
Campbell, James E., 13, 15, 36–37
candidate behavior, 26–28; of Bush in 1988,
83, 101; of Bush in 1992, 70, 102; of Bush
in 2000, 70, 104; of Carter in 1976, 90–91,
98; of Carter in 1980, 80–82; of Clinton
1992, 70, 102; of Clinton in 1996, 70; of
Dole, 74–75; of Dukakis, 82–83, 101; of
Eisenhower, 76–78, 92–93; of Ford, 70, 98;
of Goldwater, 78–80, 95; of Gore, 70; of
Humphrey, 70, 96; of Johnson, 95; of
Kennedy, 83–86, 94; of McGovern, 74, 97;
of Mondale, 80–82, 99; of Nixon in 1960,
70, 94; of Nixon in 1968, 86–90, 96; of
Nixon in 1972, 70, 97; of Reagan, 80–82,
99, 100; of Stevenson, 76–78, 92–93
candidate-based stories, 52
Carsey, Thomas M., 17
Carter, Jimmy, 1, 2, 37, 46, 70; campaign ads
of, 51, 61, 68, 98–99; as insurgent candidate,
38, 39, 72–73, 80–82, 83, 90–91, 106, 113,
136, 163; newspaper coverage of, 51, 61,
98–99; speeches of, 51, 61, 68, 80, 90–91,
98–99
Carville, James, 136
challenger, 1, 4, 23, 134; campaign effects of,
121, 140, 143, 157. *See also* outparty
Cherry, Lynne, 15
Chrystal, Alec K., 160–161
Civil Rights Act, 88
civil rights, 12, 86–88, 90
clarifying campaign, 31; content of, 68–69;
effects of 115, 123–129, 131–133, 156; and
winning, 70
Clinton, Bill, 1–2, 23, 35, 71, 75, 163; campaign
ads of, 61–62, 68, 102–103 campaign effects
and, 126; as clarifying candidate, 38, 39;
newspaper coverage of, 51, 59, 61, 102–103;
speeches of, 51, 61–62, 68, 75, 102–103
code of conduct, 2
coding scheme, 54, 56–57
Cohen, Martin, 53
Cold War, 59, 74, 77, 82, 94

communism, 12; in 1952 campaign, 76–78,
114, 136, 147; as context, 165
conformity, 11
constraint, 1–2, 4, 33, 67, 105
consultants, 9, 10, 26, 46
content analysis, 15, 74; implementation of,
46–49, 52–58
context, 1, 4, 11, 27–28, 105, 109, 113, 122,
135; and content analysis, 54; creation of,
159–160
convention, 1, 43, 49–50, 78, 80, 88
Converse, Phillip E., 11, 17, 21, 24, 159
Cook, Timothy E., 15
corollary, 32, 33, 69–70, 74, 76, 105, 106, 145,
147
cost of living, 85, 92
crime, 17, 28, 82–83, 87–89, 101, 127, 132
criteria, 14, 16, 67, 89, 108, 136
cue, 13, 18, 24, 40, 71
cynicism, of the media, 53, 60; of politics, 27,
66, 90

Daisy Spot, 47, 79
debates, 9, 15, 43–44, 46, 53
debt, 85
deduction, 32
democracy, 12–13, 59, 162
Democratic Leadership Council, 75
difference in distances, of candidate and voter
positions, 144–151; and vote choice 151–155
discourse, 15, 46, 49–50, 60, 62, 66, 70, 116,
159
Dole, Robert, campaign ads of, 51, 61, 68, 103,
campaign effects and, 127, 140; as insurgent
candidate, 38, 39, 67, 73, 74–75, 106, 135,
136; newspaper coverage of, 51, 61, 103;
speeches of, 51, 61, 68, 75, 103
Downs, Anthony, 12–13, 14, 16, 17, 18–19, 22,
26
drugs, in 1988 campaign, 101; in content
analyses, 54–55; in media coverage, 60
Dukakis, Michael, 1, 9, 26, 46, 113; and campaign ads, 51, 61, 68, 101; campaign effects
and, 128; as insurgent candidate, 38, 39, 73,
82–83, 105, 106, 136; newspaper coverage
of, 51, 61, 101; and speeches, 51, 61, 68, 82,
101

economic gap, 85
economy, 1, 4; advertising effects on, 118,
120–121, 123; and campaign typology,

31–33, 36; in clarifying messages, 69–71; as context, 27, 29, 31, 160; and forecasting models, 13, 37, 107–109; in Gallup Polls, 29; and individual level effects, 113, 118, 120–121, 123, 126–133; in insurgent messages, 75; when mixed, 34; presidential manipulation of, 160; and myopia, 162; and retrospective voting, 21–22; and uncertainty, 126–133; in voting behavior literature, 12, 16 education, 3, 55, 64, 82–83, 88, 101–104, 135

Egypt, 78
Eisenhower, Dwight, 2, 76–78, 80, 91, 135, 136; campaign ads of, 51, 61, 68, 92–93, as clarifying candidate, 38, 39, 71; newspaper coverage of, 51, 61, 92–93; speeches of, 51, 61, 68, 78, 92–93, 147
Electoral College, 69, 90
elites, 11, 23, 116, 164
employment, 21
Enelow, James M., 17, 19
energy, 22, 164, 165
equal rights, 89
Erikson, Robert S., 36, 161
error, in forecasting models, 13, 14, 16, 107–108
Estrich, Susan, 9

Fair, Ray C., 13, 36
Fallows, James, 59–60
Farah, Barbara G., 83
fear, of communism, 77, 84; of nuclear weapons, 79; of SDI, 163; in the 1960 Campaign, 84, 165; in the 1968 Campaign, 87–88, 163, 165
Federal Election Commission, 9
Ferejohn, John, 161
fidelity, of candidate and media content, 62, 64, 65, 165; of content and voter perceptions, 116–119
Finkel, Steven E., 15
Fiorina, Morris P., 13, 16, 21, 22, 159, 164
Ford, Gerald, 1, 90–91; campaign ads of, 51, 61, 68, 98; and campaign effects, 126; as clarifying candidate, 38, 39, 71, 147; newspaper coverage of, 51, 61, 98; speeches of, 51, 61, 68, 91, 98, 126
forecasts, 13–14, 23, 36–37; and campaign type, 39; explaining the errors in, 107–109
Formosa Strait, 77
Fowler, Linda, 15, 44
frame, 62–63, 65

Franklin, Charles, 14, 17, 18
Freedman, Paul, 15
Frey, Bruno S., 160

Gallup Organization, 28–30, 37, 63, 79, 89, 91
Gans, Herbert J., 49
gas, 164
Gaudet, Helen, 10
GDP, 36, 38, 161
Geer, John G., 15, 46, 53, 54
Gelman, Andrew, 13, 23, 40, 139
Geneva, 81
Gerber, Alan S., 44
Gilens, Martin, 53
Glazer, Amihai, 17
Glenn, John, 80–81
GNP, 36, 107–109
Golden, David G., 160
Goldstein, Ken M., 15
Goldwater Library, 47
Goldwater, Barry, 47, 81; campaign ads of, 51, 61, 68, 95; as insurgent candidate, 38, 39, 68, 72, 78–79, 105, 106, 136, 148; newspaper coverage of, 51, 61, 95; speeches of, 47, 78, 79
Gore, Al, 46; campaign ads of, 51, 61–62, 68, 104; and campaign effects, 127; as clarifying candidate, 38, 39, 67, 69, 70–71, 105, 160; newspaper coverage of, 51, 61, 104; speeches of, 47, 51, 61–62, 68, 104
GOTV, 45
Green, Donald P., 44, 45
Greenwood, Lee, 46
Grier, Kevin, 161
growth, 35–36, 38, 75, 80, 107, 161–163

Hagen, Michael G., 83
Hammond, Thomas, 17
Hart, Roderick P., 15, 53
healthcare, 28, 55, 62, 82, 83, 85, 102, 103, 130, 135, 164, 165
heresthetics, 27, 32, 38
Hershey, Margorie R., 83
Hess, Stephen, 48
Hetherington, Marc J., 15, 23
Hibbs, Douglas A. Jr., 13, 34, 36, 161
High Hopes, 83–85
high-information voters, 142–143, 147–148, 152, 154–155
Hillygus, D. Sunshine, 17
Hinich, Melvin J., 17, 19

Holbrook, Thomas M., 15, 36, 37, 43–44
Homeland Security, 165
hope, as campaign appeal, 57, 84, 85, 87, 91
horse-race coverage, 52–53
Horton, Willie, 83
Housing Act of 1949, 85
Huber, Gregory A., 44
Humes, Brian, 17
Humphrey, Hubert, 11, 88–90, 148; campaign
    ads of, 51, 61–62, 67–68, 96; as clarifying
    candidate, 38, 39, 71, 147, 162–163; news-
    paper coverage of, 51, 61, 96; speeches of,
    51, 61–62, 67–68, 88–89, 96
hydrogen bomb, 79

ideology, 25, 46, 125–126, 130–133
immigrants, 164
immigration, 165
incumbent, 1, 4, 16, 30–39, 105; campaign
    effects of, 121, 143, 160–165; messages of,
    134, 140; and retrospective voting, 13,
    21–24; and war, 30
independents, 148, 150, 155, 166
in-depth analyses, 49, 52–53
individual-level effects, 34, 113; of advertising,
    120–123; of candidate messages, 118–119;
    from clarifying campaigns, 125–133, 156; on
    differences in distances, 144,146, 152–154;
    on the economy, 132–133; from insurgent
    campaigns, 134, 137–138, 141, 144, 146,
    152–154, 157; on most important problem,
    137–138 141; on uncertainty, 125–130
inference, 18, 76, 131
inflation, 22, 31; in content analyses, 55–57;
    in Jimmy Carter speeches, 80; and tradeoffs
    with unemployment, 160
information, political 24–25; conditioning
    effects of, 141, 146, 153, 154–157
insurgent campaign, 32; content of, 71–74;
    about the economy, 74–75; effects of,
    134–138, 144, 146, 149, 153–154, 157; and
    losing, 76–83; and winning, 83–91
insurgent issue, 33, 72–73; of Bush in 1992,
    70, 102; of Bush in 2000, 70, 104; of Carter
    in 1976, 90–91, 98; of Dole, 74–75; of
    Dukakis, 82–83, 101; of Goldwater, 78–80,
    95; of Gore, 70; of Humphrey, 70, 96; of
    Kennedy, 83–86, 94; of McGovern, 74, 97;
    of Mondale, 80–82, 99; of Nixon in 1968,
    86–90, 96; of Stevenson, 76–78, 92–93;
    and theoretical compliance, 72–73

integration, 89
inter-rater reliability, 56
Iraq, 80
isolationism, 76
issue ownership, 17, 38
issue positions, of candidates, 2, 4, 17, 18, 19,
    21, 25, 26, 75, 78, 81, 88, 90, 105, 123–135,
    147, 149–150, 164; of voters, 11, 17, 18, 19,
    20, 21, 26, 147, 149, 150, 156
issue, see insurgent issue
Iyengar, Shanto, 14, 15, 16

Jackman, Simon, 17
Jamieson, Kathleen H., 47
Johnson, Lyndon, 11, 30, 79, 87, 89, 148; cam-
    paign ads of, 51, 61, 68, 79, 95; as clarifying
    candidate, 38, 39, 69, 70, 71, 105, 160; news-
    paper coverage of, 51, 61, 95; speeches of,
    51, 61, 68, 95
Johnston, Richard, 15
journalists, 1, 3, 9–10, 50; and issue coverage,
    63
Just, Marion R., 15

Kahn, Kim F., 15
Keech, William R., 160
Kelley, Stanley Jr., 12
Kennedy, John F., 1, 2, 54, 70, 135, 162–163;
    campaign ads of, 51, 61, 68, 94; as insurgent
    candidate, 38, 39, 68, 73, 83–86, 113, 136,
    164–165; newspaper coverage of, 51, 61, 94;
    speeches of, 51, 61, 68, 84, 85, 94
Kennedy, Robert F., 87
Kenney, Patrick, 15
Kern, Montague, 15
Key, V.O. Jr., 16, 159
Kinder, Donald, 14, 16
King, Gary, 13, 23, 40, 139
King, Martin Luther Jr., 87
Klein, Ethel, 83
Korea, 30, 46, 76–78, 92, 135, 147
Kovach, Bill, 59
Kramer, Gerald, 13, 16, 36, 159
Krasno, Jonathan S., 44

landslide, 11
Lau, Richard R., 15
law and order, 90, 96
Lazarsfeld, Paul F., 10–11, 159
leadership, as a campaign appeal, 46, 53,
    55–58, 87, 90, 94, 98, 99, 100, 101, 135

learning, 14, 31, 69, 114, 124, 126–128, 131–134
Lewis-Beck, Michael, 13, 36
Libya, 80
Lohmann, Susanne, 17
Lowery, David, 161
low-information voters, 142–143, 147–148, 150, 152–155
Luna 2, 84

MacKuen, Michael, 15
Marcus, George E., 15
Marshall Plan, 76
Massachusetts, 82, 83, 85
McCain, John, as insurgent candidate, 38, 163
McCarthy, Joseph, 76
McCombs, Maxwell, 14, 16
McGovern, George, 11; campaign ads of, 51, 61, 68, 97; campaign effects and, 127; as insurgent candidate, 38, 39, 67, 72, 74, 106, 135, 136, 140; newspaper coverage of, 51, 61, 97; speeches of, 51, 61, 68, 74, 97
McGuire, William J., 17
McPhee, William N., 159
McRae, Duncan C., 160
media coverage, 14, 48–49; amount of, 50; coding of, 53–57; content of, 51–53, 58; and candidate discourse, 58, 63–65; of domestic policy, 65; of economy; 65; of foreign policy, 64; of traits, 64; by year, 60–62
media exposure, 25, 132–133
Meet the Press, 21, 25
Mendelberg, Tali, 83, 88, 89, 90
message, *see* candidate behavior
Middle East, 77–78
Miller, Warren E., 3, 11, 17, 21, 24, 159
missile gap, 1, 84–86, 91, 94, 166
missiles, 84–86
mixed economy, 34
Mondale, Walter, campaign ads of, 51, 60–61, 68, 100; as insurgent candidate, 38, 39, 72, 80–82, 135, 136, 163–164; newspaper coverage of, 51, 60–61, 100; speeches of, 51, 60–61, 68, 81, 100
Montgomery Bus Boycott, 88
Moon, 84–85, 165
Moscow, 81
most important problem, 28–30, 63, 74, 137–143, 157
My Lai Massacre, 87
myopia, 161–162

narratives, 131, 165–166
NATO, 81
NES, *see* American National Election Study
Neuman, W. Russell, 15
New Deal, 75
New Frontier, 84–86, 94, 164–165
New Hampshire primary, 44
New York Times, 1, 4, 21, 46, 48–53, 64–65, 92–104, 186
news, *see* media coverage
newspaper, 24, 38, 70–71, 81, 86, 93, 114–126, 154
Newsweek, 53, 59
Nie, Norman H., 17
Nixon, Richard, 1, 2, 84–86, 91; campaign ads of, 51, 60–62, 94, 96–97; and campaign effects 128, 140–141; as clarifying candidate (1960, 1972), 38, 39, 67, 68, 69, 70, 71, 83, 105, 160; as insurgent candidate (1968), 38, 39, 68, 73, 86–90, 113, 136, 148, 163, 165; newspaper coverage of, 51, 60–62, 68, 94, 96–97; speeches of, 51, 60–62, 68, 94, 96–97
Nordhaus, William D., 160
Norpoth, Helmut, 36
North Africa, 77
nuclear arms, 80, 95
nuclear bombs, 78–79

Obama, Barack, as clarifying candidate, 38
oil, 22, 74
open-ended responses, 115, 116, 120–121, 124
Orangeburg Massacre, 86
outparty, 16, 35; and forecasts, 36, 108–109. *See also* challenger

Page, Benjamin I., 17, 18
Paletz, David L., 15
parties, 9, 12, 14, 16–19, 21, 22–25, 31, 36, 47, 80, 160, 164
party identification, 3, 11–12, 17, 24, 151; conditioning effect of, 149
Patterson, Thomas E., 15, 53, 59
PBS, 65
peace, 21, 27, 30, 56–57, 74, 78, 80–84, 93–94, 107–108
performance gap, 85
persuasion, 17, 20, 23, 25, 150, 152
Petrocik, John, 17, 26
Pledge of Allegiance, 1, 82
polarization, 161

political business cycle, 160
Political Communication Lab, 47, 50
political party, 24, 45, 148
political sophistication, 17, 147, 155, 166
Pomper, Gerald M., 17
Popkin, Samuel L., 15, 16, 131, 165
Poterba, James H., 160
Powell, G. Bingham Jr., 17
power, 12, 18, 28, 32, 43, 63, 65, 78–79, 106–107, 116, 122, 145, 150, 160; in campaigns, 75, 78
predisposition, 24–25, 156; as filter, 149
presidential approval, 14, 36, 107, 108
presidential campaign, of 1952, 76–78; of 1956, 76–78; of 1960, 1, 10, 83–86; of 1964, 78–80; of 1968, 62, 86–90, 163; of 1972, 127–128, 165; of 1976, 1, 62, 90–91; of 1980, 10, 13, 80–82; of 1984, 10, 56, 58, 80–82, 135; of 1988, 1, 9, 26, 82–83; of 1992, 2, 10, 62, 74–75, 134; of 1996, 67, 70, 75, 127, 165; of 2000, 9, 60, 62, 67, 127, 128
Presidential Election Discourse Dataset (PEDD), 46
prices, 21–22, 164
priming, 14, 16–18; effects of 136, 140, 142, 164
prison furlough, 1
prosperity, 27, 29, 30, 32, 55, 77, 82, 93, 113, 165
proximity, 17, 145, 150–155
public opinion, 4, 14–16, 18–23, 63; on campaign issues, 28, 34; on the economy, 29, 31; on insurgent issues, 33–34, 135, 152; and polarization, 164; on war and foreign policy, 30
pundits, 1–3, 9; interpretation of 1992, 23; interpretation of 1968, 83

race, 127, 132, 151; and the 1968 campaign, 88–90; and the 1988 campaign, 82
rational choice, 12, 14, 17
RDI, 34, 36, 107
Reagan, Ronald, 2, 13, 80–82, 91, 135, 136, 163–164; campaign ads of, 51, 56–57, 58, 61, 68, 81–82, 99–100, 126; and campaign effects, 126; newspaper coverage of, 51, 61, 99–100; speeches of, 51, 61, 68, 80, 81, 99–100, 126, 162–163
recession, 1, 75
RePass, David E., 17
retrospective voting, 13, 16–19, 21–22, 38, 159

Revolving Door ad, 82–83
Rice, Tom, 13, 36
Riker, Bill, 15, 26, 27, 32
riots, 86, 87
Rivlin, Douglas, 58
Robinson, Michael J., 14
Rock the Vote, 45
Rosenstiel, Tom, 59
Rosenstone, Steven, 13
Runkel, David R., 9
Russia, 1, 76, 126, 128, 133
Russians, 54, 60, 70, 77–79, 81, 84–86

safety, 17, 28, 96
salience, 17; effects on increasing, 152, 163
SALT, 91
SALT II, 147
SALT III, 81
Schattschneider, E. E., 27
Schneider, Friedrich, 160
scripts, 131
segregation, 86, 88–90
services, 124, 126–128, 133
Shaw, Daron R., 15, 44
Shaw, Donald, 14, 16
Sheehan, Margaret, 14
Shepsle, Kenneth A., 14, 17
Sherr, Susan, 47
shortcut, 18
Sides, John, 17
signal, 16, 18, 31–32, 89, 120, 131
Simon, Adam F., 17
Smith, Tom W., 28
Social Security, 23, 85, 135, 164, 165
South Carolina State College, 86
South, 86–87, 89–90
Soviet Union, 76, 79–80, 135, 162
space exploration, 84–86, 165,
Sparrow, Bartholomew H., 15
spatial model, 18–20, 22, 26, 38, 116, 156
special interests, 91
speeches, 4; by Bill Clinton, 134; database of, 46–48; by Gerald Ford, 126; Goldwater's missing, 47; by John F. Kennedy, 84 162; number of, 50–53; coding of, 53–57; content of, 57–63, 68, 91; about foreign policy, 63–64; about traits 63–64; about the economy 65; about domestic policy, 65; and theoretical compliance, 67, 69; by Barry Goldwater, 78; by Ronald Reagan, 80–81; by Michael Dukakis, 82; by Richard Nixon,

85; by Martin Luther King, 87; by George Wallace, 90; of candidates by year, 92–104; individual-level effects of, 117–123, 156–157

spending, on campaigns, 9; on defense, 55, 92–104, 124, 130; on domestic services, 124, 130; on household, 164

Spiliotes, Constantine J., 15, 17, 44

spillover effects, 130–131

Stanford Mediaworks, 47

Stanford University, 47–48, 50, 114

states' rights, 90

stem-cell research, 164

Stevenson, Adlai, 84, 147; campaign ads of, 51, 61, 68, 92–93; as insurgent candidate, 38, 39, 68, 72, 76–78, 106, 135, 136; newspaper coverage of, 51, 61, 92–93; speeches of, 51, 61, 68, 76–77, 92–93

Stevenson, Randolph, 13, 23

Stockholm, 81

Stokes, Donald, 11, 17, 21, 22, 24, 159

Stranger, Jeffrey, 58

strategic arms reduction, 80

strategy, 1–2, 9, 15; context and, 26–27; of George H.W. Bush, 75; of insurgents, 33, 164; in news coverage, 49, 53, 59; of Ronald Reagan, 81;

structural conditions, 11, 27, 32, 55, 83, 109, 113, 159, 166

Suez Canal, 77–78

taxes, 23, 30n; in 1976 campaign, 91, 97; in 1988 campaign, 101; in 1992 campaign, 102; in 1996 campaign, 103; on cigarettes, 164; in content analyses 55–57; and insurgents, 74–75, 105, 119; spillover effects, 130; in Stevenson campaign, 92

television, 16, 45–47, 64, 66, 132; see also advertisements

test-ban treaty, 79

Tet Offensive, 87

theme, 26, 28; in 1960, 162, 164; in 1968, 97; in 1988, 82–83; and content analyses, 54–57; of campaigns, 58, 92–104; for insurgents, 71;

theoretical compliance, 67, 105

Tien, Charles, 36

tone, 2, 49; of campaign advertisements, 53

traits, 58, 60–61, 64, 117–120

trust, as a campaign appeal, 1, 91, 96, 98

Tufte, Edward R., 13, 16, 36, 159, 160

typology, 4, 33, predictions from, 35, 45–46;

and behavior of candidates, 67, 71, 106, 113, 147; and corollaries, 76; and forecasts, 108

uncertainty, 14, 19–21, 32–34; effects on 125–133, 155

unemployment, 22, 31; in content analyses, 55–57; in Jimmy Carter speeches, 80; in 1972 campaign, 97; and tradeoffs with inflation, 160

University of Pennsylvania, 46

urban unrest, 89

utility, 12, 18–19, 167–168

valence issue, 22, 163

Vavreck, Lynn, 13, 15, 17, 23, 44, 53

Verba, Sidney, 17

Vienna, 81

vote choice, 3, 13, 16, 17, 20, 35, 49, 114, 140–144, 151–155, 161

Voting Rights Act, 88

Waldman, Paul, 47

Wallace, George, 90

War in Vietnam, 1, 12, 74, 78, 87, 91. See also war

War Room, 2, 35

war, 30, 40, 107; Cold War, 59, 74; and content analyses, 54; Eisenhower and, 77; in Korea, 30, 76, 78; nuclear 79, 81, 147; in Vietnam, 1, 12, 74, 78, 87, 91

Warsaw Pact, 81

Washington outsider, and Carter Campaign, 1, 91, 98

Washington Post, 35, 49; polls in, 164

Watergate, 90–91

Wattenberg, Martin P., 15

West, Darrell, 15

Western Europe, 77

white pride, 88

Whitten, Guy D., 17

Williams, John T., 161

Wink, Kenneth, 13, 15, 36

Wisconsin Advertising Project, 47

Wlezien, Christopher, 36

women, 89; rights of, 12; role in workplace of, 124, 126, 129–130, 133

World War III, 81

Zaller, John R., 17, 23, 24–25, 36, 66, 116, 142, 161